Running with the Fairies

Running with the Fairies: Towards a Transpersonal Anthropology of Religion

By

Dennis Gaffin

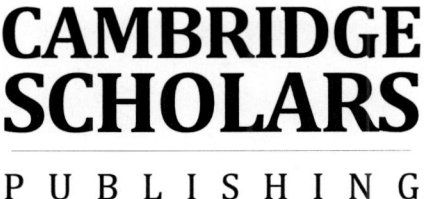

Running with the Fairies:
Towards a Transpersonal Anthropology of Religion,
by Dennis Gaffin

This book first published 2012. The present binding first published 2013.

Cambridge Scholars Publishing

12 Back Chapman Street, Newcastle upon Tyne, NE6 2XX, UK

British Library Cataloguing in Publication Data
A catalogue record for this book is available from the British Library

Copyright © 2013 by Dennis Gaffin

All rights for this book reserved. No part of this book may be reproduced, stored in a retrieval system, or transmitted, in any form or by any means, electronic, mechanical, photocopying, recording or otherwise, without the prior permission of the copyright owner.

ISBN (10): 1-4438-4287-7, ISBN (13): 978-1-4438-4287-7

'Prince Enters the Wood'

'**The Prince Enters the Wood**:
 All light and white as a fleecy cloud, / A female form floats gracefully'
© The Trustees of the British Museum.

In *An Old Fairy Tale Told Anew,* an 1866 illustration by Victorian fairy painter Richard Doyle. He was uncle of Arthur Conan Doyle who wrote the mystical *The Coming of the Fairies* and the Sherlock Holmes stories.

The gaze of the rider on horseback is alerted and altered by the light of the fairy, inviting him into the woods, where his adventure begins.

TABLE OF CONTENTS

Acknowledgements ix

Foreword xi

Chapter One.. 1
Introduction

Chapter Two 25
Overview
    What are Fairies?

Chapter Three 37
Opening Up
    From Childhood to Eureka
    Connections – Adult Fairy Experience

Chapter Four.. 65
Lightness, Drama, and the Natural World: Attitude and Preparation for Fairymindedness
    Lightness and Drama
    Fairyfolk in the Natural World
    Minette's FairyLands

Chapter Five 77
Fieldwork and Personalwork

Chapter Six 91
Perspectives and Writings on Fairies

Chapter Seven.. 105
No Bad Fairies

Chapter Eight... 113
The Unconceptual

Table of Contents

Chapter Nine 123
Realization
    Awareness of Fairy

Chapter Ten 133
Incarnation and Reincarnation

Chapter Eleven 145
Mission, Purpose, Responsibility

Chapter Twelve 153
Fairypeople Traits
    Physical Traits
    Sensitivities and Personality

Chapter Thirteen 167
Healing and Well-Being

Chapter Fourteen 189
Individual Transformation

Chapter Fifteen 207
Fairyfolk Together

Chapter Sixteen 217
Ireland: The Fairy Portal, Artistry
    Music, Art, Creativity

Chapter Seventeen 231
Consciousness, Evolution, Planet

Notes 251

Bibliography 273

Index 291

ACKNOWLEDGEMENTS

I want to acknowledge the support of others who made this work possible.

For technical support I would like to thank the staff at Cambridge Scholars Publishing and Ken Fujiuchi at the State University of New York College at Buffalo library. Phillips Stevens, Jr. of the University of Buffalo was most helpful in his support and with incisive comments on an earlier version of the writing.

Grants from the Research Foundation of the State University of New York supported fieldwork, and a sabbatical from the Department of Anthropology of the Faculty of Arts and Sciences at SUNY College Buffalo gave me additional time to pursue on site research.

In Ireland I am most grateful to all the newly made friends since the turn of the millennium in the County Donegal hamlets of Doagh and, four years later, Baile an tSleibhe. I would especially like to thank Brendan, who allowed me to stay by myself without charge at his classic Irish cottage down a walking path overlooking the beautiful northwest coast. There I burned peat fires, read by candlelight, typed up field notes, and transcribed interviews.

I am greatly indebted to all the real life characters in this book, but most of all to Kay Mullin, to whom I became a sort of apprentice. She nourished me in many ways: with delights from her garden of fruits and vegetables, with rooms to sleep, and, most of all, with a wealth of gentle, spiritual wisdom. It is quite clear that my seemingly happenstance meeting with her has dramatically shaped my life and made this work possible.

Back in North America I am most grateful to my partner and colleague Ana Bodnar, not only for her joining and assisting me during recent stays in Donegal, but mostly for her moral and spiritual support of this daring work and unconventional journey. Thanks always Ana.

FOREWORD

The contents of this book have potential to resonate with people of a variety of ilks.

For students of spirituality and religion, anthropologists, psychologists, and academicians of various sorts, I suggest to begin reading with Chapter One. This heavily-footnoted scholarly introduction lays the academic, theoretical, and methodological background for this work.

For those less academically inclined, I suggest initially skipping the Introduction and starting to read at any point which might stir one's interest or imagination. Chapter Two gives a general overview of the subject of fairies. Chapter Three details how fairyfolk, humans who experience the world of fairies, came to connect with the Fairy World. Chapter Five discusses the process of fieldwork and personal change. Chapter Six discusses previous popular and mystical perspectives and literature.

For those wanting to listen to fairyfolk's often extensive verbatim philosophical and psychological discussion of their spiritual experiences and perspectives, see the many chapters by subject. Most chapters contain occasional analyses and cross-cultural comparisons. Skipping around different chapters might also prove intriguing. For example; those interested in reincarnation could jump to Chapter Ten; those interested in spiritual transformation alongside interpersonal relationships might skip to Chapter Fourteen; those interested in music and art Chapter Sixteen. And so forth.

Thanks.

Chapter One

Introduction

Within anthropology, sacred experience of spirit entities for European peoples has remained largely unexamined, despite Plato's recognition of "daemones" as intermediaries between gods and men. Anthropologists have long researched indigenous peoples' and Eastern religions' views of and experiences with supernatural beings, but ethnographers have almost ignored Europeans' experiences of angels, fairies, nature spirits, other-than-human persons (Hallowell 1960) and god-like beings of non-human origins. Such research has been risky for social scientists wanting to maintain their reputations in the academy (Salomonsen 2004, Turner 1994, Lee 1987, Winkelman 1982). And to give respectful ethnographic treatment of people who believe in and experience entities such as fairies might dethrone the intentional or unintentional sensibilities that the standards, logics, and spiritualities of organized Christianity, Judaism, and Islam (or Western science) are somehow at the "center." Even though there are supernatural entities and spirit beings in the mainstream and mystical sects of these monotheistic religions, the attention of anthropologists has been directed almost entirely to the existence of spirit beings in "other" cultures. Only theologians, e.g., Garrett (2008) for angels, and folklorists, e.g., Narvaez (1991) for fairy lore, have paid disciplined scholarly attention to Western spirit entities.[1]

The general anthropological and scholarly perspective which has demanded "scientific" explanation, and frowned heavily on "going native" in the arena of religion has been analyzed and well documented by Greenwood (2009), Harvey (2006, 2002), Spickard, Landres and McGuire (2002), Howard and Mageo (1996), and Young and Goulet (1994). They trace the history of rationalist, structural-functional, psychoanalytic, content analytical, and symbolic approaches which in general "explain" or explain away religious and spiritual phenomena. Yet now there is growing acceptance of the work of anthropologists who themselves experience mystical states or spiritual entities in the cultures they study or live in. Edith Turner's brave work and article (1994, 2009), recounting her encounter with an African spirit, alongside the experiences of Harner

(1980), Grindal (1983), Lee (1987), Luhrmann (1989), several authors in Young and Goulet, eds. (1994), and others, and Irving Hallowell's (1960) recognition of the reality of "other-than-human persons" in Ojibwa ontology, are becoming important to what has come to be called a dialogical, participatory, experiential, or transpersonal anthropology.[2]

Although at the time of the fieldwork which is the basis of this book I was unfamiliar with much of this anthropological work and experience, I too came to experience an alternate state of consciousness as a consequence of my fieldwork in County Donegal, Ireland. Presumably it was facilitated by my own cognitive and affective receptivity, and because, among other things, I am a theist. Here, at the outset, I want to reveal any possible biases I had which may have influenced this ethnography. Thus, as I discuss in more detail below, my own propensities, faith, and previous experience made me receptive to others' own claims and experiences of the Divine or semi-divine, and receptive to new experiences and cultural permutations on the theme of God/Divinity/Creator, and lesser beings.

Actually, the respectful and participatory treatment of European spirit beings by an anthropological scholar is not recent. In 1911 Oxford University Press published *The Fairy-Faith in Celtic Countries*, by Ph.D. anthropologist Walter Y. Evans-Wentz, an Oxford fellow. Evans-Wentz was an American who had studied at Stanford with William James and William Butler Yeats, and then later at Oxford with R.R. Marrett. He dedicated his book to Irishmen Yeats and to George Russell (pen name A.E.), both of whom were mystics who believed that fairies exist. They believed that fairies are nature spirits, elemental beings of non-human origin, who can enter and exit the corporeal world of humans, can communicate with humans, and appear in various forms akin to humans or animals of various sizes. And in contrast to the vast majority of believers in fairies in Ireland, they believed that fairies are creations of a divine God.

For his doctoral research, Evans-Wentz traveled through Ireland, Scotland, Wales, Brittany, Cornwall, and the Isle of Man to collect experiences and stories of fairies (*sidhe*, Irish Gaelic, pronounced shee) and related entities. He, himself, believed that fairies existed. Possibly his belief in them had been learned early in his life from his parents who were Theosophists, who generally posited the existence of several kinds of spiritual realms and entities beyond conventional Christian cosmology, and that he was familiar with the work of Madame Blavatsky, Annie Besant, and others.[4] Clearly he was not only open to Irish and other

European folk conceptions of the make-up of the universe, which included fairies, but his anthropology was "participatory" (Greenwood 2009).

Psychologist and philosopher William James had published *The Varieties of Religious Experience* in 1902, positing a "stream of consciousness," a part of which is glimpsed by different individuals and cultures in varying religious experiences across the globe. Although discussions continue about the extent to which James' understandings fully accepted the existence of planes of reality beyond the human, he is well known for being, at a minimum, "sympathetic" to religious experience and promoting a "radical empiricism."[5] At the time such an approach which recognized the reality and truth of spiritual experiences and worlds for individuals of different cultures clearly deviated from the general Western academic notions that mystical experience, interaction with deities, and other religious experiences were products of "primitive" or childish cognition. This latter approach within anthropology, and academia in general, which demanded scientific explanation, rather than theological acceptance, became the norm within anthropological circles. But Evans-Wentz believed in Irish and Celtic mysticism, and treated the Fairy Faith as a particular manifestation of the world-wide phenomenon of animism.

The Fairy-Faith in Celtic Countries has never received any lasting anthropological renown. It has been popular only among some folklorists and "New Age" thinkers. Indeed Evans-Wentz is primarily known for, and is famous for, his later editing of the first translation of the *Tibetan Book of the Dead* (1927) and for other significant works (1935, 1951, 1954) on Tibetan Buddhism. These have long been heralded by scholars as pioneer works in religious studies and the anthropology of religion. Like Tibetan Buddhism in general, as opposed to the Fairy Faith, anthropological scholars, particularly in the last thirty years, generally treat *these non-Western* understandings as legitimate perspectives worthy of continuing study and nonjudgmental respect. And, even though Evans-Wentz termed the Fairy Faith as mysticism, and had the support of others such as Andrew Lang, John Rhys, and later Carl Jung, no subsequent serious academic scholar, to my knowledge, has diligently treated it in discussions of Western mysticism, spirituality, or religiosity.[6] This is despite the fact that Evans-Wentz parallels fairies to "nature-spirits," as Tylor (1871) in *Primitive Culture* called such discarnate beings, to the elemental beings of medieval mystics, and to the "middle-world" of fairy-like entities found in many cultures across the globe. These include Persian and Turkish *peris*, Islamic *jinns*, Tibetan *dakinis*, Chinese *apsaras*, Jewish *mazikeem*, Seneca

Jo-go-ah, Cherokee *yunwi tsunsdi*, Australian Arunta *alcheringa*, and many others.

Moreover, Evans-Wentz was not simply a sympathetic student of Tibetan Buddhism. He became a practitioner: he studied extensively under a lama, wore robes, ate vegetarian, and intended to spend the rest of his life in India, but World War II broke out. When back in the States, in San Diego, he was active in Buddhist and Eastern programs of various sorts. Thus, despite the general culture of academic anthropology which eschewed scholars "going native," and demanded scientific, usually structural-functional or symbolic explanations for the existence of religious beliefs and practices, Evans-Wentz was a scholar who was native in his theosophy and did "go native" into the Fairy Faith and into Buddhism.[7] Even though he stated outright in *Tibetan Yoga & Secret Doctrines* (1935:219) that certain kinds of usually invisible, sacred Tibetan Buddhist elemental entities, *dakinis, are* fairies, only dakinis have received attention as "legitimate" or believable concepts or entities worthy of serious religious scholarly attention. (See e.g., Simmer-Brown 2002, Katz 1992, Willis 1987, Kalff 1978.)

Thus we need to revise the notion that until quite recently anthropologists have been non-participatory (Greenwood 2009). Despite Evans-Wentz's unorthodox anthropology, in writing and in lifestyle, in 1931 Evans-Wentz received an honorary Doctorate of Science from Oxford. (Carl Jung received the same award seven years later.)

As mentioned, there have been some academic discussions of anthropologists' own recognitions of and experiences of various kinds of spirits, nature-spirits, discarnate beings, other-than-human-beings and other intermediate entities or energies between humans and God, the Creator, or the Prime Mover. As Wilkie (1994:164) states in Young's and Goulet's edited book on the anthropology of extraordinary experience, in a discussion of the "spirited imagination," the autonomy of spirits, and the make-up of the "inner worlds,"

> Some spirits are indeed figments of the human imagination, yet there are others who have been around much longer than human beings. Among spirits there is a vast hierarchy, from simple energy-forms and nature spirits to angelic and higher forms of divine and galactic intelligence. These may be terrestrial or celestial, intimately associated with human life or not, but all are aspects of the one Universal Being, conceived of as the totality, inner and outer, or as its creator.

And Young's own article (1994) does give some anthropological credence to spontaneous visions, the kind of visions my informants below have, and does say that "visions are not that rare. They occur in all cultures and to people from all walks of life" (190). But even though he considers his and others' visions as "real," they exist because humans create energy that produces a tangible form. This approach still eschews the possibility that entities exist independently of the human mind, which mystics and indigenous peoples *know*. The mystics' certainty is not proof of the phenomena, no matter how certain the individuals are. Yet, however unverifiable, that knowledge and conviction are anthropological data.

Almost all of the recent anthropology which examines contact with "spirits" or spirit-worlds is attached to concerns with altered states of consciousness and/or shamanism. Most scholars treat shamanism or other worldly experience with non-humans as a consequence of cultural expectations and specific ritual methods – e.g., drumming, dance, fasting, entheogens – which individuals use to create a trance, ecstatic, or visionary state as a portal to another world. (See Hume 2007). The issue of perception is key here. Preparatory rituals and/or ingested substances are used to alter ordinary perception, a universal biological-physiological trait of humans.[8] Under certain induced and/or environmental conditions and (learned) cultural expectations or models, - which includes affect – these experiences can result in an altered (or alternate) state of consciousness and perception.

Emotion influences cognition which influences perception. Ingold (2000:161) explains the incorporation of emotion into cultural models:

> ... cultural models – to the extent that they are fully internalized – do not merely describe or represent the world, they also shape people's feelings and desires. That is to say, they can have 'motivational force' (D'Andrade 1992:28). As Claudia Strauss argues.... The realm of cognition is inseparable from the realm of affect; thus cultural models should be understood as 'learned, internalized patterns of thought-feeling' (Strauss 1992:3).

Thus perception is channeled not only by cognition but by emotion, and helps to explain how individuals' cognitive orientations and emotional preparedness influence their resonance with and adoption of beliefs and their openness to experiences. Yet the epiphanies and first time surprise sightings of fairies by people who did not theretofore believe in fairies, as some fairyfolk discuss in Chapter Three below, challenges the full acceptance of this notion. The sight or sensing of fairies or fairy energy by the *fairyfolk* of this book is usually spontaneous or nearly spontaneous, without much or any specific ritual preparation.[9]

In this book *fairyfolk* refers to human beings mystically ensconced in the experience of and belief in the Fairyworld. The Fairyworld is a non-corporeal, spiritual realm in another dimension of reality where fairies reside and from whence they sometimes come into humans' corporeal plane of existence.[10]

Running with the Fairies deviates from the usual, recent subject matters in the anthropology of religion, not only in its focus on European, particularly Irish, interaction with spirit entities, but also in general in not placing the topic directly in the realm of shamanism or of states of consciousness altered by substances or protracted rituals.[11] I agree with Sheppard's (2007) critique that studies of shamanism have usurped much of the attention of transpersonal anthropologists. Although most studies of altered states of consciousness and shamanism seek to "explain" phenomena such as the appearances of spirits, this book remains primarily descriptive. It is a presentation of those who understand and experience fairies and fairy "things." It places them not only in the context of transpersonal anthropology but, in addition, in comparative contexts of mysticism and transpersonal psychology.

Harvey (2003:9) suggests "At best, a spirit appears to be a being rarely seen except by shamans." But the fairyfolk in this book are not specially initiated or trained shaman or shaman-like persons, nor, like most shamans, are they engaging in "performance" for others. Shamanic spirit contact is much a social phenomenon among human beings. The contemporary anthropological focus on shamanism as performance and as the province of specially trained individuals can potentially distract us from understanding fairy experiences and fairy consciousness as essentially individualized and mystical.

Also, shamanism is much about the mastery of spirits and the use of spirits for the purposes of healing individuals or groups in times of medical need or emotional stress. (E.g., see Jakobsen 1999.) Despite the fact that fairyfolk sometimes understand fairies as helping humans in everyday tasks or (metaphysical) realizations/awarenesses, fairyfolk do not control or use spirits (fairies) in this shamanic way. Fairyfolk understand fairies as more independent entities, subservient to Nature and God, which help humans to accomplish tasks and to understand the sanctity of nature and the closeness of God.

Mageo and Howard *(*1996) do elevate studies of terrestrial appearing spirits into a discipline, and endeavor "to bring spirits back to their rightful place in theories of religion, beside the gods with whom they coexist"(2). But all the articles in their work treat the phenomena in the context of indigenous Pacific societies. Moreover, the focus is psychological and sociological explanation for particular kinds of indigenous spirit beliefs and experiences in the context of cultural change. It does not really address the mystical experience of non-ordinary realities. While certainly helpful in clarifying many issues, it avoids a participatory anthropology, as evidenced by the fact that none of the articles make any reference to E. Turner's (1994) own experience as described in "The Reality of Spirits." Thus *Spirits in Culture, History and Mind*, while clearly respectful of native spiritual experience as real for natives, avoids a transpersonal approach which would make more room for the possibility of specific individuals' and cultures' supernatural experience as particular venues for sacred phenomena across cultures – indigenous, East, *and* West.

Hallowell's (1960) introduction of the term "other-than-human-persons" in discussing Ojibwa entities is most helpful in discarding the Western academic and linguistic dichotomy of natural versus supernatural, especially of human (body) versus spirit. Hallowell appreciates native understandings of the continuum of entities, ranging from humans to person-like non-humans to gods or God. In Western contexts fairies (and angels) may well be thought of as other-than-human-persons, spiritual other-than-human beings. Thus I wish to go beyond anthropologist Laughlin's (1994c) call for a transpersonal anthropology required for a full description of the experience upon which the cosmologies of many non-Euro-American societies are grounded to include European and Euro-American settings.

In Pagan Studies (Harvey 1997, Blain, Ezzy, and Harvey 2004), and in studies of Witchcraft (Ezzy 2004, Orion 1995, Luhrmann 1989), anthropologists are beginning to examine Western nature-spirits with minds open to the reality of the experience for subjects and anthropologists. In his book on animism, Harvey (2006), critical of earlier anthropological stances on the subject matter, also discusses Pagan and Eco-Pagan animism. And Greenwood (2009), who equates magical consciousness with mystical mentality, discusses contemporary Western, but unconventional spirit(ual) experience. These studies can lead into my ethnographic study here of experience with fairies and modern fairyfolk in Ireland. Indeed Harvey (2006) does devote three pages to discussing fairies and other elemental spirits among (neo-) Pagan animists, but concludes:

> The most important point about these beings is that they do not necessarily attract a lot of attention in, and only rarely become central to, the everyday life and pursuits of animists. Their existence may well be taken for granted and unremarkable – literally not remarked upon – and their presence, at least in particular places and particular times is casually expected. (124)

The casualness and "unremarkable" nature of fairies in Pagan animism he describes is far from the Fairy Faith described here. This is not only in that the fairies are seemingly in the background, rather than the foreground, but he also says that Pagan animists are generally non-theistic.

Butler's (2011) article in *Ireland's New Religious Movements* does briefly mention belief in fairies as characteristic of some neo-Pagans, who "relate to ... traditions connected with fairies" (123) and who have fairy "associations" with particular sites. But in the (only) example she gives of a woman speaking of an experience at a particular site who Butler says has an "awareness of associations between a goddess [Anu] and the fairies" (129) the woman does not mention fairies. Moreover, Butler indicates that "not all neo-Pagans express belief in deities or in supernatural entities" (such as fairies or God). And Letcher (2001, 2006), in another notable, brief exception to the general lack of scholarly treatment of fairies in the anthropology of religion, does say that for British Eco-Pagans "fairies are regarded literally not metaphorically" (2006:182). But his treatments are also of (Eco-)Pagans, and discussion revolves around the politics of enchantment of the landscape for protest movements. One of his articles (2001) is published in *Folklore*, and doesn't quite get fairies out of the realm of folklore into religiosity or mysticism. And one of Taylor's (2010) informants, a mystical radical environmentalist, who practices what Taylor calls "dark green religion," does mention "Fairies" (97) in passing, but there is no other reference or discussion of fairies or fairy-like beings in this book on nature spirituality. And Butler's (2011) article is the only one in the volume which Cosgrove, et. al. (2011:5) say "represents both the 'state of the art' in terms of research on new religion in Ireland and an empirical overview of some of the major *types* of new and alternative religiosities"(italics original).[12] Thus it becomes clear the Fairy Faith is not really discussed by scholars of (neo-)Paganism and alternative religion. Let us return to animism and theology.

Harvey (2006) helps to liberate the term animism from its previous Western biases and I follow his "new usage of animism [which] arises from respectful relationships with indigenous and other cultures in which boundaries are permeable and putative 'opposites' are necessarily engaged in various ways" (xiv). Yet the fairyfolk in this book are not Western animists in the same sense as witches, Neo-Pagans, and other New Age persons or groups, the subjects of some recent approaches to an enspirited earth (e.g., Blain, et. al. 2004, Greenwood 2000, Harvey 1997). The informants in this book recognize the reality of fairy nature spirits as part of a wider monotheistic theology. The Fairy and other Realms are planes of existence under the direction and discretion of a Creator, and thus fairyfolk are not polytheistic, but theosophical. They see and experience Fairy as both earthly and divine. Their animism is theistic.

Although Pagans and fairyfolk are both nature-oriented, unlike Pagan groups fairyfolk generally do not eschew or avoid Christianity or Judaism or theological perspectives in general. Nor do they regularly participate in collective rituals or seasonal festivals, train themselves in shamanic journeys, congregate in groups, seek feminine energy nor focus on goddess alignments. (Fairies are said to be both male and female). Although believers and experiences in Fairy are sometimes considered "New Age types," their modes of being actually resemble conventional religious and mystical orientations. Also, the mystical Fairy Faith is not a New Age movement in that it is not really a social movement. Prince and Riches (2000) argue that a central feature of the New Age is its opposition to "mainstream", being outside the Church. Although some fairyfolk may participate or sympathize with some New Age concerns, the Fairy Faith does not entail the central characteristics of the "New Age" (Townsend 2004).

Thus in several ways the beliefs in and experiences with fairies are not substantially different from some long-standing beliefs in angels, nature spirits, and elemental beings in the cosmologies of older orders and mystical sects of Western, Eastern, (and indigenous) religions. The Fairy Faith is not necessarily an alternative to organized religion: some of my informant fairyfolk in Ireland invoke Jesus Christ in their conversation and attend church, as well as all of them think fairies are messengers of God. Except for a few earlier mystics such as Kirk (1776), Yeats (1962), and Russell (A.E.) (1965), this latter understanding is a change from the old Fairy Faith in which fairies were not perceived as divine, and were generally feared and avoided. (See Chapters Six and Seven and Briggs 1976). The Fairy Faith might best, I suggest, be termed a "theistic spirituality" (Vincett and Woodhead 2001).[13]

Thus the nature-spirit spirituality of fairyfolk is directly connected to a high-god, unlike Paganism which is generally polytheistic (Harvey 1997). Also, the Fairy Faith is much less institutionalized and is best conceptualized as a form of mysticism in which fairy experience occurs as a consequence of direct mystical experience in what might best be called vision or apparition. Such alternate consciousnesses do not ordinarily occur in our "monophasic" society (Laughlin, McManus and Shearer 1983:144) which

> narrowly confines experience and knowledge to a narrow range of phenomenological phases. For our culture generally, the only phases of

consciousness appropriate to the accrual of information about the world are those acceptable as "normal waking consciousness".

In Laughlin's terms, fairyfolk's experiences would be a product of "polyphasic consciousness," and when seeing or sensing fairies or fairy energy humans "cross phases" of consciousness.

In his treatise on mystical experience, visions and the famous 19th century Hindu mystic Ramakrishna, Indian psychoanalyst Kakar (1991) identifies four kinds of visions: nightmarish visions (hallucinations); conscious visions, which include visual insights; mystical illusions; and indescribable, unconscious visions. Although I did not use such terminology in discussing fairy experiences among my informants, I conclude that fairyfolk, when seeing a fairy, are experiencing conscious visions with visual insight. Kakar (1991:22) describes conscious visions and visual insight:

> Welcomed by a prepared mind, they fall on a receptive ground. Conscious visions may be symbolic representations of an ongoing psychic process, the symbols taken from the mystic's religious and cultural tradition.... Other conscious visions are visual insights, images full of conviction and sudden clarity, couched either in a universal-mystical or in a particular, cultural-historical idiom.

Seeing fairies is in part a consequence of the "cultural idiom" of fairies in Irish, Celtic and European history and consciousness.

Visions, in Western discourse through the ages, have been experienced by mystics, religious ascetics, and some laymen, such as William Blake. In Catholicism, officials of the Holy See deem, sometimes many years later, only a very small portion of claimed visions to be a consequence of the reality of an actual, real apparition, usually a Marian apparition. Some visions of medieval European women, such as Teresa of Avila and Hildegard van Bingen, have been upheld by the Church. (See Christian Jr. 1981 and and Petroff 1986).[14]

The *Catholic Encyclopedia* describes three types of visions, one of which is called an extrinsic "corporeal vision" which is a spiritual vision experienced in a normal state of consciousness. In Eastern Orthodoxy "vision" (*theoria*) refers to experiencing the "energies" of God, and fairyfolk who sense fairy energy would be akin to this. In anthropologist E. Turner's (2009:150) terms, fairy appearances would be spirit manifestations "which constitute the deliberate visitation of discernable forms that have the conscious intent to communicate, to claim importance in our lives." But, as indicated earlier, visions of fairies have not been discussed in much detail, theologically, psychologically, or anthropologically, except by Evans-Wentz and a few non-academics discussed in Chapter Seven.

A fairyfolk's "extraordinary claim" (to most Westerners), the seeing and experiencing of fairies, perceived as "real for him/her," can be investigated through ethnographic data "even though it has no basis in science" (Stevens 2011).[15] My purpose here is not to debate the "truth value" (Young and Goulet 1994:328) of religious or spiritual entities, not testable beyond the words and experiences of informants. Their experiences do not scientifically prove the independent objective reality of fairies, but lead us to understand the conditions under which such beliefs and experiences occur and to explore the religious and psychological concomitants thereof. Because I too came to "feel" fairy energy also demonstrates that conditions and preparations exist that also can lead the anthropologist to come to belief and conviction. But I recognize and accept the limits of traditional scientific investigation. (For further discussion of these issues see Greenwood 2009 and Harvey 2006, 2002.)

Beginning in Chapter Three I primarily present the words, experiences, and beliefs of fairyfolk rather than on the "Fairy Faith." This approach honors individuals and avoids a reified notion that could imply that there is a canon independent of individuals or that the Fairy Faith is an autonomous religion unconnected to the theism of Christianity (Judaism or Islam), rather than an elaboration of (Celtic) Christianity. I do not want to obfuscate the experiential, mystical dimension. As Harvey (1997: viii), I

> take seriously people's self-understanding and self-presentation…This is different to theology in which the focus of attention is a set of beliefs held by religious people, usually those who claim the authority to define what should be believed.

As a form of mysticism or experienced religiosity outside the realm of conventional theology, Fairy Faith is, and incorporates, a religious "other" (Knecht and Feuchter 2008).[16] It entails an expansion of conventional Western cosmology and theology, rather than a discarding of mainstream religion. The practitioners of the Fairy Faith thereby influence or transform both conventional Christianity as well as the conventional secular Fairy Faith, as the former for the most part did not consider fairies as real for anyone and the latter did not usually consider fairies as divine.[17] Combining fairy/nature spirits with Christianity, fairyfolk connect with God, historically associated with formal structures of religion, and with numinal beings (spirits), generally personally experienced and counterhegemonic (Levy, Mageo and Howard 1996).

One would be hard pressed to even call fairyfolk members of a "neo-tribe" (Maffesoli 1991; Bauman 1992), a temporary association, a sociality or group drawn together by collective identification to "perform that sense of belonging" to a group (Letcher 2004). At best the fairypeople and fairy conscious people discussed and quoted at length in the following chapters form some kind of amorphous "cell" or network of mystics. Some of them have found one another for occasional sociality and sharing of perspectives and experiences, rather than for a collective practice or experience of visions with other humans.

The nature and degree of mystical experience vary, and students of religion and mysticism have differentiated styles. William James (1902) wrote of a distinction between "sporadic" and "cultivated" mysticism, and similarly Arthur Deikman (1996) distinguishes between "untrained-sensate" and "trained-sensate." As the terms suggest, the former is more spontaneous, while the latter is disciplined. Generally speaking, as I have observed and discussed, fairyfolk have experiences of the first variety, although occasionally some individuals, fairyfolk like Jon, one of my major Irish informants discussed and quoted below, occasionally attempt to contact fairy energy in special areas in the wilds. Yet his and other fairyfolk's mysticism is not of the kind that one would associate, for example, with Sufi mystics or disciplined Yoga practitioners, whose routine often includes training and sustained, regular discipline.

Soderblom (1981) calls one form "mysticism of the infinite," in which an elevated awareness and ecstatic experience in unity with a divine entity remove perception of everyday sensory experience, and may entail trances or visions. This has also been called nature, theistic, monistic, or soul mysticism. The other form Soderblom calls "mysticism of personal life," in which a person in deep faith meets the divine entity in the middle of everyday life's normal consciousness, and could be called "mild." All these differentiations are not necessarily either/or distinctions. Most fairyfolk, as I have stated, have mild, usually untrained experiences or visions.[18] All fairyfolk, however, experience noesis, a deep conviction of knowing of the reality of fairies or fairy energy.

Husserl (1931) used the word "apodicticity" to refer to the sense of certainty in direct experience of any kind and when certainty comes from pure intuitive knowledge he called it "eidetic intuition."[19] I myself have never seen a fairy but, in occasional alternate states, I "feel" fairy presence or energy, a form of eidetic intuition. It is a kind of mild "high" of metaphysical connection with invisible being(s) or energy fields. That feeling and understanding incorporate a lightness, sanctity, otherworldliness, alliance, and contentedness, often as a mild smile crosses my face and my mind. It entails an attitude of less gravity or attachment to quotidian or corporeal concerns. From my own experiences and from spending considerable time with the individuals discussed below, their literal sighting and intuition of fairy presence have convinced me that for them the presence of fairies is real – authentic, that they are truly experiencing a spiritual reality, as humans everywhere are capable. As indicated earlier, their perception is a consequence of their biological capability which is manifested in specific ways and forms which the (sub)culture has in its repertoire. Simply put, for someone to call an entity a fairy means that they know the (English) word and some associated cultural expectations of meaning and experience.

But, again, the contemporary Fairy Faith I describe here is not a deliberately organized collective or leader-led organization, nor a "revitalization movement" (Wallace 1956). Movement refers to a social gathering, the social impetus, which is undeveloped here, as well as some definitive canon, formal or informal. And Wallace considers movements as "conceived in one or more hallucinatory visions by a single individual" (272). The Fairy Faith is not led by a single individual. Perhaps we can refer to the newer Fairy Faith here as a loose congeries of people who have "vitalization" or "revitalization" experiences. Divine fairy sensibility and experience is a (re)vitalization experience in that it 1) does re-invoke the historical Celtic reality of fairies 2) invokes the divinity of fairies, generally absent from the older common Fairy Faith, 3) vitalizes and re-vitalizes the individual in having life and spirit enhancing mystical experience and 4) re-vitalizes usually-forgotten childhood sensitivities and experiences of fairies (Chapter 3). These changes in the history of fairyology are similar to changes in other belief systems which emphasize, in different periods, different spiritual principles or entities, and differing functions of such entities.[20]

The newer Fairy Faith is one instance of many in history in which there are individual and sometimes collective changes in the organization or elaboration of the "tiers" of the cosmos. These changes and additions are ontic (ontological) shifts in individual awarenesses. The history of changing conceptions and experiences of spiritual entities over the ages, for example with angels (Garrett 2008), demonstrate that there can be a fluidity in the location of god-like beings or spirits in the geography of the cosmos, and changes in the very geography of the cosmos. Each person or group's "cartography"- mental map - of the cosmos may vary, even within established religious orientations. Knowing and experiencing Fairydom alters the "map", giving it more detail, just as Kabbalism does in its delineation of the emanations of God, or as Theosophy chronicles additional realms of the universe beyond Christian and Western convention. Once and when you come to know another etheric, astral, or spiritual plane or tier, you can then experience it, and perhaps even pay more attention to that plane than others. And in the new Fairy Faith, as informants below attest, awareness and experience of Fairydom may come unexpectedly as a revelation and thus "explode" or shift their previous mental map of the universe.

The fairyfolk below represent an elevation or change in the common emic classification of fairies from often troublesome, mischievous spirits to god-like beings. In Levy, Mageo, and Howard's (1996:14) terms, for fairyfolk here, fairies, rather than, or in addition to, being spirits, are also god-like beings. Fairyfolk believe and know, in contrast to most Irish of the past, of the Divinity of fairies and these divine beings are significantly present in their worldview and experience.

The existence of Fairydom, and fairy consciousness thereof, in its elaboration of the Godly in nature, simultaneously incorporates an ascension and a descension, an immanence and a transcendence. Fairydom is both earthly and heavenly. Fairydom as it manifests in nature on earth is but another divine realm of God's creation.

In this context of experiential, mystical experience, it becomes apparent that the word or idea of "faith" can be misleading. "Faith" implies the notion of personal belief as well as extra-personal institutionalization. (There is no formal institution, literally or figuratively, of the Fairy Faith, no "church" - see Chapter 15.) Moreover, as Goody (1996) suggests, faith implies at least some doubt, as otherwise a person would not need faith as something between conviction and doubt. Kay, one of my primary informants, states that the existence of fairies is a "fact" in the same sense that ordinary physical reality is a fact. Her and others' knowledge of the Fairy Realm is not a matter of faith reified, not a matter of conceptualized belief learned from others, but of inner, personal, received knowledge.

The fairyfolk of this ethnography did not walk around saying that they "believe" in fairies, but rather they spoke of their experiences and understandings concerning them. This accords with the recognition that "emphasis on personal declaration of belief in the tenets of a faith is not only not universal, but in fact is not widespread among other [non-Christian] faiths, particularly religions in small-scale homogeneous societies" (Stevens, Jr. 2011:32). And Glazier (2011), summarizing earlier work, quotes Smith (1998) who says belief statements are almost "impossible to refute" (32) and, when speaking of others' beliefs are "less precise" and, perhaps most importantly, "believing... is not and has never been a primary focus for most religious people" (34).[21]

In alignment with this perspective, Abraham Heschel (1959), one of the leading Jewish philosophers and theologians of the twentieth century, describes faith:

> Faith is not assent to a proposition but an attitude of the whole person, of sensitivity, understanding, engagement, and attachment. It includes faithfulness – loyalty to the higher moments of insight even during long periods of ordinary living. (17)

> The essence of Jewish religious thinking does not lie in entertaining a concept of God but in the ability to articulate a memory of moments of illumination by His presence. (70)

> Awe rather than faith is the cardinal attitude of the religious Jew.... In Biblical language the religious man is not called "believer," but *yere hashem* [the awe of God].(53)

Thus for Heschel faith is more a consequence of experience than belief. Replacing Heschel's words "Jewish" and "God" and "His" with "fairy," a particular manifestation of God, we understand that human fairyness is the ongoing awe-full presence of particular fairy experiences in the life of fairyfolk.

Thus Fairy Faith is more mysticism than religion. Yet Mullin's (1997) *The Wondrous Land*, a non-academic book, is subtitled *The Faery Faith in Ireland*. It uses the words "Fairy Faith," only, I suggest, because that phrase – The Fairy Faith - has been a historical convention, as was put forth in Evans-Wentz's own 1911 book title. Fairy sensibilities described below comprise "faith" only in the outsiders' sense that for the often skeptical, if not scoffing, non-experiencer of fairies, faith is a term which describes a mindset that the outsider would consider beyond verification. Thus "faith" in this case is not really emically descriptive: it does not describe the ontology or epistemology of fairyfolk who experience fairies, but of the outsider materialist scientist. This also epitomizes the problem that conventional religious authorities have with personal mystical experience and some mystical sects within larger organized religions, e.g., as with Gnostics within Christianity, Sufis within Islam, Kabbalists within Judaism, as the nature of their religious experience is primarily spiritual, i.e., individual, rather than coordinated through established human hierarchies.

The often overlapping concepts and language, sufficient or not, in discourses on belief, faith, and spiritual or religious experience can be elusive. Belief or experience can also be quite contextual or situational, dependent on a place, a time, a background, both in inception and reappearance. As the fairy sensibilities of my informants have sometimes waxed and waned, I too have lost a portion of my fairy sensibility, a lessening of the experience and frequency of experience of the intuiting, feeling, of the presence of fairy energy while in an alternate state of consciousness. This also includes (cognitively) remembering less, and paying less attention to, the very existence of the Fairy Faith. I have it less consciously in my thoughts and experience. This is salient for me in the context of being back in the US, back in scientistic academia, back in the modern, busy, technologically-oriented world. If you walk less in the woods or nature, then of course you have less opportunity to sense nature beings.

Various approaches and theories to the nature of religious or mystical experience exist, and more keep getting published.[22] Space here limits a thorough examination of the complexities of belief and experience, but it is not one to be avoided and some of the issues will be woven throughout this work through the words of fairyfolk and in my occasional analyses and cross-cultural comparisons. The existence and authenticity of fairy experience are central to both my informants' mode of being and to me in conducting and relating a participatory anthropology. I am most indebted in this regard to Rodney Needham's (1972) *Belief, Language, and Experience* in conceptualizing what "belief" is, and how I myself came to believe and experience Fairy.

For a long time in Celtic countries, and in Scandinavia, fairies and similar nature-spirit beings were commonly seen and heard about. But Western organized religion, scholarly discourse, and modernity – in their denigration of fairy belief as "folk religion", folklore, or superstition and technological/urban development - in its destruction of natural habitats and contemplative wild space - have diminished the number of people who accepted fairies as real.[23] Yet there are a good number of people, (often formally educated professionals) in Ireland, from whom I learned about Fairy Faith, who experience fairies. Ironically, or perhaps better said, synchronistically, it was happenstance, rather than intention, that led me to work with these people while I was doing a very different kind of research in Ireland. I fell into a kind of rabbit hole or web of Fairydom. Thus my approach was unintentionally participatory.[24] I did not decide to believe. This is in accordance with Needham's (1972) general perspective on belief that we do not decide to believe or actively change our minds. And transpersonal psychologist Washburn's (2000) recognition that "transpersonal cognition… is as much something that happens or is 'given' as it is something that can be achieved by steadfast effort" (207).

> We do say transitively that *we* change our minds, as though it were in our power to foresee a new idea. Yet all we know, and necessarily only in retrospect, is that we now entertain or express thoughts which are different from those that we were conscious of before. (Needham 1972: 241)

By exposure to new or different religious ideas or beliefs, as Laitman (2008:305) contends, others' ideas infiltrate our subconscious, even without intent, and thus may later reappear as our own ideas or beliefs with our conscious minds, unable to discern that the ideas are not really our own.[25]

As Needham suggests, there really is no objective foundation in the psyche's experience for belief statements.[26] And cross-cultural comparisons of the notions of belief indicate that "it is very difficult to separate what is properly experience from what is properly belief "(Levy-Bruhl 1938:10).

> The very notion of religious 'experience', in other words, is itself a singular and complex concept among others, not a neutral and undifferentiated background against which cultural concepts can be set up for inspection. (Needham 1972:172)

Somewhat similarly, Greenwood (2009), with an eye towards a participatory anthropology, makes a strong case for the legitimacy of various modes of knowledge and consciousness, and thus brackets or puts to the side the notion of belief or disbelief in investigating religion, so as to make room for a mode of magical (mystical) participation. Yet in the transpersonal anthropology and psychology put forth here, I would question Greenwood's conclusion that the question of the reality or non-reality of spirits "appears to be unreasonable," (141) that we should necessarily adopt an attitude of "spiritual agnosticism by not believing or disbelieving in their reality" (140). I think she says this because she is (understandably) concerned with a methodology that might satisfy rational materialists. It can be possible, as it was for me, the investigator, to be influenced by the environment and by others, especially as, when talking to and looking them in the eye, I felt and perceived the fairyfolk perspective and experience as deeply authentic. But the question is not whether there are those spirit beings in an "objective reality" outside people's minds, but whether the anthropologist can access a local alternate state of consciousness.

Greenwood does, nonetheless, concur more or less with Needham's, Glazier's (2011), Smith's (1998) and my own perspective that "belief" may not always be a helpful word describing religious experience.

> Whilst participating in a magical aspect of consciousness, the question of belief is irrelevant: belief is not a necessary condition to communicate with an inspirited world. (Greenwood 140)

is probably true from the insider's perspective and from the anthropologist's point of view. While it may be true that some humans on their own fantasize beings, I, like Young (1994) and some others, ascribe to the perspective of Young's Zen monk informant:

> ...many "spirits" are created by ourselves for one reason or another. There are many other spirits, however, over which we have no control. ... They are part of the natural world which has many levels, many of which are unavailable for experience by most people. Regardless of their nature, when they appear to us they *take a form which we can understand*. It is natural that an Indian might see an animal spirit, just as it is natural that a Buddhist might see a Buddhist saint, or a Christian an angel. (173) (my emphasis)

And, I should add … "natural that a Celtic Christian see a fairy." (Irish and Celtic connections to fairies are discussed in more detail in chapters Seven and Seventeen.) Although not common for members of conventional European religion, for this Zen monk, and, as he says, for others, the world of spirits is integrated with the world of humans.

This understanding that different individuals and cultures experience variations on central themes of spirits, gods, and mystical experience could be described as part of a perennial perspective. Like James' (1902) "stream of consciousness" and Wilber's (1998) "spectrum of consciousness," it posits a band along which specific mystical/religious concepts/experiences are cultural variations of a universal human spiritual/religious paradigm. If all peoples have religion, and as many have suggested, that every individual is capable of mystical experience (Forman 1998), and that there is an innate drive to seek transpersonal experience (Roszak 1975, de Chardin 1959, Weil 1972), then a starting point can be religious/mystical experience reported in ethnographic data *in situ* and *sui generis*. There need not be a psychological or sociological deconstruction of it. In this light I use anthropological, psychological, and occasionally theological discussions to support, in comparative context, the authenticity of the newer Fairy Faith which experiences fairy things as divine. I use comparison and social science as a forum not for deconstruction but for delineation and understanding of individuals' fairy experiences and perspectives, and for "walking between the worlds" of researcher and native other (Neitz 2002).

The overall purpose or perspective can then become an examination of the particular as an example of the various styles or contents that generally make up religious and mystical experience, potentially finding some cultural commonalities and variations. We may then be able to describe those commonalities and differences, rather than look for veracity in any particular religiosity. This would be an attempt towards a kind of perennial anthropology of religion, such as a perennialist approach to mysticism (Nelstrop 2009), able to incorporate myriad religious and mystical experiences.

Psychoanalyst Kakar (1991:5), who could be called "transpersonal," describes this orientation:

> In other words, my own enhanced feeling of *adequatio* [adequateness] reflects the presence of an unstated project in contemporary psychoanalysis in which the co-presence of different orders of experience is tolerated and no attempts are undertaken to explain in terms of the other without reciprocity.

Fairyfolk connect with spirits and spiritual energies which for them also exist outside the individual's imaginative ability to experience them. I use imagination here in the Jungian sense of the ability of the mind to get outside of itself and connect with, and interact with, entities, (collective) consciousness, or forces which exist outside the self, but which are amenable to incorporating into the Self. Jung's concept of "active imagination" is a process through which the ego encounters the unconscious in a waking state. Belief in and/or experience of normally not visible entities outside the self rests on the "Imagination," the ability to intuit, even synaesthetically (Abram1996) apprehend. For fairyfolk it is logical to say that fairies exist not just in the language of "mythos" (Greenwood 2009:76), but phenomenologically in the language of "logos." Thus I, and these fairyfolk, subscribe to what Stephen (1989) calls the "autonomous imagination," which Hume (2007:149) says is

> based on the assumption that a phenomenological world exists independently of the human mind, and that the complexity of such a world is described, interpreted and ordered in different ways by different cultures.

Moreover, as in true mystical tradition, Fairy connection, unlike most New Age practices and perspectives, incorporates a struggle in personal psycho-spiritual growth. That includes, while on the transformational spiritual path, facing and transforming psychological shadows (see Zweig and Abrams 1991), sometimes with experiences of suffering.

The recent rise of "transpersonal" anthropology, (e.g., Campbell 1976; Campbell and Staniford 1978; MacDonald 1981; Laughlin, McManus and Shearer 1983; Young and Goulet 1994; Laughlin 1994; Winkelman 1990, 1993; Sheppard 2006, 2007) follows on the heels of a popular recognition of transpersonal psychology, often traced back to William James, made particularly evident by Abraham Maslow, Carl Jung, James Hillman, and Ken Wilber.[27] These Western psychologies and anthropologies examine individual experiences as they connect to wider spiritual realities/forces with the aid of the imagination in the Jungian sense. Jungian analyst Bernstein (2005) has come to identify Western individuals with affective, spiritual alignments with nature or nature spirits as "borderland personalities." He suggests that these individuals have in part evolved out of the ratio-centric and cogni-centric qualities of the Western ego and have come to have "transrational" connections with nature, akin to indigenous peoples' identification with nature. [28] The evolution, he suggests, into this transrational orientation, is a consequence of the emergence of (Jung's) "collective unconscious," engaged in an identification with nature, what Levy-Bruhl (1926) termed a "participation mystique."

Humanist anthropologist E. Turner (2012) summarizes a recent perspective in which anthropologists "freeing much of the discipline from its tight positivism" write empathetically about religious experience. This kind of work looks "kindly, not critically, at the sincerity behind the religious experiences of those we study." (7) *Running with the Fairies* could be conceptualized as being a study of one form of communitas, for, as Turner describes it, in addition to a feeling of joyful unity with other persons, communitas can be a felt unity, a communing, with a spiritual being. In the chapter "The Communitas of Nature" she suggests that we "try out the thought that the spirits outside our selves are part of the world, open to anthropology, and also, therefore, are part of nature" (143). Thus later she quotes anthropologist Willis' (1999:120) curing ritual experience among the African Lungu in which he 'discovered that the state of *communitas* provides access to those transpersonal entities or forces commonly called "spirits."' (220, italics original)

Transpersonal anthropology is much concerned with altered states of consciousness and shamanism. As indicated earlier, Sheppard's (2007) critique that too much transpersonal anthropological attention is paid to shamanism is especially apposite here as fairyfolk are not, nor do they act like, shamans. They are not socially recognized trained healers, spirit masters, or spirit journeymen or women who have had near-death experiences (Jakobsen 1999). Nor do they engage in much ritual in working up to a trance or altered state. We could say that fairyfolk enter altered states of consciousness, but perhaps it is better to say *alternate* states as Laughlin, McManus, and Shearer (1983) suggest. "Altered" often infers the use of external agents such as entheogens and/or specific, if not elaborate, practices such as drumming, fasting, etc to "open doorways" to other realities or lifeworlds (Hume 2007). Nor is experience with fairies like spirit possession or mediumship. Perhaps fairy experience can be seen as shamanic only in that there is contact with the ordinarily invisible world, but shamans are manipulators of spirit entities, while fairyfolk can not direct fairies to do things. Fairyfolk "simply" have contact with these forms of divinity, intermediaries of God, and that is something that any theist potentially can have.

As Greenwood (2009) calls for a participatory anthropology of religious and mystical experience so does transpersonal psychologist Ferrer (2000). The latter calls for both the scholar's full participation and for conceptualizing mystical phenomena as a result not just of inner spiritual experience but also of phenomena outside the self. The self itself is a subject of study (e.g., Rouner 1992) and is sometimes conceptualized as a Higher Self, an aspect of self which brings in the divine. This arena of study begins with the individual's perspective or consciousness.

An effect of Fairydom is its incorporation into a person's psyche of (another) usually invisible, divine layer of the cosmos. (Jungian Bernstein (2005) might describe it as the manifesting of the collective unconscious.) In understanding one's self, and the Self, there are then internal dialogues in relation to that Fairy tier, and a psychology of identity and development - individuation in Jungian terms – which entail an additional set of relationships. Discourse thus needs to include some kind of dialogue with the self, dialogue/contact with fairies and the Fairy Kingdom, dialogue with God, and dialogue with others who experience Fairyness. Fairydom expands psychology, as does transpersonal psychology in general, to include a kind of sacred science or social psychology of interacting persons, numinal beings, and God. The fairyfolk speak of their notions and experiences of these kinds of dialogues in the chapters to follow.

What is also interesting and stimulating to me is that only after my initial fieldwork in Ireland beginning in 2000, which was not concerned with the subjects of this book, and for several years after, and after I wrote a first draft of this book, did I come to realize that more or less simultaneously and in parallel there had come to be an academic movement for participatory anthropology (Greenwood 2009), as well as a subfield "transpersonal anthropology." My own fairy sensibility, empathy and sympathy, attained after much contact and experience with fairyfolk and with an alternate state of consciousness, was stronger than I even knew when I was greatly saddened when Kay said fairies temporarily had stopped reincarnating as human beings (discussed in more detail below). (Such a halt occurs as a consequence of human insensitivity to nature and to divine realms, as is manifest in the browning of fields of the earth, the general browning of human consciousness in its domination over nature. Fairy consciousness is also green consciousness, depth ecology. (For more on this see Chapter Four.)

That "fairy sensibility" entails, as Chapters Three, Four, and Five indicate, a theistic worldview with a Creator, a strong attachment to nature, a lightness and openness of attitude, and mystical intuition which recognizes the appearance of fairy traits, outlined in more detail in Chapter Two. Changes in worldview occur, as many suggest, as a consequence of an emotional readiness often brought on by a recent emotional change or upheaval which loosens the steadfastness of a previous worldview. In my own case, prior to the fieldwork I underwent a divorce, moved to a new residence, changed many of my daily activities, and took on an added openness to travel and research. I experienced a freedom from and cessation of contact with entrenched perspectives and the scrutiny of others, and developed an enhanced interest in personal growth. Really, only in retrospect, do I now understand that those conditions provided an emotional and motivational background which must have aided the modification of my own cosmology. This kind of change has been labeled "interpretive drift" (Luhrmann 1989). And as Robbins (2009:141) summarizes: "the history of anthropological fieldwork is full of instances of the researcher being drawn into the beliefs of the people he or she is studying." And studies of religious conversion (Buckser and Glazier, eds. 2003) indicate that "shifts in belief at the heart ... of conversions [to Christian Spiritualism] are often sparked long before eventual converts come to Spiritualism." And as Glazier (2003:149) points out, conversion, in contrast to the general Western tradition "often understood as a dramatic and solitary process like St. Paul's experience on the Road to Damascus," can be "seen not so much as a leap of faith as a series of baby steps." Or as Rambo (1993:165) suggests, that while conversion can be triggered by particular events, "for the most part it takes place over a period of time."

The themes and purposes of this book are a) to elevate fairyology to a respected branch of the anthropology of religion and of religious studies, b) to promote an expansive anthropology of religion to include a fuller consideration of spirits and god-like beings in European and American religion and spirituality, c) to promote a participatory anthropology in which anthropologists and other students of religion need not be, or posture themselves as, atheistic or agnostic - not to simply suspend disbelief, but to actively participate in native views and experience, d) to demonstrate that some of the features of fairy mystical experience, historically relegated to indigenous "others," are part of Western experience, e) to explore the relationship between the anthropology of religion and the transpersonal psychology of religion, and f) to explore relationships between belief and knowledge in discourse on religiosity, spirituality, and mysticism.

In addition to locating this ethnography in the academic anthropology and psychology of religion, in several chapters of the book I primarily let people speak for themselves. This is done in an attempt to refrain from over-analysis and codifying what are, after all is said and done, direct personal and transpersonal experiences. Thus my approach is one of phenomenology, in that "it emphasizes the importance of an empathetic approach to other cultures and the need to walk in the moccasins of the faithful .... looking at religious phenomena from the viewpoint of the people themselves," but without the usual "neutral standpoint" (Morris 2006:6). Despite the pages to follow, I remain ambivalent about the extent to which one can talk about what are essentially ineffable things.

Kakar (1991:x), speaking about his writing, portrays my own attitude:

> if my endeavor.....brings the mystic down from the level of "divine" to that of human, I console myself with the thought that it may also help in raising the rest of us by making us more aware of our own sensuous and psychic potentials.

Although I do not want to exaggerate the importance of Fairy Faith in the lives of fairyfolk so as to imply that religion "is described as forming the basis for almost everything that humans do or think" (Morris 2006:11) or that it is "very much and always with us ... at every moment of life" (Idowu 1973:1), it is clear that fairy experience is fundamental to the people in this book in their worldview and after-worldview. Moreover, we must not construe the uninstitutionalized nature of fairyfolk experiences or their existence alongside other religious experience or belief as indicative of the Fairy Faith somehow being tangential to the lives of these mystics.

There is an unobservable-by-others, ethereal quality to fairy sensibilities and experience, as there are no set rituals of practice or dress. In this regard, this is like many spiritual mindsets and interactions with generally unseen gods, beings, or forces. Yet the mystical Fairy Faith adherents' understandings of themselves, the local world, and the wider universe are fundamentally entwined with fairies/nature spirits. Relationships with entities inform and guide many of their everyday choices. These include choices of companions, interacting with likeminded persons, eating natural and organic foods, living in settings close to nature, and reflecting and dialoguing about the metaphysical and its relation to their own and others' lives. Alongside emotional receptivity, these kinds of personal backgrounds and ongoing perspectives and activities provide a preparatory stance amenable to mystical experiences of this kind.

Fairyfolk's ontological and epistemological positions in the world are mystically entwined in fairy presence, seen or unseen. The truly "fairy way" provides them with a greater understanding of purpose in this lifetime, both as an individual and as a member of the collective. It also grounds them in an enlarged understanding of life, death, and reincarnation. It operationalizes their understanding that God and God's divine creations are close at hand. It is paramount to fairyfolk to improve the physical and social conditions of the planet, to improve the lives of others, and to engage in their own psycho-spiritual development. And contrary to most other modern persons' essential grounding in advanced technology, fairy sensibility grounds one in Nature. And this all incorporates a political and environmental philosophy that is perhaps best described as a mystical style of deep or depth ecology (Naess 1973). Very far from being a recreational hobby or something exterior or incidental to the person, the mystical Fairy Faith fundamentally defines who fairyfolk are.

This spirituality and spiritual psychology contrasts with the context of a world filled, on the one hand, with doctrinaire, institutionalized, or fundamentalist religion, and, on the other, secular humanistic psychological talk therapy or self-help paths. The mystical Fairy Faith, in its mild-mannered ways, provides an avenue for both psycho-spiritual development and a unique, increased attachment to God and Nature. Its lightness of being, its translucence like conventional romanticized fairy wings, should not be construed as less than quite serious. In dissolving the veils between the world of Spirit and the world of human beings, and in dissolving, as Eckhart Tolle (1999) terms it, the "pain body," an essential Oneness is discovered and expanded upon, uniting the self with its Self, with other humans, spiritual entities, God, and Creation. It is through this light, this lightness, ethereality emerges as a force for peace and environmental sustainability. It operates in the personal daily consciousness of individuals and in their working with others in informal settings, and, ultimately, helping to repair a wounded world.

Chapter Two

Overview

> Millions of spiritual creatures walk the earth Unseen, both when we wake and when we sleep.
> —Paradise Lost

Experiences of revelation and interchange with divine beings of various kinds are classical expressions of mystical experience. As noted above, one also finds real world experiences of nature beings such as fairies, sometimes considered to be divine, among small scale Native peoples, Hinduism and Buddhism, and in mystical sects of Islam, Judaism, and Christianity. These intermediaries between humans and the high god(s) populate the ethereal (or etheric) world, part of the "geography" of the cosmos. Not gods themselves, fairies, angels, *peri*s, *dakini*s, others mentioned in Chapter One, and numerous other ethereal beings are messengers, representatives, embodiments, partial manifestations, or aspects of God, the Creator, or the Source.[1] In everyday affairs these divine inhabitants of the in-between worlds are most often invisible to the human eye.

These spirit or elemental beings can, at times, manifest as observable to human vision and/or as sensorily perceptible to the mind and heart. They manifest at different geographic, cultural, and vibrational locations on the planet. Depending on the particular philosophy or ontology - understanding of the nature of reality - peoples know that these sometimes-embodied spirits can be benevolent and/or malevolent. In some cosmologies a god need not (always) be or do good, and can vacillate between being or doing good and bad. In societies where the high God, or the gods, are thought of as only benevolent, as in the monotheistic religions of the West, nature spirits like fairies which are often bad (or sometimes good) have traditionally been separate from Divinity and are not deemed divine intermediaries or representatives.

Whether they are good or evil, light or dark, is linked to the kind of morality anthropocentrically ascribed to the God or forces of the universe, as well as how the geographies of the cosmos and their inhabitants are constructed.² For example, in Christianity "regular" angels are good, but Satan is an "irregular" angel who fell from on high to a lower part of the Christian cosmos "below" the earth. Some people who liken fairies to angels, good and bad, have considered fairies to be fallen angels, (see Chapters 6 and 7), but they did not fall as far "down" as Satan, only to earth. In traditional Celtic thinking since fairies do not live in or travel to God's heaven, nor represent or provide messages from God, they can be good and bad. And fairies are generally more embodied of the earthly and elemental realms – of the spirit of air, fire, water, or earth - and are more connected to the everyday concerns of human beings.³

Also, for the overwhelming majority of Westerners ethereal spirit-beings (good and/or bad) are usually conceptualized as only mythological, symbolic, metaphorical, not-real entities, with the possible exception of angels. Thus to modern Westerners, secular or religious, fairies are only mythological, beings of fantasy for children and adults. But the experiences and understandings of the fairyfolk in this book are not part of a mythology. I have spoken with many people in Ireland (and elsewhere) for whom fairies truly exist. They are fully real. This is not a book for children, or adults, who think fairies are "cute," made-up recreational creatures. This is not a book about fantasy, but about some persons' spiritual realities.

But because fairies, commonly, historically, were usually considered mischievous or malevolent, they were seen, literally or figuratively, as part of the cosmos separate from God and did not reflect, literally or figuratively, the light of God. Therefore, in contrast to good angels in Christianity, (although some angels rebel against God), fairies classically have not been an avenue for connecting with and pursuing the sacred, or as part of the path to spiritual awakening or transformation. Transformation, defined and pursued in varying ways, especially for the devout, is the goal of spiritual/religious practice. Thus historically in the Celtic lands the often harmful fairies, although real beings from another plane, were to be avoided, rather than invoked as part of the spiritual quest. However, for a few mystics in the past, and for an increasing number of people in the new Fairy Faith, there is a significant difference in the understanding and experience of fairies, of God, and the make-up of the universe. They not only know that fairies exist, but also welcome them as luminous, divine beings. These humans who seek connection and alignment with these nature spirits of Creation are what I call *fairyfolk*.

This connection happens in encounters with the visible beings and from the physical results of their presence as in a whirlwind of leaves or the movement of objects. Or it happens in a human's intuitive recognition of an invisible, spiritual field or aura of influence, divinity, lightness, and upliftedness, which can manifest as a kind of lightheadedness. The mystical experience of interacting with visible fairies or sensing their fairy energy has brought forth realizations, (re)awakenings, and attunements to divine purpose and goodness. Since divinity, or parts thereof, can reside in more than one or two realms or consciousnesses, the Fairy Realm being one of them, fairyfolk understand that fairies are part of a wider, vast set of God's/ the Universe's sacred realms. And once one enters the doors to another realm, the possibility arises that there are more doors to be opened. This shift into realizing that there are multiple domains or planes of existence of Creation is an ontic shift, an expansion of the monotheistic Western paradigm held about the constitution of the universe.

As Kay the fairyperson harp player puts it:

> There certainly are other beings of other dimensions, other than fairies. And there are fairies in other cultures, like the *dakinis* of Tibetan culture. There are all kinds of jump-out-of-time experiences in different cultures.

Anthropologist E. Turner (2009), from her own experiences, distinguishes between a "spirit manifestation" and sensed "energy." Fairies are spirit manifestations, vehicles of wider, higher consciousness and divine connection. Turner describes sensed energy as "very like electrical energy" (313).[4] For me, and for others below, fairy energy is a vigor, an undulation, a pulsation of light from outside the ego, from the higher Self which incorporates the divine.

What is thought to be real, of course, can vary from individual to individual, from religion to religion, from mystical sect to mystical sect, derived from varying perceptions and understandings. The relativity of "reality" is a consequence of personal psychology and experience embedded in wider cultural expectations. But a fundamental tenet and experience of mystics such as fairyfolk is that there is more to know and experience of the Realms and creations of God than what is generally held in mainstream religious circles. Among some groups, this kind of opening, and search for gateways to "the other side," "beyond the veil," is part of spiritual realization, growth, and transformation. This is already so in the West, for example, among Kabbalists, who know that God's aspects or realities are multiple, tenfold at least. Seeker-practitioners attempt to experience the varying metaphysical "parts" of God. Spiritual unfolding within differing religious perspectives often necessitates divine guides and intermediaries who oscillate between the realms of the physical and of the spiritual. They lead humans to awe, to mystery, to transformation. In

Ireland the mystic *fairyfolk* of the newer variety recognize fairies and fairy energy as helpers and manifesters of God, of Spirit.

This book is about fairyfolk in Ireland who believe in and know of the reality of fairies, and other nature spirits. Their understandings have yet to be (re)incorporated into conventional or received wisdoms in the West. Furthermore, and significantly, some of these fairyfolk, what I and some Irish locals call *fairypeople*, humbly know - hold convictions - that they themselves are literally descended from the Fairy Realm through reincarnation.

This last understanding of human embodiment of and/or descent from a celestial realm is not unusual in the history of some religions or individualized spiritualities. In Hinduism there are avatars, in Buddhism there are buddhas and bodhisattvas, in indigenous systems shamans and medicine men, in Christianity saints and prophets, in Judaism prophets, in Kabbalism living souls, and in Theosophy adepts, chelas, and ascended masters. All these are living or deceased persons who have been liberated, chosen, blessed into having special access to divine realms. They have abilities to attune with spiritual energies through personal inquiry, sometimes through divine resurrection or reincarnation. Their task is often not easy, and their spiritual transformations from ordinary human beings into partly divine entities often include emotional and psychic pain and disorientation before substantial alignment with Spirit. (See Chapters Thirteen and Fourteen)

In some systems each person has the inherent ability to go beyond ordinary consciousness and attain an advanced spiritual state, as in Buddhism and Yoga philosophy. The holy person may only be enacting the possible, and in that sense s/he is like all other humans, and should be modest. They are merely channels to the beyond. Such human beings, such as saints, often represent for others the very paths and goals of religious or spiritual attainment.

In the pages to follow *fairyminded* or fairy conscious individuals, fairyfolk, including *fairypeople,* speak up of their ideas and experiences of realizing, working through, and mastering the journey of life. *Fairypeople,* or fairypersons, are a special kind of fairyfolk. They understand themselves and are understood by other fairyfolk as having themselves been fairy beings in previous lifetimes, now reincarnated as human beings. All the fairyfolk increasingly come to understand the relationship between the human and the divine, the human and the fairy, and realize that fairies are conduits of higher consciousness or energy. Some of them gently speak of their experiences and perspectives. I relate most of them in their own words, from extensive transcribed discussions and interviews.

The people who inhabit this book are all very alive. Through them we can for the first time receive an intimate portrait of the Fairy Faith as an ongoing spiritual journey. They became my friends and acquaintances during what could be called my fieldwork apprenticeship over many months and years in Ireland. (See Chapter Five.) The main characters, among others, who, in the course of reading, you may come to resonate with, are:

Kay – A spry, petite, sylph-like person, harpist, gardener and PhD clinical psychologist. Former Californian now in her seventies. Author of *The Wondrous Land: The Faery Faith in Ireland.*

Jon – an Irish fairyman and mystagogue, writer, workshop leader, former professor of psychology and philosophy, who left his academic position to concentrate on his and others' spiritual development and teaching.

Carol – Irishwoman, accomplished fairy artist, natural historian, and informal tour guide to fairy sites in County Donegal.

Marita – Irishwoman, poet, nature being, Jungian psychotherapist who sometimes invokes attunement with fairies in her clinical practice.

Minette – Irishwoman, musician and song writer. Living rurally in house not too far from "FairyLands", an area of fields, rocks, and trees she visits.

Marc – English writer, workshop facilitator, fringe theatre director and channel. Author of *Earth Will Be Reborn.*

Val – English illustrator, teacher, and aromatherapist. Partner of Marc and co-author of *Earth Will Be Reborn.*

Dennis – myself, interviewer, American ethnographer, professor of anthropology, ecologist and amateur naturalist.

These people mostly know each other or of each other. Kay has been a central person in this informal social network. She calls herself the "Fairy at RiverRun," but is often termed by others, never herself, as "Queen of the Fairies." These people have never all met together as one group, but sometimes visit, speak, or write one another, but not on any regular schedule. Each of them is strongly attuned to the Fairy Realm. Kay the harpist, Jon the former professor, Carol the fairy artist, and Marita the psychotherapist are also fairypeople, knowing that they descended from the Fairy Realm across planes of existence. There are other fairyfolk in Ireland, including Lorraine, Liz, Bob, Denis and a few others, who briefly appear below, and others whom I did not meet.[5] There are many others scattered around Ireland, Europe and elsewhere. The very informal networks are slowly growing. But fairy understandings and orientations are not dependent on being a member of a group or congregation, but in having one's own individual mystic awareness and experience, sometimes shared with others.

In the course of this book, primarily in their own voices, I trace contemporary individuals' fairy connections in the contexts of psychology, mysticism, my own fieldwork, and others' writings about fairies. After this chapter's discussion of "What are Fairies," I detail some of my primary informants' childhood and adult sometimes epiphany-like experiences of awakening to and connecting with fairies and fairyness. Chapter Three also briefly considers some theory concerning childhood imagination and cognition. Chapter Four describes attitudes and orientations – a style of being – associated with openness to connection with fairy phenomena. This includes a lightness of spirit, of attitude, and of emotion and significant resonance with the natural world of plants, animals, and landscape. The last part of the chapter describes my experience with three fairyfolk who, rather than avoid fairy contact, which was generally the Irish approach to fairies of the past, sought fairy presence in a large uncultivated field called 'FairyLands.' Chapter Five elaborates on the fieldwork experience, my personal orientation, and my own shift in consciousness. Chapter Six documents previous writings and histories about fairies and the Fairy Faith, which leads into the next chapter's more detailed description of the newer fairy consciousness which knows fairies as good, divine beings. Moving onto spiritual understandings and practice, in Chapters Eight and Nine we describe what fairyman Jon, former professor, calls the "unconceptual", the intuitive, non-rational, heart-centered modus operandi for metaphysical alignment with the Fairy Realm. That is a state of awareness/non-awareness which other cultural and religious groups sometimes invoke as the altered state to be attained through forms of prayer, meditation, chanting, ecstatic dance, fasting, and protracted rites of passage. Reincarnation in Fairy Faith cosmology, sometimes reincarnation across planes of existence, back and forth between human and Fairy Worlds, is examined in Chapter Ten. All part of a much larger picture, Chapter Eleven discusses the mission or purpose of fairies and fairyminded humans.

This leads to the experiences and realizations that fairyfolk receive, and the kinds of physical, emotional, and mental traits that predispose or follow from being attuned to fairy energy. Discussions ensue about the effect of fairy connection on people's own mental well-being and the healing dimension of that connection, the process of individual transformation, fairyfolk's connections with one another, Ireland and the artistic sensibilities of fairyfolk , and ultimately the role of the Fairy Faith in the evolution of consciousness and the unfolding of the future. Throughout the work, by way of described experiences and journal extracts, I briefly chronicle my own increasing resonance with the Fairy Realm and fairyfolk.

The issue of authenticity of belief, of person, is quite intriguing, especially in the arena of religion or spirituality. Some theorists exhort that we often believe in God, for example, because we are afraid of the possible consequences of not believing. My explorations into the Fairy Faith, and my friendships with the fairyminded and fairypeople, illuminated the notion of authenticity for me. I have been struck by these people who have well-developed faith and knowledge of divinity. As we proceed, to minimize interpretive academic "translations," the book at times contains the lengthy relaying of exact words and verbatim interviews and conversations. I feel that their own words and experiences speak the loudest.

Rabbi J. Steinberg, author of *The Unlikely Nature of God,* argues that spiritual and human progress can be measured by how enveloped humans are in the various consciousnesses or realms of the divine, (in traditional Kabbalist terms the ten Sefirot of God). In Indian Vedic philosophy one can strive to move to and through *samadhi*. Jon, the ex-professor fairyman calls these various realms "frequencies."

In psycho-spiritual terms, people who resonate with the various frequencies are resonating with different expressions of what Jungians and others might term the elaboration of the transpersonal, and with what Ken Wilber (1998) calls different bands within the spectrum of consciousness.

For the sake of clarity, I repeat. *Fairyfolk* are either a) fairy-conscious, fairy-minded individuals who know that fairies really exist and have seen or felt, intuited the presence of fairy beings or energy or b) *fairypeople,* in addition to knowing the reality of fairies "on the other side," know that they themselves were fairies "on the other side" in a previous incarnation.

Carol, the fairy artist, calls fairypeople like herself "earthbound fairies." (As my informants say, some fairypeople are not aware of having been reincarnated as humans or even of their own fairy energy.) The Fairy Faith notion of reincarnation, ordinarily an Eastern concept, demands attention and is explored, as mentioned, in Chapter Ten.

Fairy-conscious (or fairyminded) people, although not descended from the Fairy Realm, identify well with fairypeople about fairy things. As we will see below, fairy-conscious Bob and Lorraine, although not fairypeople, well recognized in Kay (and others) her reincarnated descent from the Fairy Kingdom. All these people's understandings of the reality of fairies and fairypeople is important to their own mystical spirituality and their interaction with the earth, and beyond.

Colloquially, in Ireland, fairyfolk, but especially fairypeople, are sometimes simply called "fairies," ordinarily a term reserved for non-human beings who have the power to become visible and invisible to humans. Thus a "fairy" in common usage may also refer to a human who has strong connections with the Fairy Realm. In Ireland's past the people who interacted with fairies and fairy things were also said to be "running with the fairies".

The word "fairy" is also used as an adjective to describe lightly magical, fairyish, fairy-related, fairy-like, fey, enchanted, sometimes amusing things, behavior, or places. Fairy as an adjective is somewhat unspecific or elusive. It is mostly used by people with an understanding of or sensibility to fairy traits, a recognition that really only comes with experience. (Recognition is re-cognition, which generally demands knowledge or familiarity with something.) Fairyness or fairy-like qualities of humans are also fluid and vary in degree. In a discussion of being a shaman and shamanistic Campbell (2003:134) describes this kind of variability: "Thinking in terms of a quality allows thinking in terms of degrees – something or someone can have a lot of it, or a little of it, can have it for some time and then lose it again." For a human being "fairy" is an evolving quality, a way of looking at the world, a way of experiencing and understanding.

A fairy or fairyish place is one that has a kind of light aura about it: it stands out as a location where a fairy visited or might visit, a very natural place of beauty or glamour with an untrammeled-by-humans character. It could possibly be a very organic, enchanted building inspired by a fairy or fairy conscious person.

Williams (1991:471), a folklorist who systematically studied the historical uses of the word "fairy" in its various forms, concludes:

From the earliest date fairy seems to be used both as a typification of experience (i.e., denotationally or referentially, applied to a real experience) and as a metaphor for experience (i.e., associatively, connotatively) meshing both kinds of meaning, as can be seen from the unclear etymology.

Significantly, *one does not have to have seen or communicated directly with fairies to recognize the presence of fairies.* I am a case in point. I have not seen a fairy, but, in an acquired occasional, brief alternate state, under the right mental and environmental conditions, I intuit, sense, their energies.

Fairy energy is light and near. In Western monotheism God is usually conceptualized as All-seeing and All-knowing and thus God's purview and energy are more complex, more encompassing, more dominating. Fairy energy has less graveness and less *gravitas*. Fairies and fairy energies are more like fleeting companions on a human-like scale, part of a friendly community, actors or essences sometimes on the stage with humans. Unlike fairies the western all-knowing one God is not an actor in the playing out of the universe, not a character in Her/His own play. Some people use the capitalized word Fairy (or Faerie) to indicate a whole realm of beings such as fairies, elves, and other kinds of nature spirits, and their energies. My informants say that the many who doubt or scoff at the existence of such a realm(s) have grown up among perspectives and forces that hinder ability to connect with the Fairy World. Such conditions hinder access to the mental state or alternative consciousness fairyfolk experience. Materialism, egoism, strict monotheism, and the hierarchical church often overshadow the possibility of this kind of spiritual understanding. And, in North America the atmosphere, literally and figuratively, does not substantially allow for the mystical spiritual experience of alignment with the Fairy Realm. Kay and others say that the cosmic geography of the various worlds is constructed in such a fashion that fairies and fairy consciousness arise primarily in Ireland and the Celtic lands. The veils, the membranes between the Fairy World and the human world, are thinnest there, where there is more porosity between the physical body, the mind, and spiritual energies and beings. (See Chapter Sixteen.)

For Celtic peoples nature was not matter, but rather it was a luminous and numinous presence which had depth, beauty, and possibility. Many an Irish author has described the Celtic Christian approach to nature and landscape as one in which there was no real divide between this world and the "other" world of divine and spiritual beings. John O'Donohue (1997), noted author of the international bestseller *Anam Cara: Spiritual Wisdom from the Celtic World* proclaimed: "The Celtic eye has a great sense of that interim world between the invisible and visible" and "In the Celtic world… there was a wonderful sense of how the visible and invisible moved in and out of each other."

What are Fairies?

Rojcewicz (1991:503-4) summarizes ancient, classic Western notions of "daemones" and fairy-like experiences:

> In Hellenistic times an anomaly like a strange aerial display or confrontation with one's "daemon," did not mean a violation of natural law, but its reverse. Anomalies and synchronicities established the fundamental order of nature and history, and were a "sign" of some overall design in reality. They were "portents" and "messages" from nature (i.e., the gods) and were not so interesting in themselves as for what they portended for the future.

Among fairyfolk today there is a recognition of fairies as intermediaries of God to help and guide individuals to understand themselves and the earth around them. All my informants asserted that fairies have some powers over human affairs and phenomena of nature, and are often thought to be producers of bountiful harvests. Some fairyfolk and others think or know that human ideas and activities are often (invisibly and unknown to the humans) prompted or directed by fairies. These numinal beings are akin to guardian spirits, nature fertility (demi)gods, spirit allies, or vitalizing, metaphysical life forces.[6] They often give or help develop wisdom in humans, although the specific functions of fairies historically often have varied from region to region or person to person. Winkelman (2004) suggests that spirit experiences are "natural" to humans.[7]

Fairies are luminary beings that have a sidereal quality, often having a misty or foggy physical presence. They often assume discernible forms of luminous, glowing light and possess "quasi-physical natures that challenge common sense wisdom. Because of their subtle malleable bodies, fairies are extremely protean. They pass effortlessly through material objects and instantly dematerialize" (Rojcewicz 1991:485).[8]

Fairyfolk generally consider fairies to be "below" the angels and are of the spirit of earthly things and close to humans' daily concerns. Fairies range from light, airy celestial beings to heavier, earthier entities. But among the fairy conscious there is no fully shared understanding for exactly describing, defining, or classifying fairies or other elemental entities. Many have suggested that exact knowledge of the make-up and nature of the non-human realms is not possible for mortals. As transpersonal anthropologist Laughlin (1994a:117) declares, the certainty that direct experience during transpersonal or contemplative experience gives, the apodicticity, "does *not* require categorical "crispness."[9] Difficulty in categorizing fairies is also a consequence of their own ability to allow us to see only what they want us to see, an ability that in the past has been called fairy "glamour" or "pishogue." Several people I interviewed had various perspectives on beings which inhabit the Fairy Realm, differences between fairies, elves, gnomes, and nature spirits in general. Some people think elves are fairies, whereas others think elves are not fairies. The word fairy is often used to invoke the panoply of invisible nature spirit beings of Celtic and European traditions. Today, among fairyfolk there are a variety of elemental kingdoms, one of which is the Fairy Kingdom. Kay was informed by her channel that there are about twenty elemental kingdoms, of which fairies comprise one.[10] Kay is not sure if different types of fairies include one whole kingdom or whether the air fairies – the sylphs – are a kingdom unto themselves. Like many others', her breakdown of the Fairy World is more or less fourfold, based on the anciently conceived four elements of air, water, earth, and fire, the elemental worlds of Paracelsus and others afterwards. (See Chapter Six.) [11]

Kay relates:

> I use the word fairy for the whole elemental kingdom. But specifically it is a word for air fairies and sylphs, when I am talking about my own particular group. The earth fairies are generally square and solid and relate to the earth. But it is confusing how I and others use the word 'fairies.' But I don't know how to get out of it. So if I say elementals, I mean fairies. When I say fairies I sometimes mean air fairies, and sometimes mean the whole group.

Fundamentally, this lack of crispness is of little consequence to the matter at hand. Who has what specific understanding does not matter much, for we need not get too attached to definitions or exactitude. As many spiritual teachers have said, rigidity and identification with form or dogma can hinder greater awareness. As anthropologist of religion Lambek (1996:242) points out:

> In training our own sights on spirits we have to ensure that our apparatus is not too powerful, overexposing its subjects.....
>
> These margins of the cultural world are not just beliefs in unruly forces, but unruly beliefs in such forces. Anthropology has tended to focus on that which is most systematic or most elaborated, hence to provide the

most elegant analysis or fullest reading. But the unsystematized is not necessarily unimportant, either for the locals or for refining our own theoretical understanding of religion and culture. Indeed, this *absence* of system may be part of what Weber meant by enchantment.

And in the same volume, Feinberg (1996:100), studying spirit encounters on the Solomon Island of Anuta, declares that, not unlike the vagaries of local Irish delineations of what a fairy is:

> ... people of Anuta recognize a plethora of numinals, ranging from a few that might well be described as "godlike" to a number that could be termed "spirits." In general however, they emphasize categories that shade into one another, avoiding terms or concepts that imply absolutes.

Since Evans-Wentz's 1911 doctoral dissertation work, elaborated in *The Fairy-Faith in Celtic Countries,* fairypeople or the fairyminded have not been systematically interviewed in depth. Or, as far as we know, even been interested in relaying the details of their spiritual understandings and mystical experiences. We do not know if the experiences of fairyfolk of previous centuries, (with the exception of a few esoteric writers discussed in chapter 6,) were part of a path to the Divine, or whether fairies were part of psycho-spiritual paths for transformation in personal or collective growth. We do not know how the Fairy Realm of the past affected the fairyminded or fairypeople's inner lives and wider worlds. Now, here, for the first time, we can get a detailed glimpse of these modern mystics' fairy connections and traits and what it can mean to "run with the fairies."

Chapter Three

Opening Up

> Aerial spirits, by great Jove, designed to be on earth the guardians of mankind.
> —Hesiod

From Childhood to Eureka

How does one become awakened to fairies as divine, spiritual beings? What brings fairyfolk to sense fairies? How does one realize that she or he is a fairyperson?

Most of the people with whom I have interacted describe a central experience, a specific moment or set of moments in which they came as adults to epiphanies, moments of realization of fairy energy or presence and/or of their own fairyness. Wallace (1956) would call these changes "mazeway" reorganization. (The Greeks used the word "metanoia" for moments of cognitive and spiritual insight.) Fairyfolk also often discuss their earlier childhood connections and sightings of fairies. The fairyfolk I worked with usually explain that they lost their connections after childhood and that their early adulthood and subsequent years blotted out their sensibilities to these celestial beings. Their later Eureka experiences brought them back to an awareness they had had as children.

Carol, a native Irishwoman, is a natural historian and artist painting fairy subjects. She worked at the famous Glenveagh Castle in County Donegal in the northwest of Ireland and takes people on walking tours of the land around Glenveagh National Park. She has been commissioned to paint murals on buildings and on the walls of houses, and sells her watercolors at various locations in Ireland. Carol lives alone in a secluded house off a long dirt road in a remote, deep valley of Donegal.

With a slightly larger-than-usual frame for a woman, she speaks loudly and confidently, sometimes boisterously, with a simultaneously deep and high voice. With dark hair and dark eyes, and mildly angular features, she is earthy, but jubilant. Both her personality and her art work are colorful, literally and figuratively. She seems to prefer muted pastels and earth tones in her dress and her watercolors. Carol told me that for a fairyperson she is very practical, and in recent years has found a balance between her fairyness and practical needs.

While I lived in Ireland I met with her many times, sometimes with others, and she took Kay and I, and a couple from Germany, on a tour of a part of rural Donegal where she or others had spotted fairy-beings.

Here Carol speaks openly about her many fairy sightings and experiences as a child and as an adult. She said that she was also a fairyperson when she was a child:

> I had this thing of thinking that I was invisible. My mother used to tell me that I could walk into rooms without being noticed. That is something I would definitely associate with the fairy world.

I questioned her about childhood experiences:

Carol: When I was a child I used to see a being I called Watty.

D: Could you look upon him or her at will?

C: No. I couldn't do it just anytime. I had a particular place in the garden where I could connect with this person.

D: Do you have a sense of the form or the kind of fairy he or she was?

C: Yes I do. I have a kind of memory of it. He was definitely old in appearance, and perhaps I felt that way about it because of the clothes he was wearing, and things like that.

D: You mean he had grey hair?

C: White hair, definitely white hair. He was ancient.

D: So you haven't seen Watty for a long time?

C: No, I haven't, actually. I think it is because probably that was his state then and that was his energy field. If fairies come into my life I just allow them.

D: Do they guide you or direct you to do certain things?

C: Absolutely. Even if I didn't want to do something, I would end up doing it.

I asked her how she came to realize as an adult that she was a fairyperson:

> It happened to me when I first came up to Donegal. I thought it was the first time I was in Donegal, but actually I felt like I had been here before. For a long time, I suppose around the age of twelve or thirteen, I had tried to disassociate myself from any of those fairy things and blocked them out. It made my life very depressing, very frustrating. Later as an adult when I first came up here I went down to Garten Loch [Lake]down there, by the shores full of stones, just by the edge. Whatever possessed me, I decided I wanted to jump. I *needed* to jump on top of this particular rock. But I completely missed it and fell on my ass in the water. And I started laughing, you know. *I realized then. It was like it broke some kind of spell or something that I was under.* It was a great feeling.[1] It all kind of started, not even to make sense, but I began to feel much more content with myself, accepting of what was going on in my life. (italics added)

Marita, another fairywoman, knows that she derives from the Nature Kingdom of fairies. She is a Jungian psychotherapist in her mid-fifties, who lives in the midlands of Ireland and occasionally travels, by herself or with a friend, to visit Kay in Donegal. Marita is a striking, dark-haired, sturdy-framed, buxom woman who wears dark eye make-up. She carries and dresses herself in a fashionable, feminine fashion. I socialized with and interviewed her at Kay's house in Donegal, and also drove down to her office in County Westmeath at her home, which she shares with her aging father. During interviews she was forthcoming.

When she speaks, especially of fairy things, a distinctive shine appears in her eyes. Although generally a bold speaker, in the course of her talking when she speaks directly of sensing fairies, she sometimes lowers her voice almost to a whisper, and assumes a gentle child-like innocence and glamour, a state of enchantment.

She gave me an account of how, at the age of 35, she was sparked to her reawakening to fairyness through a book. That book was *Insights into Reality* by Flower Newhouse (1975), a Christian mystic I discuss in Chapter Seven. Marita said the book opened her to an inner world she had known as a child. That world was very familiar to her. She lamented that that familiar world had been lost in her growing up. But in explaining the experience with that book she brightened up and recalled "Oh my Gosh, I am not alone anymore! That place inside myself, it's authentic." She sparkled in her recounting of her reawakening over fifteen years earlier, and her discovery that someone else knew of the fairy spaces and places that Marita called "other dimensional."

I asked her about her childhood consciousness of Fairy. Marita seemed clear:

> I was conscious until I was about 18, maybe. I use a specific moment of when I was about six and a half of an experience that I had to connect me with the fairies. I had so much peace from nature and somewhere of another dimension outside the human reality. That experience I kept to myself. Even at that age I decided not to tell anyone, and particularly not to tell my Mom and Dad because I knew that they wouldn't understand..... But that experience was what I went back to in times of great difficulty and aloneness. *Knowing that there was more than what was in my human environment.* And I could close my eyes and go back to that place. And pray. I would often pray that that might come back to me again, that I could somehow know that place through the pain. The pain was great of separation from the Fairy Realm.

Marita said the experience with Newhouse's book was definitely a "Eureka" experience and that for two solid days afterward she entered, re-entered, back into herself that fairy connection with herself, and with nature. She said it was "incredibly joyful":

> And it was very connected. There was a connectiveness. That was the reality. That connectedness again ... through the book ... really of someone putting this actually into written communication. And I think it was the written communication that really brought me then back into my own journey, into the Fairy Realm... It is very, very difficult to put words onto these things. Very joyful....And I shared it with my best friend at the time, who was also with me in that experience.

The experience moved Marita so much that she traveled to California time and again to be with Flower Newhouse and people of like mind.

> I think that as a fairy, as a nature being, that one serves the Divine, God. We aspire as a little fairy or nature being to be angelic. I think that for the child the Fairy Realm is a real world. Somehow that magic, like fairytales, is in the unconscious of every child.... And it's a real world for me now. It's not a child's world anymore. You know the child has met the adult in me and knows. It always was a real world for me, but as an adult human I didn't share it until I met Flora Newhouse and opened that book, because I didn't feel safe.

Kay was the fairyperson with whom I spent the most time. I met her seemingly by chance through a friend during my earlier landscape studies in Donegal. Kay introduced me in one way or another to several other fairyminded folk and fairypersons. She is The Fairy at RiverRun: RiverRun is the name of the house and acreage she owns. Her property sits alongside a little river not far from the indented rocky coast of northern Donegal, and near the rugged land surrounding Muckish Mountain. She is a light haired, light bodied, light boned woman in her seventies who originally lived in California as a Ph.D. practicing psychotherapist.

Kay has dedicated much of her recent life to the pursuit of fairyness, to her own spiritual development, and to gentle promulgation of fairy consciousness. In part she has done this through her book *The Wondrous Land: The Faery Faith in Ireland* (1997). She does not give workshops or advertise herself, or lay her fairy worldview and knowledge on others. But she has come to be known. Her book, newspaper articles, a documentary partly about her by a woman Nora who we will meet later, and word of mouth have brought her a modicum of notoriety, within and outside fairy conscious circles. But her ego is not large, and she is an unassuming person. We came to be trusted colleagues.

I stayed in an apartment she owns connected to her own dwelling, and later a trailer on her property. Kay's house and contents, along with fairy murals, has a distinctly organic flow, with colors coordinated in soft, harmonious earthy and light pastels. Without really intending to do so, I more or less became an apprentice to her simply by my concerted interest and by spending many, many hours, days, weekends, and months around her. She is a fully authentic human being and mystic.

I occasionally worked in her extensive garden which produces numerous flowers, berries, and vegetables. She pleases herself and her guests with its products. I sometimes helped her prepare dinners for us and her visiting friends. We have drunk more than a few bottles of wine together and have visited others together in Ireland and Northern Ireland. Sometimes her fairy and other friends stay with her for visits and talks about all kinds of things. She is the nexus of about twenty people in Ireland who are actively in some fashion fairypeople or fairyminded, although there are other people in Ireland and elsewhere who more or less subscribe to the same perspectives. (There are others still who claim fairy consciousness and make money selling "fairy" items.) The very loose group that she and I interacted with are similar to her in their lack of interest in commercial aspects of their fairy connectedness. She thinks of this book as part of her (our) mission in disseminating information about Fairy.

Sometimes Kay gets letters, e-mails, and visits from people wondering how to more fully realize themselves in their own fairyness. As a former clinical psychologist and as a sensitive human/fairyperson, her grasp of human nature, psychology, and the spiritual path is grand. She is sometimes sought after for advice and welcomes inquiries from people interested in spiritual and fairy ways. At seventy-something, she remains light on her feet and vivacious, sometimes traipsing heartily through the woods to get to special sites.

She is inquisitive, highly-educated, and in English and Irish jargon "brilliant." If you met her, saw her, experienced her house with all its colors and walls painted with fairy scenes, heard her playing the harp, observed her working in her garden, and interacted with her you would clearly understand, or get a glimpse of, the fact that she is a sylph-like person – a human with characteristics of an air fairy that lightens and enlightens the world about her.

Kay relates that in her childhood she remembers events that were "very fairy." She remembers seeing fairies as a very young child and thought that it was "natural" that the woods were full of creatures.

Kay: As a child it seemed like the whole woods was alive with fairies, or shapes. My memories are pretty fuzzy about it. But I did have a fairy companion when I was three or four. He would sit on the window sill and entice me to come out and play with him. He did have form. He was like a green man, and he had a green suit on. I tried to tell my mother about it, but I couldn't get it out. I tried to tell him [the fairy] that he wouldn't be interested in playing with me because he was a much older boy. He was, in my way of looking at things, about nine or ten. He was on my side. It was like we were ancient companions. Such incidents are called hallucinations, but they weren't.

I would have a connection to mystery. And I would transpose time…. Yes, and also as a child I did not feel that I belonged to my parents. It was like I didn't belong to this planet, this world. I was just a stranger here. I mean I still feel that. But it wasn't depressing or anything like that because I was different. It wasn't bad. I was just different somehow.

D: It must have been a formative experience to have a fairy friend when you were so young.

K: It didn't happen that often, but it happened often enough for me to remember. I never thought as a child that it didn't happen. I just didn't have the vocabulary. I mean, nobody would have denied it. My parents would have never denied any mystical experience. I didn't tell them about it because I couldn't express it or I just thought it was natural. I have never censored these experiences I have had.

Kay is sometimes hired to play the harp at social gatherings. The harp, as much literature suggests, is quintessentially fairy. For Kay it is more than a coincidence that she started playing the harp when she was a child of eight or nine, long before she knew about fairypeople as reincarnated fairies.

> And I came upon the harp at a neighbor's house, and it was like magic. The woman was about thirty, and it was her harp, and she played it for me. I was astonished... So my parents got me a harp. It was a little harp and I took lessons all through high school and through college. Then I got married and moved to California, where I spent the rest of my married life. I didn't resume playing again until twenty years ago. So there was an interim in there where I lost it. But I always missed it, even just to look at it..... The music that I play would be considered fairy music. But even before that, even before I knew my fairy connection, I would choose fairy music to play.

Kay had an early knowledge of fairies as a young child, when she saw the fairies, had a fairy companion, and was in the woods often, but moved through much of her adult life without conscious connection:

> There was no societal recognition of it. It just didn't work into the lifestyle of the times. And then I was married to someone who didn't have a clue about it, even who I was. But neither did I!

She continued to relate that much later in her life, when she was about 55, while still in California, she was talking to a channel, Jeremiah, with whom she had spoken several times before. The channel said that Kay's granddaughter was an exceptional person "if allowed to be" and that the granddaughter was from the Fairy Kingdom. Then Jeremiah said that Kay was a fairy[person] herself, had originally in a previous lifetime been a fairy in another dimension. Kay explained the timing of the information:

> He didn't tell me before that, I am sure, because he would have said it wasn't appropriate or it wasn't the right time. I wouldn't have been free to fully digest it and act on it anyway until I got close to retirement. You know I would have gone my whole life without having the kind of knowledge I now have about it... I didn't know about my fairy identity until I was told, about twenty years ago.

After she learned about her fairyness, at the moment of being told, she relates:

> It made sense: it wasn't something just superimposed upon me. I felt awake. Part of spiritual tasks is to recognize our stance, our reason for being here. Who we are. Where we have been. Where we are going. It is always helpful to recognize one's lineage.

Kay has met some fairypeople who know that they have come from the fairies, whose awareness is also sharp. There are not many of them, but she says they are certainly mostly in Celtic countries. "It is very rare for somebody in America to be so knowledgeable," she declares, because it is so accepting in Ireland, where, she says, "It is nothing weird." She repeated that it is not common, but then again not incomprehensible, that in America someone would know of his/her fairy background. Indeed the major reason she moved from America was for Ireland's spiritual openness and acceptance, to more fully pursue and integrate her fairy background and nature.

Jon, a native Irishman and former Ph.D. professor of psychology and philosophy, recently resigned from City University of Dublin to pursue his spiritual path full time. He also writes and leads workshops. He is a kind of mystagogue, fluent in mystical and psycho-spiritual "talk" and experience. A little shorter than the average man, with a slightly smaller than usual frame, he has somewhat angular features with few wrinkles, short-cropped hair, and an impish smile. He seems ageless. With light blue eyes, light brown hair, at times he looks other-worldly, half-human, half starry-eyed android. He reminds me of a classical drawing of an elfman portrayed in books like Brian Froud's illustrated *Fairies* (1979) and *Good Fairies/Bad Faeries* (1998). Jon engages in lightly ritualistic movements, as he sometimes walks with palms up in front of him. He feels energies. Sometimes he kneels in the woods and/or folds his hands together touching his chest, directing energies in and out of his heart.

Jon said it had been about fifteen years since he had full awareness of his fairyness, born out of an experience of insight at the Hill of Tara, an ancient Celtic archaeological site set in the rolling, hilly landscape of the Midlands. The experience led him to remember. He knows that as a young child he experienced fairyness, but it went away as he grew older. But now he feels a "linked resonance" with his childhood and fairyness, but not in "conceptual language". It is a link that is "spontaneous and discovered."

Debbie is a sculptor of fairies and maker of fairy dolls who lives in Northern Ireland. A native to Northern Ireland she is a tall, lithe, red-headed woman with a bouncy disposition. I heard about her while living in

Donegal, and later visited in her home and studio. There I saw an other-than-human fairy doctor sculpture with which I resonated. I commissioned her to sculpt another fairy doctor for me, which now sits on a bookshelf in my farmhouse in Western New York state. Historically, fairy doctors were human beings known in Ireland for their healing skills, said to be imparted to them through fairies. She sent me the fairy doctor sculpture, (and a birdman sculpture) via post after I returned to the States.

She wrote me about her childhood, her inspiration for the fairy doctor, and the relationship between her childhood and later life. In figuring out how she came to invent and sculpt a fairy doctor:

> I vividly remember an experience which was more than a dream and occurred long before I knew of the Fairy Faith. It happened twice, once when I was 7 and once when I was 14. On both occasions I was having a bad bout of illness. As you may well have experienced yourself sometimes during sickness, you can find yourself in a kind of altered state somewhere between sleep and waking [3] – the kind of state spiritual practitioners try to induce through meditative techniques. In just such a state my fevered mind stilled and I suddenly became brightly aware of a "man" standing at the foot of my bed. Both times were the same except that on the second occasion when I was 14 he was not alone. He turned up with a horse-headed faery man on one side of him and a very faery being on the other who had no humanistic characteristics. In later years this reminded me of the Triple Alliance of human, animal, and faery allies which Robert Stewart writes of in *Power Within The Land*. The Faery Doctor was dressed very much as I have made him since.
>
> I was not frightened or disturbed in any way by seeing such queer figures in my room in the dead of night. There was nothing shimmery about them, they were very physically apparent. There was a silent, energetic communion which flowed from him to me. And on both occasions when I woke the next morning my health was greatly improved.
>
> It would be very easy for me to have psycho analysed myself in light of this experience and come at it with all sorts of mental arguments about it. But I have had some very key experiences beyond the norm and have never felt any need or desire to do that. I have just accepted the reality of such experiences and how they affected me. I have never seen them that way again but I have "felt" his presence, and thinking about all this made me sit down and work it out, and I realized that there has been a pattern of this at key moments in my life.

The childhood experiences and thoughts of fairy coming or coming back to these people is mostly joyful, divine, and integrating. Their personal narratives of spiritual insight and unfolding are also wrestlings. Sometimes they well up the pain of having been different, of being separate from people and God, or disconnected from a dimension that is powerful, life changing, life enhancing. In all these people's lives there was a period of years, often many, when their fairy connections were covered over by environmental and personal blockages. Rationality, it seemed, had disallowed the spirit of fairy consciousness to fully emerge.

Following his *A Sociable God* (1983), Ken Wilber (and others) might say that childhood connection with fairies is a state of consciousness, the early self of childhood. Part of a set of developmental stages of consciousness through which humans often proceed. That childhood connection would be prior to the early adult *psychological fall* which Wilber describes as "a self-reflexive awareness ... that we are living in a fragmented, torn, alienated world that appears to be separate from Spirit"(21). I suggest it is this "fall" that covers over the child's connection with fairy spirit. But the connection with spirit reappears later for fairypeople and the fairyminded, not as a return or regression to childhood immaturity, but as a stronger, adult connection within a more developed stage of consciousness.

With respect to the frequent phenomenon of Western children believing, or saying that they believe in and interact with entities such as fairies, Piaget (1932) and others have posited this phenomenon as an early stage in the developmental sequence of types of thinking. Thus a popular perspective in the West is that children's early cognitive stages are a form of undeveloped, "primitive," pre-rational thinking, which some psychologists and early anthropologists of the past have even attributed to adults in traditional, so-called primitive societies. This Western-biased, rationalistic approach judging children and other cultures as less advanced cognitively or intelligence wise is no longer held by psychologists and anthropologists.

Yet still children today are often conceptualized as "primitive" thinkers. Belief and interaction with fairies, however, both as discussed in this book as operative among intelligent, highly educated adults, (and as demonstrated by fairy belief by many Western adults in the past), rules out the notion that fairy belief is a consequence of unadvanced thinking. Moreover, as suggested above, it is clear that belief in and interaction with deities or intermediate deific beings is part of many non-Western cultures' orientations *throughout life*. Thus it is likely that the adult training of Western children which eschews children's belief in alleged fantasy beings is greatly responsible for what Wilber (1983) calls the "psychological fall."

Recent Western research suggests that children do indeed have a "theory of mind," an intuitive ontological understanding that the mind and reality are "both distinct and related," which includes the understanding that mental entities have different properties than physical things (Wellman 1990). In other words, they understand the differences between themselves, and other physical, abstract or ethereal entities, and are intelligently and naturally interacting at various levels of awareness. "It is clear that preschoolers can distinguish between three "worlds: (1) that of experienced reality; (2) the realm of the imagination, where the individual conjures up beings, objects, and events; and (3) the world of fantasy and fiction, found in fairy tales, cartoons, and so, where agents other than oneself carry out magical, anomalous, or supernatural acts." (Boyer and Walker 2000:145) "In explicitly supernatural contexts, or when appropriate 'natural' explanations elude them, they [young children] frequently resort to 'magical' explanations" (146).

Psychoanalyst Sudhir Kakar (1991), in contrast to many earlier analysts, especially Freud, who conceptualized mystical and religious experience as pathology, or reduced mysticism to sublimation, regression, or illusion, treats mystical experiences as "legitimate." He suggests that mystics have access "across to a period in early life – 'oral' in classical nomenclature, when the border between the psyche and soma was much more porous than is the case in adulthood" (21). This "porousness" may explain the fairy sensibility in these and other people's attunement and connections to the fairy world.

Children's and some culture's use of "magical" explanations, as my informants and others suggest, is stifled by empiricist, rationalistic adults whose own cognitive and cultural development included the stifling of magical explanations, and whose own paradigms are limited, "monophasic" in Laughlin's (1983) terms. The absence or repression of such experience does not mean that the "magic" is not there: it just means that much magical thinking withers under such conditions, which does not happen in cultures or groups where beings like fairies are real for children and adults (Boyer and Walker 2000). For example, Mills (1992) discovered that when east Indian children talk to entities that adults cannot perceive, the adult assumes that the young child is talking with a very real entity who exists in the realm of spirit, or is part of the child's past life.

Connections - Adult Fairy Experience

Carol is most definitive and straightforward about her abilities and experiences. I asked Carol if she can detect a fairy tree. She uttered dramatically:

Oh yes, absolutely. You can feel the energy. Oh yeah. Absolutely, without a shadow of a doubt. You know you are in a fairy place. You can even walk into it. I have come across many useful places like that, cause the energies can be really strong. I can feel a lot of fairy consciousness and energy boundaries in different places.

Carol, as mentioned above, took Kay, me, and a visiting couple from Germany on a car tour of one of the more remote sections of Donegal. There she has experienced and seen a variety of elemental beings and fairies. She drove us around and pointed out where she had had fairy sightings. We stopped at a few places to look more closely at the exact locations. Driving along a back road, and then just inside the woods we talked, and I taped the conversations.

Carol: I have to go very slowly [in the car] here because one of the major fairy sites is down here, and I want to bring these flowers to it. It's one of those places that appears and disappears for me all the time....Two years ago I saw a green man in here one afternoon during one of my walks. He was just sitting down. He had very long hair and was completely covered in green, like moss green. I was totally transfixed. I stood there for a long time looking at him. He was kind of smiling at me. Then I went on, and wondered if I would see him again. I had been walking. So I went on and told Bernie, a friend of mine from Scotland, about it when I got home. And of course she was laughing at me. So I said "Let's go for a walk this evening. Maybe he is still there." So we went. And we walked around and we saw him again! I couldn't believe it. She couldn't believe it either. We both saw him.

I was delighted, because it is very unusual when you get confirmation from somebody else. He was just in here, in these woods here. It was quite a surprise. Normally you wouldn't come across those kinds of things so close to the road or near a house. But since then neither of us has seen him.

So that was nice. And Bernie remembers it till this day. It was a very special occasion. The green man was kind of a big fella. A big tall, bearded fella, a very chilled-out looking kind of person. He was totally green.

Kay: He was just sitting there?

Carol: Yea, he was just sort of sitting down, the first time I saw him. The second time I saw him he was more physically accomplished.

Kay: He was formed? Or was he vague?

Carol: Oh no, he was very formed. Very obvious. He had to be obvious for Bernie. Bernie wouldn't accept it on faith. The fact that she saw him as well, so very clearly, was brilliant.... You don't drive the car and commune with the fairies at the same time. Although they have stepped in and out of vehicles of mine.

D: They opened the car door?

Carol: Well, no. Sometimes I haven't even noticed them getting in. Once I felt something was pulling at my hair, and I kept looking to see what it was.

D: Did the same fairy reappear at another time?

Carol: Yes, for a short while. One fairy stayed around for about a month or two, and it did take things from around the house. I knew it didn't belong to my house, and it probably wasn't comfortable in that particular house.

D: You said that when you were a child you had a particular fairy around, Watty. This fairy in your car was not "your" fairy. Are fairies always associated with a particular person?

Carol: For me they are associated with place.... But the landscape has changed so much.

Here Kay speaks of some of her earlier adult spiritual experience, which contributed to her later understanding of herself as a fairyperson.

D: The other night when Kerstin was over she was sharing the experience she had with the [shadowy being] woman she saw on the island in the river, before she knew that other people had seen her. With her eyes closed, Kerstin saw a vision of a woman with red hair in an archway. You said that you had had similar experiences. But you said that you actually physically saw someone, or something, with your eyes open?

Kay: Probably I was referring to the specific time that I actually did see a spirit person. That was quite a while ago: I must have been in my 30's or early 40's. ... I was alone in my bed and I had been reading a newspaper. I guess I fell asleep. (Previous to that I had been to an ashram with our school class. We did a lot of meditating there. I figured that that had something to do with clearing my channels, clearing my "pipes.") I woke up and I knew that I was awake because I could feel the newspaper. I told my psychologist that it was just a dream, but it was clearly not just a dream. I woke up, and at the end of the bed there was a considerably large multi-plumed bird that looked kind of a like an ostrich, and it just sat for a second. It scared me. And then, almost at the same moment, over in the corner of the room, there was a woman. This woman was fully clothed in some kind of white garments. I think she had a sash around her. She was very Nordic looking, with long blonde hair, and Nordic features, nothing Irish looking. She had in her hand a cross, a blazing cross. (Later I identified it with a Celtic cross.) And it was not like it was on fire, but it was firey. And I was surprised to see it. But she looked at the bird, and just dismissed him as if he were mischievous. She wasn't angry. And then she looked at me, or I looked at her, and she said something telepathically that she was my guide. She said she would be with me until the end of being. She didn't say until the end of time, she said *the end of being*. And she just kind of smiled at me, and then she kind of zapped me, and I just went right back to sleep... It was completely blissful. ...

There was something wrong with the lights, I can't remember exactly what. I had just put in a new light bulb when I was reading. And when I tried to turn on the light, it wouldn't turn on. The light bulb was apparently burned out by the energy. OK. And before this happened, when I first woke up, the room was ice cold. (It was spring or summer). I have heard since then that when people have visitors that somehow when they pop in they drain the energy. They absorb the warmth. But when she left, the room was warm. It wasn't cold any longer.

D: You mentioned that Jeremiah, your channel, said Shendu was a guardian spirit of yours.

K: That was at least fifteen years before I found out that I was [reincarnated] from the Fairy Kingdom. I have never seen Shendu visually, even with my eyes closed. However, I have a sense of him. I have a sense of his presence and I can imagine what he looks like. In that sense I have a visualization of him. I also have times where I actually see things when my eyes are closed. That is a different kind of vision.

D: What is the visualization like, is it of something inside your head or outside your head?

Kay: It is like eidetic vision. You close your eyes, and you actually see something. Like when you are dreaming, but you are not dreaming. In Ireland and in the Caribbean are the only two places where I have had eidetic visions..... If I could paint, I could paint Shendu, out of some memory of what he is like. And it might change over the year. I might have a different idea of what he looks like from ten years ago. He is supposed to be the guardian between the dimensions, between the fairy dimension and this dimension.

D: For everyone?

K: I don't know about everyone, but he guards the gates, so to speak.... And I have had a sense of the passageways that he guards, or the bridges that you meet him on. They are usually underground caverns or bridges. The bridges are usually over water. He is very stern about who he is going to let into the fairy realms. Hardly anybody passes. It is not easy to get by him.

Here Kay speaks of the relationship between herself, fairies, and the divine:

K: Well, you know, from my concept of myself, to know my fairyness is to be so spiritually aligned with the divine that that there is no separation possible. I couldn't possibly be a fairyperson without being aligned to the divinity that I am. It just wouldn't be possible. The actual sense of being connected to the Divine, and being absolutely sure of that, is because in all the psychic and visualization experiences I had before [before I realized that I was a fairyperson]. I knew of the existence of the divine and identified fully with It. Then to come to identify as being a fairy[person] too, it became more further linked. There couldn't be anyway of being anything else. Logically how could you be anything else? How could you believe in the divinity of consciousness and say somehow you're a fairy[person] that was not linked to that? It wouldn't make any sense. *It is not even anything to think about. It just is. It is beyond thinking.*

D: Is the Fairy Faith a religion?

K: No, I don't think so. It is a belief and experience in spiritual realities. It's a belief and experience in mystery and transcendent reality. So if that is a definition of religion then it might be a religion. But there are no rules, no dogma, no structure to it. It's quite individual. Each person's Fairy

Faith would be different than the next person's, woven into their personality and experience and family structure, and what they are allowed to be.

I asked Kay about the method or style of "connecting" with fairies. She said that there are different kinds of connections, but not necessarily because you have seen a fairy. Some people who have seen fairies have no fairy connection at all, and simply have seen fairies for some reason, as fairies sometimes like to show themselves. So seeing a fairy isn't necessary. It's one of the possibilities. One of the characteristics of fairyness is to be able to see fairies, but *"just because someone sees fairies doesn't mean that they're more fairy than somebody who hasn't seen them."*

She went on to say that there are several ways of sensing fairies, and seeing is just one. A "very strong" other way of sensing the fairy is to hear them. When you talk to people, musicians, for instance, some say they got their musical inspiration from the fairies. In some cases they actually hear it. In addition to visual or audient experience of fairies, there can be "an intuitive awareness." "A sense of them being around." She said that it is hard to define, but is real.

I asked her if she could see or talk to a fairy at will. She responded:

K: It's more like…like I become aware that they are there, rather than willing it. It's more like *they* will it. They make me aware again. Like one time…In the other house I was on the computer and there was some form that just went through the bed. The bed was there, the desk was there, and I was there. And I just looked around and this form went into the bed. It was a definite form and I initially thought that it was a cat or something like that. Of course, cats don't move through beds. And then I went outside and there was a swoop of leaves that came down right at my feet and swooped up and came down again in a circular pattern. That kind of thing isn't usual. It was very subtle and one could say that it wasn't anything at all, but those events that are things that are "nothing" at all, happen. And there are enough of them that they can't be explained any other way than as the doings of fairies. With my other connections to them it doesn't seem that those kinds of things are just fantasy.

But I don't go out into the woods and will them to show up and they show up.

D: Historically there have been particular places, sites known to be fairy haunts, locations where fairies hang out. Does that mean that the likelihood of becoming aware of Fairy is increased by going to those places?

K: If the places become too identified, they lose their magic. It's more like a place you discover is fairy, rather than going back to the place thinking "we'll go to this place because fairies are there." The place may still have fairy qualities to it, but they may not. They don't immortalize a place like that. I don't think I've ever heard anybody say that. When fairies have been seen they usually, but not always, have been seen in fairy places. But they have also been seen at that place by somebody else, so it becomes expected that people go there and see a fairy. Like if you look down in a river you're going to see a heron, because a heron hangs out there. But fairies are very elusive. They don't show up when you want them to. They don't have a set pattern.

Marc and Val are an English couple who visit Ireland frequently. I met them at the house of Minette, a friend of Kay's who lives in the Midlands. I drove from Donegal to stay at her house with all of them for 2-3 days. When I was visiting at Minette's, sitting out on the large lawn by the garden, we all talked for quite some time about fairy experiences and connections with fairies. Neither Minette, Marc, nor Val consider themselves fairypeople (reincarnated fairies), but they have fairy consciousness, the ability to resound with fairies. They are fairyminded, as I call them. Marc and Val and Minette were friendly, down to earth, and sincere. They all talked to me with intelligence and authority about the realms of existence, without being pompous or condescending.

Marc is a writer, artist, channel, fringe theater director, and workshop facilitator. He worked with his partner Val on his channeled book *Earth Will Be Reborn* (2007). In one of the chapters he writes of the Faerie Realms, elemental energies, who sing from the hollows of "crystal" hills and "the hearts of mountains" and who hold no animosity towards humanity. Val is a teacher, illustrator, and aromatherapist. (I discuss Marc, Val, and Minette in more detail in Chapter Five.)

I asked Marc and Val how they evoked fairies or fairyness in their lives and creative work. They echoed Kay's statement that you can't will fairies to appear.

Marc: You can evoke something, but you can't force something. That's where some people have erred, where they're literally forcing some things to happen and making and pushing things. It's a different approach. I think the approach we're looking for is where we are opening something and allowing it to happen. We are present, but we are not forcing or controlling.

Val: I think of it as a dance. You open. As you open, you shine. As you shine you are breaking out. You don't know who your celestial partner is going to be. There can be great surprises. That's what I did last time, I just sat there and sent out these things and this huge dance occurred. I put the invitation out for a dance, and I got a response, and whoever responded we all danced together. An amazing dance happened and then it just came to an end. That was a very different way of working than I had done earlier in my life, because before I would ask things. I don't do that anymore. *You just shine...* There are lots of different ways of doing it as well.... That was an invitation to join me in a seed of a dream, if you like. When the dance is at full height I actually let go of it. It wasn't mine anymore... But there are other times when you might actually want to see something special, so you might invite a certain energy within, to work with you or to work through you. But what you're doing is just feeling what is being done, and how it's being done. It's still a dance. They're not controlling me, and I am not controlling them or anything like that. So it is still this dance element, it's an invitation. It's never a command. I couldn't command anything.

Marc: We see the Fairy as very iridescent and shimmering. It reminds me of Minnette's drawings, where she has the silver and gold threads from the Fairy Realm that she was tapping into. They are the threads that run through it. The fairy threads are translucent and shimmery. It's like they are the aspect of the self and the world that are most fugitive and most difficult to grasp onto. But they are here all the time. But you can't own them or grab them.

Minette is a musician and songwriter who lives with her husband in a large house on some acreage. Her old stately living room is dominated by a large piano where she writes and sings. She has made CDs. Her work is fluid and interactive between herself and Fairy, and the songs she sings and plays on a recording I heard are light and airy.

D: When you go out to the fairy site, Minette, do you go to certain places to feel the fairies?

Minette: No. I don't go exactly to feel the fairies. But I might do what I did today, and just go put my hands on the trunk or the branch of the fairy tree to feel the pulse of the energy and to see what comes into my mind. Obviously, whatever is going on in my life at the time would be part of the experience, and some helpful and very loving comments come to me. In a way I take it all on trust. At the same time I just know that it is true, and they're just around all the time.

Back in Donegal I asked Marita about her connections to the fairy world. She told me about a being she called Anya, whom she experienced over the years.

D: When Anya came to visit you the other night was it because you intended to experience her?

Marita: No. It was just something that happened at the time, before I was going to sleep. I consciously was trying to connect with that part of myself that was light and fairyish. And that was just the kind of energy that came closest to me at that point. I honor that part of myself, and I pray for the connection back into myself.

D: Do you do that intentionally at certain times?

Marita: Yes. When I have been closer to nature it happens more. So it is like when I want to reconnect more, I spend time in nature. It happens in phases for me, but definitely more after being in nature. Depending on where that nature is, it always gives me a big spurt inside myself, and sometimes I drop back again. It comes and goes.

D: Can you tell when you are in a particular place in the woods that it is a fairy site by just sensing it or seeing something?

Marita: Yes.

D: Is it the physical landscape or is it something else?

Marita: It can be both, a combination of both. It is very much physical landscape, but nature is getting so disturbed more and more, and the fairies are moving away from disturbed places, so now you really have to go farther away into nature to commune, to really commune with Nature.

I asked Marita if there were things that happened in her daily life, in the house, or wherever, that she knew as fairy events, visitations or tricks.

She replied that she didn't feel them much in the home that she lived in because there is not an acceptance of that in her house because she lives with her father. But when she goes out she can sometimes feel the fairyness. (Sometimes she and her client go outdoors from her office.)

M: Something magical calls….. "Let's…" I hear that voice. [Now speaking softly] "Let's go out to the garden. Let's just connect. Let's take little baby steps. Let's pick a daisy. Let's see what…" … It comes in as, I suppose "Go, go, go out into nature." That is the way I hear it most, but there are many, many ways….

Marita says sometimes she goes to a particular bookshop at the Hill of Tara:

M: A lovely place, a lovely fairy and angelic bookshop. And there are all these little fairies in the shop. And I go in there and play. So I go to places like that. Fairy rings and such.

Marita explained that sometimes she feels fairies with her clients and she "plays" with that dimension in her work. When there was a "vulnerability" somewhere with her clients and/or herself, she would spend the last part of the therapeutic session…

> Just feeling, feeling, feeling… "What is in the grass?" Feeling "What is under it?" Feeling "What is in it? Is there a shamrock? Is there a clover? What is there?"… The gentle, gentle, gentle…. Feeling… The fairies are being connected… Feeling….. [Almost inaudible] A safe place… *If you let it.* That is how the fairies come to me, in my daily life.

I interviewed both Jon and Kay together at her house one day. I asked about fairies having preferences for particular kinds of landscape, ones more beautiful or treed than others. Kay said that fairies are not judgemental, they simply have an awareness of where they belong. "A longing for where they belong," Jon added. He also said that there was a fairy for every natural environment. Thus there were thousands of them.

Jon, whom Kay said was the most fairy person she knows, is a fairyperson of a different ilk. I spent time with him at Kay's or traveling with him and Kay around parts of Donegal, walking beaches and cliffy coastlines, and communing in the woods. Jon seems middle-aged, but only in some generalized sense, and as indicated above, has an ageless, almost otherworldly, sometimes androgynous look. His eyes shine, especially when talking, and he has a confident, impressive, and easy presence and demeanor. A sort of wiseman comfortable in providing spiritual, mystical knowledge and guidance, he does not want to be categorized, nor to categorize other things or people.

When in Donegal he sometimes goes out alone to a particular woodland place to commune. He moves easily and enjoys his time in the glade, often using his arms and hands in varying positions to capture energies out of the air. His contact with energies or beings on the "other side" of our daily physical reality is not exclusive to the fairy dimension. The day after he came back from the glade he spoke about his experience:

> Yesterday there was intense emotion involved, and it is really difficult to explain this or verbalize this. But the essence of it I think is that in calling these dimensions together I was coming into direct contact with aspects of my own divine self that I have been in contact with for a long time. This is the way, beyond any kind of model of encounter that's based on a sense of visual perception. It's my pure direct knowing..... *My understanding of what it means to be a full human being, made in the image and likeness of God, is to have the capacity to realize the various frequencies of divine energy and beings.* And to differentiate the expression of God and creation within oneself. So I think when you come to the point of being able to imagine and approach that, it must be that you have served some time in these various realms so that you develop the capacity within you to bring all of these diverse lines together. Although I do have a strong sense of a fairy dimension within my own consciousness, I'm not especially bound up with it. I do have an affinity with that dimension and make contact with it, as well as with others.

In later chapters Jon speaks much more.

The "intense emotion" of which Jon speaks may be, according to Kakar (1991:20), in speaking of visions, an example of a

> central common feature: intense affect they generate, an affect that endows them with their characteristic sense of noesis. The affect, so strong that it is experienced as *knowing*, partakes of some of the quality of the symbiotic state in infancy when the child knew the mother through an interchange of their feelings, when affect and cognition were not differentiated from one another. (author's emphasis)

Here I question Kay more about the nature of her connections:

D: Do you communicate with fairies in general, or specific fairies?

Kay: Yes, but it's like I try to hear something I can't hear. It's not vocal. A lot of it is intuitive, a sense of their presence. Sometimes they are around. You are simply aware that they are around, or they are giving you advice or suggestions or help, or direction not to go in that direction or to go in that direction.

D: So I spill this cup of tea, or you spill this cup of tea. Is that because there was a fairy that led that to happen?

K: Sometimes, perhaps. Sometimes their humor is great. I mean some of the humorous coincidences that happen to me are fairy done, fairy doings. They are sometimes so obscure that only other fairypeople usually know about what I am talking, and experience those kinds of things. Fairies are very elusive.

D: How do you differentiate between something that happens that is connected to fairies versus something that is independent of fairies. We said sometimes the teacup tips over and you know that it is a fairy that made that happen, sometimes it is not. How do you know when it is a fairy?

K: You don't always for sure, but *the fairies' way of communicating has a distinct flavor to it.* And it is generally joyful, and it is generally humorous, and it is generally an "I told you so" kind of thing. It stretches your imagination. I mean they are gentle, but they are not pansies. But there is a sense of laughter, a sense of joy, a sense of humor, and sense of color and light and harmony.

D: The fairies communicate with you, and sometimes you don't see them, but sometimes you do see them, like when you are working in the garden. Is that right?

K: Generally no. If I do see them, then I don't see them as fairies sitting on a post or something like that. I see them as an impenetrable force or vaporous form. Sometimes in color.

D: Sometimes you see definite physical features of a fairy?

K: Usually no. Usually they are in this vaporous or colored form, or sometimes lightness.

D: Do you talk out loud when you sense or see a fairy?

K: No, because you don't need to. It's telepathic.

D: Is there dialogue? Do you get communications from a fairy and then communicate back telepathically. Is there then sometimes a response in turn from the fairy?

K: It can be dialogue, but it isn't a very long dialogue. I always appreciate their humor and I sometimes get something back in a sense of "yes, we appreciate" or something like that. Or I get an idea or an affirmation or confirmation. But the dialogue doesn't have to be a humorous dialogue, and it can be spaced over time. You can pick up the dialogue on the same subject later, maybe in an hour, maybe a week or two.

D: When you communicate with a fairy from the other dimension what language do you use?

K: It is all really ESP or thought projection. I mean I don't hear the fairies. Some people say that they speak, but I don't hear them in that sense. It is telepathic.

D: What kinds of things do you telepathically communicate about?

K: Sometimes messages come to me, unexpected and unanticipated and quite often. So I would say that that would happen more often than the other way around, and that can be any kind of thing, just to take note of whatever it is that lets me know what is going to happen. That is just another assurance that this communication system is real. …Like there was a commercial truck coming around yesterday that I used to buy frozen poultry and fish from. It was about two years ago that I used to buy these frozen items from them and then they went out of business. Yesterday I was thinking, and I didn't have any particular reason at all to think about it, but I just was thinking that I wonder whatever happened to those people because they really did help people obtain good quality produce. And then here comes the truck… But those things happen to me so often. That is just an example of it. There is no possible way of having any physical knowledge of that or even any interest in it. So why did that thought come to me? Other thoughts come to me quite often, maybe three or four times a day that I have knowledge of something that is going to happen, or that somebody is thinking of me and so I am thinking of them. So this was fairly concrete to show that I got evidence... So that helps me realize that the communications from outside the physical dimensions are real. The fairies give me advice on everything, they give me advice on cooking something, and I hear a voice, but it is like an exterior voice.

D: Are there times when you solicit advice?

K: Yes, but it doesn't come directly, it may come in some form that I have to pay attention to. The answer may come in anything. It may come in a book somebody brings me, or it may come when somebody tells me something, or I read something or hear something or see something, or something happens in the car.

D: Do you know that they sometimes change or move things in our physical reality?

K: Yes

D: What kinds of things have you noticed that they physically change in this dimension?

K: It's been a while since I can pinpoint that, but they not only change things around but they put some things in prominence. I can't tell you how they do that. But it's like they help you notice something that you might not have noticed something that is beneficial for you, or something that you might enjoy and think is beautiful.[4]

D: If you were in a store, supermarket, or a clothing store, something would stand out, even though they didn't physically move the item, the dress? But they made you notice a certain item or dress?

K: I would be looking for something. Let's just say a dress. They would know that I would like anything that looks like a fairy garment. So they would tell me where it is and I would find it. I would find it if I am supposed to have it, and they would point to me where to go to find it.

D: So you would ask them where the shoes are and it would turn out that you would find them.

K: Well, I wouldn't ask them so much as I just would want some sort of shoes to go with my purple dress. They know I like the color purple and they would just simply help me find it. They would direct me to it. A thought would come up "Why don't you go into this store," and there would be the purple shoes.

D: Are you conscious of them telling you to go into the store?

K: It's more like I was listening to my intuition and suggestions.

D: So you get promptings from fairies to do things. Do you get promptings about doing things beyond particular tasks, about things to do with your life in general?

K: They, as so-called individuals, may be task-oriented.... So many directions in my life have been guided by the fairies, not just coming here to Ireland. Of course I didn't always listen, and didn't know I was supposed to listen. They certainly got through enough of the time that I can trace the pattern of my whole life and see what parts of it were fairy directed.

D: When you say fairy-directed, do you mean directed by a particular fairy or do you mean Fairy with a capital F, some kind of general amalgam of fairies or fairy energy?

K: I don't know. I couldn't answer that. I know that the direction that they guided me in has been essentially the same, with the same kind of guidance. Whether that is a group of fairies, an individual fairy, or different fairies doing different facets of the tasks, I don't know. Do I have a fairy helping me with my music, who is different from the fairy helping me with my cooking, and another with the garden – all fairy type tasks – I don't know. I would imagine so. I know other fairypeople think of having specific fairies with different kinds of personalities. Or even one kind of mascot fairy, or something like that. I don't yet have a sense of that, although it may well be true. *That I have fairy guides, I do not have any doubt about that.* But how they are organized I do not know. Fairy guides seem to have more of a sense of humor than other kinds of guides do. And they have more capriciousness to them, and they are more spontaneous. Less heavy. More joyful....You know the fairies could even be responsible for those tits [chickadee birds] being out there, because the fairies were seeing that I was getting too obsessed about what I was going to do. Those birds are in a highly unlikely place.

D: Yes, the nest is in the wall right in front of the door you always use, and there is no green there

K: Yes, and it is low. Usually birds are higher.

D: I find things tend to happen just when I am getting a little cocky about my ability to control or know my life events. Almost every time when I get cocky something happens to me to remind me that my ego is too strong. It is like somebody saying to me "Who do you think you are, thinking you can do this?" [Laughter]. Increasingly I find that things go on that teach me about myself, when I forget about there being things to teach me

K: I understand, exactly.

D: Could you categorize the kinds of issues, or problems, or events, that you get messages from fairies about?

K: I don't think they are necessarily that selective. I think they more or less deal with me as what concerns me at the moment, to assist me. More like servants, more like they are there to answer what I need at the moment. They may be giving me directions that I am not aware of, that I think on my own. They may be more in charge than I allow them to be. And the direction that I am actually going in is being more guided than I think it is, because in the past that has certainly been the case. And in the long past, *I wasn't aware that I was being guided at all, but I was being guided, and I was obeying that guidance without realizing it,* and that might be happening now also.

D: You raise an interesting question, how you or I or anybody is unaware of the extent to which fairies or other entities are actually guiding our lives. You just may be a more conscious person of the degree to which fairies guide you.

K: Yes. And those of us, in looking back in retrospect, would be aware of "How in the world did I know how to do that?" And we may not be aware of it because we are in the middle of it. I also may be doing things under guidance of which I am not aware.

The subsequent summer my partner and colleague Ana came to Ireland. She asked some similar questions:

Ana: Sometimes when I was with Dennis I told him I felt something come into the room, and Dennis said he felt something too. Sometimes at random moments, even in my city living room, something happens. Now, after being with you, I am more inclined to say it is a fairy coming in. Could that be a fairy?

Kay: Yes, it could be a fairy. Or it could be an energy of some other kind. There are other entities from other realms that are not fairies. *Probably a great deal more than we know.* Here in Ireland, it is more likely to be a fairy than in Toronto.

A: That happens to me out of the blue. Some energy out of another dimension.

D: If it were not a fairy, do you have a sense of what other elementals or entities would be in North America or in the city, or in my house?

K: Not anymore than you would. Perhaps they are devic energies.

A: I guess it depends on who one prays to, who one is connected to.

K: The fairy energy is different from other energy. It has a particular quality. It is more musical, like the image you have of music, like it would have a color. When I have seen fairies or fairy energy, they are light forms, which is really just light. They have a glow and the colors are diffuse.

A: When that happens, is that when fairies are crossing the divide? Is it that the fairy has always been there or is it that the fairy has crossed into this realm. That is, is it always there, and we just don't see it, or does it appear from the other side?

K: I think it crosses, when it is allowed to, when the energy permits it.

A: And they come in dreams too?

K: I think it might be particular to the person. *The fairy energy might manifest as anything, actually, rather than just manifesting as a fairy.* In my dreams I have had fairy communications, but that doesn't mean that that is the only way they communicate.

D: It seems like it is simply the realization or awareness of a particular vehicle, like a fairy. It doesn't preclude any specific religious or spiritual orientation. There is no exclusivity on the part of the fairies, or of the Fairy Faith…It is not like you have to be a Fairy Faith person in contrast to say Christian or Buddhist or Hindu. Fairies appear to be helpers for whatever one is.

K. The fairies know your essence, and so they know how to help you. What works is specific for each person.

A. The path is about finding a specific path. The core of spiritual life is to manifest our form. It is beautiful to hear, from a fairy perspective, that the support is for whatever one's essence is.

Kay, like others, has had fairy experience and does sees fairies when eyes are closed and when in a hypnagogic state, but mostly as a conscious vision when fully awake and open-eyed, as an "audible" telepathy and sensing intuition.

All these fairyfolk have come to insight about fairies through experience and openness. Abraham J. Heschel (e.g., 1951, 1955, 1962, 1965), a leading Jewish theologian of the 20th century, read widely by Christians, wrote:

> Insight is a breakthrough, requiring much intellectual dismantling and dislocation. It begins with a mental interim, with the cultivation of a feeling for the unfamiliar, unparalleled, incredible. It is in being involved with a phenomenon, being intimately engaged to it, courting it, as it were, that after much perplexity and embarrassment we come upon *insight* – upon a way of seeing the phenomenon from within. Insight is accompanied by a sense of surprise. What has been closed is suddenly disclosed. It entails genuine perception, seeing anew. He who thinks we can see the same object twice has never seen. Paradoxically, insight is knowledge at first sight. (*The Prophets* (1962) xii)

Thus the fairyminded and fairypeople have come to know the Fairy world.

Chapter Four

Lightness, Drama and the Natural World: Attitude and Preparation for a FairyMindedness

> It's very hard to take yourself too seriously when you look at the world from outer space.
> —Thomas K. Mattingly II
> Apollo 16 astronaut

Lightness and Drama

In the previous chapter people mentioned how fairy energy and connection is light and joyous.

I had asked Minette whether she was a fairyperson, a fairy in a previous incarnation. She responded:

> I don't think so. But I don't think it matters about identifying that. All that matters to me is a kind of light there is to fairies. It's too important to get very serious about it... I mean the human state. We live in play. We live on a grand stage. This is the great creation show. We're living it. We're sort of playing parts in it. We are all playing parts in the play, but not all of us know that we are playing a part.

Connecting to fairy is not "heavy." One cannot be too resolute about it, for in so doing, as Kay declares, "you lose your sense of humor and capriciousness, and if you lose that, you lose your contact with the fairies.... The fairies are constantly trying to break up your rigidity, and your dogma."

In the rest of this short chapter, based on the words and experiences of these fairyfolk, and some of my own realized sensibilities, I try to describe an attitude and practice of being which fairyfolk often carry.

Fairy consciousness, although serious in its sanctity, can simultaneously be very light.[1] It can be about delight, frivolity, flightiness, giddiness, frolic, irreverence, light mischief, the laughter of surprise (or the surprise of laughter), and "turning one's head around." Light not only refers, as in many mystical orientations, to the divine influx or spiritual opening, inflow, emanation, or acknowledgement of insight in enlightenment, but also here refers to a quality of buoyancy, airiness, or levity, as in lightening. This is as opposed to earnestness, weightiness, over-seriousness.

Humor and levity, a lightness of mind, is also important in other spiritual traditions. It is not uncommon for respected masters, teachers, and elders of Yoga, Zen Buddhism, and the Native American Way to use humor as a teaching tool, to break up preoccupation and ego-centeredness. Laughing at one's self can be helpful for spiritual growth.[2]

This kind of lightness does not diminish sacredness of fairies and fairyfolk. Kay, Carol and others assert that fairies, sacred beings, serve essential tasks as servants to help humans in specific daily tasks, in general education and counseling to humans concerning the environment, and to bring greater awareness of fairies in Nature and Spirit. Fairyness, all my informants agree, is also quite serious in that the heightened sensibilities of fairies, of fairy-conscious humans, and of fairypeople make them all prey to the cold dispassion in human disrespect of nature, to human insensitivity, and to greed. And fairypeople, like others, but often more than others, face distracting challenges in accomplishing the tasks of physical and psychological survival within spiritually unsupportive environs. Having feet in both physical and metaphysical dimensions can make for insecurity in quotidian affairs. (See Chapter Twelve.) But still, lightness of heart and mind permits continuous opening to realms beyond the ego and helps one be flexible.

The very consciousness of an added dimension of fairy beings can provide a buoyant, amusing awareness of things. As Kay reiterates, "One of the ways fairies break up your strictness and lack of joy is with humor. And humor knocks out the brain, disengages you." This light, lifted-aboveness doesn't discard the seriousness of the sacred. It can highlight it, embody it, and, at the same time, transform towards greater spiritual heights. Fairy lightness - enchantment - is akin to ecstatic or numinous experience in other religious orientations.

A common theme among some fairyfolk, as Minette was saying above, is the notion that life is a drama. It is important, she iterates, to realize that our own lives, and the lives of fairies and other beings, are parts of a grand play of the universe. I think she means that sometimes people get lost in the parts they play, the scripts that have been outlined for them, and even the improvisational scripts they create within the larger Masterpiece. Realizing the reality of fairies, being open to a wider script of consciousness, enables fairyfolk to look at themselves, and often laugh at themselves, and connect outside the human play within the larger drama of the earth, history, and spirit. For fairyfolk, fairies are ethereal metaphysicians who help heal the wounds of humans' separation from Nature and God.

Obtaining this kind of perspective on one's self and the world includes the realization that a person plays roles not only in their own daily life, but also in other planes of existence, even in possible past or future lives. A self-reflexive perspective beyond and above oneself can lift one into an understanding of the multiple physical and metaphysical parts one plays in a Great Drama. The realization of more than one or multiple planes of existence enables humans to understand that they may have parts in more than one realm of consciousness. Thus sometimes one get can outside of one's self on one plane and relate on one or more planes at once. This reflexivity and meta-knowledge can lighten the load on one or more levels as one "looks down" on oneself. (In other spiritual/psychological traditions, as in Yoga philosophy, this has been called the Witnessing (or Observing) Self.)[3] The physical and metaphysical roles one plays are multiple. Knowing that can make for seeing one's and others' roles as drama.

Transformation is also the playing out of changes in the self and in self-knowledge. In so doing one changes (dramatic) positions in the cosmos.

Cultural ecologist and environmental philosopher Abram (2011:270), incorporating a similar dramaturgical perspective in which humans can be the self-reflexive *dramatis persona* in what Minette above calls "the great creation show," describes how in more oral, technologically simple cultures:

> ...the world is articulated as story. The surrounding cosmos is not experienced as a set of fixed and finished facts, but as a story in which we (along with the moon sliding in and out of the clouds, and the trout leaping for a fly) are all participant. For the relation of a tale to its characters is much the same as the relation of this earthly cosmos to its inhabitants. Just as there is an interiority to the perceived world (carnally enfolded as we are by the round expanse of the terrain and the curving vault of the sky), so the characters in a well-told tale live and breathe within the voluminous interiority of the story itself. In other words, we find ourselves situated in the land, with its transformations and cycles of change, much as protagonists are situated in a story. To a deeply oral culture, the earthly world is felt as a vast, ever-unfolding Story in which we – along with the other animals, plants, and landforms – are all characters.

Transpersonal psychologist Hillman (e.g., 1985, 1996), who promotes a polytheistic psychology which recognizes multiple images and entities and "can embrace conflicting directions" (Moore 1989:37), states "indeed psychic life is *show*, both the comedy and agony of drama, and *schau*, each appearance an imagistic essence, a showing forth; revelations, theophanies" (quoted in Moore 1989:43). As Moore summarizes "The polytheistic soul is richly textured and texted. It has many qualities of character and is the *theater* where many stories are enacted, many dreams mirrored" (38) (my emphasis).

Similarly Heschel (1959:99) speaks of a cosmic drama:

> The intuition of that all-pervading unity [the universe] has often inspired man with a sense of living in cosmic brotherhood with all beings... But over and above that there is another kinship: the kinship of being. We are all – men, stars, flowers, birds – assigned to the same cast, rehearsing for the same inexplicable drama. We all have a mystery in common – the mystery of being.

En-lighten-ment can bring a light-headedness, a liftedness to one's spirit that can allow insight and enlightenment to happen. This can be joyous.... Joy is a seriously necessary and healthy human emotion/state. This joy of lightness can lessen the everyday burden of life as well as the burden of the spiritual quest.

In Western psychological terms, connecting with such non-corporeal, egoless beings as fairies is through letting go or temporarily putting aside the human ego, letting go of preconceptions, emotional baggage, and personal patterns which inhibit such awarenesses. This letting go, I suggest, *is* a lightness. Some philosophies, and associated practices for spiritual growth, as in Yoga and Buddhism meditation, revolve in great part explicitly around the self-reflexive journey to remove ego interference.

There need not be a contradiction between mainstream religions and the Fairy Faith. For believers and mystics a reality that logically may not follow from a strongly held reality is OK because logic is not the standard. The removal of logic permits authentic spiritual experience. Laughter, coming from the play and playfulness of the lightness of temporary detachment, rises above the weightiness of being overly attached to one's reality. It's both serious and amusing. The transcendent can be amusing, and amusement can be transcendent.

Fairyfolk in the Natural World

I am convinced that openness to fairies also depends upon one's attraction to nature: being comfortable alone in the woods and seeking communion with trees, birds, and nature. All the fairyfolk I met actively immerse themselves in the quiet outdoors.

Kay is an avid gardener who grows much of her own food. Jon goes to isolated spots in the glen and on remote walks to connect with divine energy. Carol hikes alone and leads tourists on hikes in Donegal mountains. Marita goes out into nature when she feels need to reconnect with Fairy.

Debbie, the fairyminded sculptor of fairy figures, gets her inspiration directly from nature. She wrote:

> I spend a lot of time watching the abundance of wild birds here drawn by the Lagan River… The sparrows had looked half starved when we moved in, not surprising when there was not a worm in the garden. … Fattening the birds became my mission and bringing in the wrens and robins and much loved blackbirds. There is an abundance of crows and magpies, and they all seem to muddle by surprisingly amicably – even when one of our lazy cats just sits there in the heather bush watching, amused by their ingeniousness. I remember once watching a big old tatty crow hide his stash. I could have watched his antics all day… When I was a child we emigrated to Canada and it took me a while to get used to different birds. Same names, different size and I kind of missed the birds I grew up with and were part of my consciousness! I remember once I was alone in the woods I used to haunt at the back of our house, closed in on all sides and above by thin little aspen trees with a golden canopy. A sound made me stop in the stillness and in a heartbeat a blue jay flashed through the trees before me and left its magical blue trace on my mind's eye.

Marita like Kay, who knows that in a past life she was a fairy, finds direct experiences of nature crucial to her being herself. Here Marita talks explicitly about her connection to nature:

> As a child I was very close to the woods. Really, really, really very close. And I am still very close to the trees and still go there. Anyone who knows me is fascinated by my connection with trees, with forests. I think my connection is in the forest and the forest floors. But I also can be very, very joyous in gardens, in beautiful gardens. But I think the closest I am to fairies is in the woods.

The locale of past and present fairy experience, in sightings or sensing fairy presence, is almost always in quiet, natural environments, away from the noise and the construction of populated areas.

I spoke with Nora, a local woman and filmmaker, who told me that as a child she had quite a strong sense of connection to fairies, and that later in life a psychic had instructed her to develop those sensibilities, expand her fairy consciousness. But Nora didn't, even though she had a yearning for Kay's and others' ongoing connectedness to the Fairy Realm. After several years living in Dublin and by allowing her busy-ness and company business to interfere with her unfolding of fairyness, she lost this connection to nature, to the natural landscape and its inhabitants. She lamented the loss.

Here Kay talks about fairies, fairy consciousness, and nature.

Kay: In the past people did have a solid connection to fairies and the Fairy Realm, and more spirituality in general. And people did not have mechanistic theories of physics. Also, most didn't live in urban environments. There are almost no stories about meeting with fairies in cities. All of these encounters were out in the woods or the fields.

That is the march of civilization. I have heard over and over again that fairies disappeared with the advent of electricity. It is probably a metaphor, but it may actually have some reality to it too. It may have something to do with whatever electricity does, making it difficult for the fairies to hang around.[4]

D: Why are there fewer fairies in the Midlands or the flat country?

K: To me it's obvious, because that is just not where the fairies hang out. They hang out where there is texture and beauty and something happening in nature, like the lakes and the trees and the mountains and sea.... The landscape for them has to be diverse and beautiful. Flat land and/or cities are just not where they hang out.

One of the people I interviewed said that music came from the fairies when he was out in nature. He heard music and turned it into fairy music for his composition. The artist went on to talk about the fairies and he said that he generally leaves them alone, like the rest of the wildlife. So you would probably find the fairies where you would find other wildlife. You wouldn't find wildlife in a cultivated meadow, or a cultivated pasture.

D: So fairy paths or fairy lines would not be found in the Midlands for the most part?

K: I think there are ley lines all over the world, but if the fairies travel, if that is what they do, somehow they travel in connection with ley lines. Fairies can go through matter. Their paths can go through matter and can go through trees. There are lots of stories of fairy paths going through houses and people would have to do something to divert the path or move.

The day Carol took Kay, me, and the two visitors from Germany on a fairy tour of northwest Donegal, Kay's and Carol's connections to nature were apparent. They were unafraid to climb around places in the woods or scramble up banks by the roadside. Even in her seventies, Kay is light on her feet and easily climbs hills and leads the way through forest paths.

One of the sites on the tour was a fairy tree, with old gnarled roots partly encasing a boulder. It definitely appeared as a small niche within the wider glade and had an appealing aesthetic quality to it. Fairy trees or sites, reputed to be frequented by fairies, often have rock and old trees embedded in one another, with little crevices, overhangs, or hiding spots. Kay explored it well and said that she could live up on the flat of the rock surrounded by trees.

We also stopped at "Fairy's Purse," a somewhat unusual looking, large boulder set near the middle of a small clearing in the woods. Although large boulders like that often appear on survey and archaeological maps of the area, this boulder, Carol said, as she looked at a detailed archaeological survey, did not appear on the map. (Carol herself has worked with archaeologists).

While we were exploring the site, some of us circumambulated the boulder in an attempt to "understand" or feel the energy of the place. Kay found blueberries growing in a shallow crevice along the top of the boulder, and started eating them. At first I thought she was eating lichen or moss. She also passed one or two berries to Carol and to me. Kay called the blueberries "fairy food." ... At this boulder, Carol explained, you can make a wish for financial success by leaving a present. The last one to leave, I threw a euro coin by the boulder.

The close identity between nature and nature beings like fairies, the discovery and experience of nature spirits in untrammeled natural spots away from "civilization," and the sightings of fairies in remote parts of the landscape are common in Celtic folklore. In non-Western indigenous societies with shamanic experience, vision quests and the like, in the nature mysticism of Western mystics and transcendentalists such as William Blake, Thoreau, and Emerson, and among modern deep ecologists, contemplative solitary time in Nature is often the stimulus and the locale of mystical experience and revelation. The discovered wisdom and knowledge of sacred experience emerges and reveals itself in the purity of Nature. In the Faeroe Islands, when I did fieldwork in the 1980's, I constructed a map of the locations of *huldufolk* ("elves") whom villagers said only lived in the nooks and crannies of the outlands and hills, away from human habitation (Gaffin 1996).

In recent years the meaning and sanctity of particular locales in nature, (and of Nature in general) in indigenous peoples' landscapes, has taken a major role in cultural (and archaeological) anthropological works such as those by Nelson (1983), Meyers (1991), Basso (1996), and, for Westerners, by Milton (2002), among others. Fairyfolk's discovery of fairies as other-than-human persons in the environment is not unlike those of indigenous peoples where the natural and the supernatural are not clearly differentiated. Alaskan Koyukon views on nature in which the natural world is quite animated is one strong example (Nelson 1983).

The centrality of nature and of specific places where fairies were or are seen or sensed is central to fairy consciousness, as people quoted above have confirmed. Fairy places – particular trees, boulders, and landscape niches – with fairy past or present fairy energy, are foundational to fairyfolk's location in the cosmos.

K. Basso's (1996) *Wisdom Sits in Places*, discussing Cibecue Apache attachment to place(s), summarizes this possibility for the profundity of place in human awareness:

> As numerous as they are both singular and specific, and fully realizable across great distances, relationships with places are lived whenever a place becomes the object of awareness. In many instances, awareness of place is brief and unselfconscious, a fleeting moment (a flash of recognition, a trace of memory) that is swiftly replaced by awareness of something else. But now and again, and sometimes without apparent cause, awareness is seized – arrested – and the place on which it settles becomes an object of spontaneous reflection and resonating sentiment. It is at times such as these, when individuals step back from the flow of everyday experience and attend self-consciously to places – when, we may say, they pause to actively sense them – that their relationships to geographical space are most richly lived and surely felt. For it is on these occasions of focused thought and quickened emotion that places are encountered most directly, experienced most robustly, and, in Heidegger's view, most fully brought into being. Sensing places, men and women become sharply aware of the

complex attachments that link them to features of the physical world. (106-7)

For fairyfolk, the locales of fairy sightings and fairy energy represent and epitomize the make-up of the layered cosmos, the closeness of God's messenger/representatives, the wisdom and attitude of sanctity, and even the individual's location in the cycles of birth, life, and the afterlife. (See Chapter Ten on incarnation and reincarnation.)

As I have argued elsewhere (Gaffin 1996:232), "like traceable links of kinship, different places and people's experience with them provide personal and cultural grounding." For fairyfolk, the fairy places in nature bind fairyfolk to a profound sense of physical, natural, and metaphysical emplacement, a "ground" of being, and in a sense and experience of interacting with and belonging to the immanent and the transcendent world of Nature, Fairies, God, and the Cosmos.

Minette's FairyLands

As mentioned above, at Kay's suggestion, I had traveled down south to Minette's in County Wicklow, an area known for its rolling granite hills and beautiful gardens. It is a less rustic, more built-up area than the wilder west and northwest coast of Ireland. But there are still many undeveloped areas. Minette's house sets apart from others on a country road, and is surrounded immediately by garden, potted plants, and trees set within a region of cultivated farmland as well as uncultivated land.

Somewhat tall, Minette is a bouncy, vigorous middle-aged, forthcoming woman with light brown hair and eyes. She has a sweet voice, and sings her own lilting Celtic and fairyish tunes. She carries herself in proud posture, and is welcoming and comforting.

Marc and Val were also at Minette's. Marc is a serious looking, less than middle-aged, masculine looking Englishman, regular build, dark hair and eyes. Once he begins to talk you get a sense that he is a learned person, with clear diction and purpose. A writer and workshop leader, he is also a respected channeler who has received many words from other Sources and has published a book of his channelings.

Val is Marc's partner, an Englishwoman of artistic temperament who is also well versed in psycho-spiritual experience and dialogue. Medium brown hair, slightly taller than the average woman, she is feminine but hearty, and, like Marc, carries herself confidently. She speaks with facility of her artistic practices and the relationship between art and spirituality.

All three of these fairyminded folks do not think that they themselves are fairypeople, i.e., reincarnated fairies, like Kay, but they strongly experience the Fairy Realm. Val said that although she is not fairy, she once lived where fairies were very strong, so she connected. Marc is knowledgeable about Celtic peoples and skills, and in contacting elementals. He well recites the classic, mythical history of how 2000 years ago invading Milesians conquered the then-reigning ancient race of Ireland, the Tuatha de Danaan. The Tuatha de Danaan, as many Irish assert, had the fairy ability to retreat into invisibility, to disappear behind the veil. They were forced to spend nearly all their time behind the veil. This, as the story goes, was the origin of Irish fairies, not just the now commonly conceived tiny or one or two foot high ones, but human-size fairies also.

Marc said fairypeople have, like all of us, threads of the past. But the fairy past of fairypeople, (humans reincarnated from the Fairy Realm), can make them especially melancholic at the loss of human identification with and respect for nature and connections to the Fairy Realm. This has all been painful for the fairies, for even the cutting down of a tree is felt by the fairies. But music and art, he said, often keep fairypeople alive. Yet Marc said "now the fairies are winning" in their increasing appearance, even if secularly as reminders on fashionable clothing and on trendy toys and decorative objects. He said they are "dancing around."

Not too far from Minette's house is an expanse of uncultivated land, within which there is an unbounded area she calls "The FairyLands". The second day the four of us ventured there in the morning. As we approached an extended area of brush, trees, and boulders I followed Minette's instructions to go first, alone, to find The FairyLands. I was drawn to one of the far corners of the uncultivated area, proceeded there, and waited for the others near some short, but old trees. I walked around what I thought was the fairy area.

It turned out that where I was waiting for them was by the exact spot that Minette calls the Fairy Tree, where Minette and her guests visit.

After Minette and the others had joined me she respectfully put her hands around what she said was the fairy hawthorn tree, old but not very tall. (Hawthorn trees for centuries have been thought to be residences of fairies.) She held it for a while to absorb its energy. Once, she said, she distinctly saw a pink triangle in the air by the tree. Without discussing our intentions, we all individually did ritual circumambulations or postures and ponderings to soak up the vibrations, to sense and commune with fairy energy, within a visible circumference of the tree.

Minette had said there was a healing stone by the Fairy Tree, but I mistook the one in front of it as the one, and I sat on it. She said that was "interesting." Actually I did not want to venture a few feet further under the thick canopy of the thorn tree, as it seemed a bit intrusive and scary. After a few minutes I did put my right hand on the stone, thinking that maybe it would help my right bicep a week or so sore from carrying heavy bags of peat down the footpath to the Donegal cottage I was living in. I forced myself a little to touch the healing stone because of her suggestion that I do it. Withdrawing my arm, lo and behold, my hand was pricked in two or three places. Thinking it might be an omen of sorts, I said to myself that the fairy tree or energy was intentionally pricking me, or as Val later called it, "slapping" me. By imbuing the pricks as a kind of unwelcomeness I self-justified my originally not feeling right about touching it or going deeply into the space. But, later, Marc said that the fairies were infusing me with some of their resin.

So the pricking experience there, according to Marc, was the reverse of what I initially thought to be a unwelcoming gesture. It was a prick into loosening my cosmology, opening a space in my mind and heart. (Several fairyfolk have said that fairies sometimes lead us to realize that the opposite of what we think is really the truth.) In retrospect, I now think that that pricking experience, with my openness to these people and the experiences, and under the influence of their mystical epistemology, was an unthinking instant that awakened me to fairy things for myself. Increasingly I have come to realize that spiritual growth and unfolding is sometimes psychically and emotionally painful. Pricking, and the realization of being wrong, are themselves metaphors for the challenges and pains of self-discovery.

Back at the house, at lunch, Minette said that I had "passed the test" for fairy sensibility, having found the location she was heading for. She said that the fairies letting me in was a "good sign," since on my own I had gone directly to the site of the fairy tree and stones. In our discussion and joint experiences we all bonded further with each other, with Nature, and with Fairy.

She said "I'm told you need to find your own way to fairy." She meant it literally in terms of finding the fairy place in her FairyLands, but also, as we discussed, that a person generally needs to find his/her own way to connections with the Other Realms. A person cannot really be instructed into experiencing the sacred. It must come from within.

Sensing fairies or fairy energy, forms of learning and growing spiritually can occur when conditions are favorable. When the ego is not so dominant and an intuitive sensibility arises, personal attitudes and emotions, alongside specific environmental and cultural influences, enable new experiences and interpretations of the world to take root. Barriers between the physical and spiritual worlds can fall away. Those experiences often take place in the wilds, locales undeveloped by human hands.

Chapter Five

Fieldwork and Personalwork

> Wonder rather than doubt is root of all knowledge.
> —Abraham J. Heschel

I had always been rather scientific minded, and had been trained at leading universities in social science research, research method, and academic writing. In Western scholarship fairies have been on the far end of the scientific spectrum of reality, usually as items of folklore and uneducated, "foolish" superstition. But as a cultural anthropologist, and presumably an open-minded person, I have been interested in other worldviews, religions, philosophies. In my experiences overseas and at home, in the 9-5 working world and in academe, I learned to avoid judging other perspectives as "wrong," to suspend disbelief, to "bracket" (Greenwood 2009) other worldviews. (Philosopher-phenomenologist Husserl coined the term "epoche" to refer to this attitude.) But this is still a fully rational (as opposed to non-rational) model. It uses the intellect to gain "understanding."

I did "believe" in God and practice religious rituals of my own Jewish background, and had inklings of spiritual forces in various practices of prayer, meditation, and tai-chi.[1] But I was an anthropologist who was secondarily a "believer," or seeker, but whose first identity was in science and professionalism.

When the study and experience of fairyfolk in Ireland initially engulfed me, I entered with the same suspension of disbelief from other situations over the years.... A few years earlier in Ireland in 1999-2000 during a sabbatical I had been researching placenames and human-to-nature relationships in traditional villages of County Donegal. I got along well with local residents, and made friends. But I was an outsider, a researcher.

The fairy path I stumbled onto in 2004, and followed, it seemed, was happenstance. Simply, as I mentioned above, a friend of mine from my earlier stay in 2000 introduced me to Kay, a seventy year old expatriate American woman living in Ireland. We resonated in some amorphous way. I decided to change my course of study towards working with people of the so-called Fairy Faith, although she is not actively interested in "converting" people to her own sensibilities. Kay must have perceived that I could be open to her knowledge of the Fairy Kingdom.[2] Unknown to me at the time, others called her "Queen of the Fairies." But she never referred to herself that way and still thinks it unfairy-like and immodest to personally assume that name.

As indicated above, many years previously as a fledgling anthropologist I had spent a year in the remote Faeroe Islands in the North Atlantic. Islanders discussed and argued about the existence and sightings of *huldufolk,* a kind of elf long experienced in Scandinavian countries. (Many Irish say the elf is a fairy.) I even mapped the locations of what some people told me were the haunts of *huldufolk* in the greater environs of the village. Like most other Scandinavian and Celtic peoples, they did not consider such nature beings as God-sent, divine entities.

But during that period in my life, I then only suspended disbelief, and did not sense such creatures as huldufolk. It was about twenty years later that Kay and other fairyfolk appeared while I was living in a rural Irish hamlet in Donegal during a sabbatical. I fell into a rabbit hole of sorts. I became enmeshed in a web of spiritual intrigue. It was enthralling. (Originally fairy meant *fai-erie,* a state of enchantment.[3]) After that I went back to Ireland for months on end, in the summers and winters between semesters at the university. A few times, for a total of about eleven months.

Although initially I did not sense the Fairy Realm, for some reasons stated earlier, I was open to, and sympathetically interested in, my informants' orientations. My journal at the beginning of summer 2004 reads:

> I am hoping that Kay and others will help me stick my hand into the fourth dimension. Right now when I look at my hands, or lift them up to the sky, in a ritual of paying attention to the sacred, I get a sense of awe, of a source or vehicle of sunlit energy to Creation. It gives me sustenance and purpose. When I look at my hands, it is almost as if they are disembodied, or not quite my own, but something attached to me, part of me, but not wholly me. My Hands.

In retrospect I have come to realize that this attitude was a form of preparation for an alternative, additional perspective and set of experiences. Under the influence of my informants, this attitude resulted in a change in my interpretation, understanding, of the make-up of cosmos. (Such a change Luhrman (1989) has termed "interpretive drift.")

I realize more so now that during my first major fieldwork experience in the Faeroe Islands in the 1980's, having been trained as an empirical social scientist, I was interested in demonstrating to myself and university academics back home that I was indeed such a scientist. As well, with my anthropological career on the line, I was at times nervous and overly serious about the process of fieldwork. That earnestness might well have disallowed me to be interested in, or have access to, alternative states of consciousness.

During and after my Irish fieldwork I have come to *imagine* shapeless vitality in the air above. This is "imagine" in the Jungian sense in which one actively imagines, mindfully, to the reality of a collectiveness or interconnectedness which supersedes the individual. It is not recreational fantasy or hallucination in which one fantasizes something that does not exist, but imagination of the mind connecting to something outside the self. Now I can sometimes, at will, sense, connect to that amorphous energy. But my consciousness of fairies in the "air" is generally spontaneous, at will, in the sense that in an instant I realize an absence of that consciousness, and then, in the contrast, connect. That is, in an instant I simply "remember" and come upon my sensing of fairies or fairy energy, and feel it not far above the ground, perhaps one or two hundred feet high.

My imaginations of this reality are not a result of active study. And without visualization techniques promoted in several New Age books. Again, my journal:

> It is helpful to skim some books because they mentioned some items such as fairy lines, of which I did not know much. But for the most part I am not interested in reading theories or stories of fairy encounters. They do not convince or help much. Interested in first-hand accounts and experiences, I am an ethnographer, skeptical of things unseen or not experienced. Visualization techniques seem forced and inauthentic and confuse fantasy with intuition and experience. There is a naturalness to the honesty and experience of the fairyfolk I am talking to, which is more in order with the naturalness of the Fairy Realm, and the coming to discover, rather than an artificial forcing. Carol had said "*you just be.*"
>
> When I detect, through my own intuition, inauthenticity in a New Age book, I merely skim or close the book..... But my own occasional thinkings, sensings, intuitings of beings or forces are real.

My original choice of Ireland as a site to explore was not accidental. Years earlier on a short vacation I was there and found the physical geography as well as the general aura suitable to my sensibilities and my anthropological studies in landscape. The 32,500 square miles of roundish island with multiple and overlapping views of the intricate coastline, mountains, hills, and plains make life itself a topographic experience. In ways hard to define, the landscape and the people are compelling and seductive. Everyone – natives, tourists, or the many "blow-ins" (outsiders who blow in with the winds of fortune and choose to settle down in Ireland) imbue the landscape with a magic beyond the beauty of the scenery. A simultaneous earthy and heady Celtic presence runs as a deep undercurrent in simple interactions with a villager or with a mountain. I chose Donegal for its beautiful land and seascape, rustic coastline, relatively undeveloped countryside, and distance from big cities like Dublin or Belfast.

During my studies in the years 1999-2000 I lived alone and walked around the countryside of the Rosguill Peninsula, where I first rented a small house on the dramatic coast in the small village of Dooey (Doagh). Back in the States I had been living for many years in the rural northeast and was an amateur naturalist, especially reveling in birds. These inclinations carried over into Ireland. As it was for some local Irish, for me nature and spirituality were entwined. Several years previously I had written natural history essays about my sometimes spiritual experiences in the woods near my farmhouse in upstate New York.

Here is a journal excerpt of those early days in Ireland, looking out the back of the house I rented. It attests to my own linkages and comfort with nature, which I argued earlier are important for a fairy sensibility.

> I saw a flock of about 25 oystercatchers [coastal seabirds] in the "backyard" and then discovered some curlews, with their exceedingly long beaks bombarding the green ground. And then there were some seagulls, a robin right by the window, a few rooks, a couple starlings.
>
> The bird sightings ground me, slow me down, anchor me, let me realize again what I enjoy and who I am, and, with these kinds of birds, where I am. In the moment of observing them, however, I am not quite conscious of it being Ireland, but just not home, as there are no curlews or oystercatchers in Mink Hollow [in Western New York State]. At the moment of experiencing them, most birds anywhere are exotic in that they take one to another plane, a plane of airy experience.
>
> Perhaps it is best said that I let them take me to that other plane, the plane where location disappears. The "place" is with the bird, with nature, a place of sentiment and emotion unattached to particular scenery. The physical landscape and its ingredients of texture and fauna are potential entry points to realms which are not site-specific because the "place" is an abstraction of nature and geography, a metonymic or metaphoric experience of something above and beyond the local.

Four years later, a few hundred feet dramatically above the rugged Atlantic coast in an isolated cottage without electricity, peat fire burning, I wrote "On occasion as I sit around, I have a sense of beings or energy nearby, part of a kind of invisible, transcendent haze or vibration."

That Donegal cottage I came to live in was just outside the six-house hamlet of Baile an tSleibhe ("Hamlet of the Mountain") (pronounced Balan Clayva) at the end of a one lane road on the Rosguill Peninsula. Brendan, a friend of my friend, loaned me the use of his uninhabited old, traditional two room cottage. It had no electric, two fireplaces for heat, and propane-fueled twin cook burners. For heat I burned turf (peat) and occasionally coal, bags of which my shoulders carried down the long footpath. For illumination there were kerosene lamps, a battery-powered flashlight, the light of the burning fireplace, and sunlight. In addition to it being sleeping quarters, there I read, typed up field notes, and transcribed tape-recorded interviews after forays into the world of fairyfolk.

I was being a good researcher and academic, diligently finding and interviewing people Kay and others told me about. Like some other sojourns and fieldwork projects, my excuse for going to Donegal was to conduct anthropological research. I think, now, that many of my travels and studies were also borne of not quite knowing how to fully connect myself with the world in the States immediately around me and through the lack of fully seeing life here and now as a magical adventure.

Consciously and professionally I was trying to conduct research on religion and spirituality, but less consciously yearning to exit an egoistic, scholarly approach to life. Thus without resistance Fairydom spiritually or philosophically seduced me while living in the closest building to the very valley that years before people in Dooey had said was a place of fairies. That valley, mentioned above, is Clochar Dorcha, ("Dark Stoney Place"), and it lies in seclusion just outside of the hamlet. In retrospect, I realize that I changed there.

When in Dooey in 2000 a neighbor, Mary McBride, a chirpy and shortish, well-dressed, single, middle-aged woman (who kept her house quite tidy), said that one of her favorite places growing up was out to Crockmore "where there is a lovely little lake near Clohar Dorcha where fairies lived." She said "you have to keep away from the trees there – we were warned not to touch them because of the fairies." At the time I hadn't been to Clochar Dorcha, nor did I think that fairies were anything but folklore. But that little valley came to be the setting of profound moments of my life.

Four years later, ironically, and seemingly by happenstance, I came to live immediately next to the little valley of Clochar Dorcha on the other, upper side. The first time in and around Baile an tSleibhe, while I was earlier still living in Dooey directly on the coast, I had been a bit disoriented, even with maps. The hamlet sits at the plateau of a small mountainous (or big hill) region above the dramatic, craggy seacoast. On short hikes in different directions you can get to places with distant views in various directions out to sea and inland. It is a beautiful, primitive locale. The settlement itself does not appear as a named entity on any map, including the Road Atlas of Ireland or the more detailed fold-out map of County Donegal. The latter simply shows three or four houses (small black squares) in an area along a continuous minor road, also termed an "other" road.

The hamlet's isolated setting, its end-of-the-roadness, its lack of modern buildings, make it almost mythological in its idyll of simplicity. The location, the lives of the people, the names of places - like the hamlet's very own name - read like a story out of an old Irish novel. Perhaps the most impressive physical dimension of Baile an tSleibhe is the rocky hinterland just above it which looks north and east out to Tory Island and Hornhead and southwards over to Muckish mountain. The latter dramatically rises above the other mountains, harboring endlessly varying cloud caps and cloud covers of various shapes and colors of gray. Above and out of sight northeast from the cottage is the mountaintop of Crockmore, with its hidden loch, of which Mary McBride had spoken. Surrounded by rustic outcrops, heather, and open space the area is a world of texture. The loch is maybe seventy-five feet wide and two or three times the length, bounded on some sides by cliffy margins, so access to all sides is not possible. The wind blows over and through the loch, sometimes making horizontal drapes of darkened ripples across the surface, like quickened schools of black/gray energy, like northern lights of rippled water. The wind blows you forward or back, even though the sea not too far below can be calm in its own shade of grayish, slate blue.

After leaving the hamlet on a first hike to the area, to walk down the mountain towards Dooey, I left the road and trail. As I wrote in 2000, long before my talking to fairyfolks:

> I walked back a bit and decided to walk over the mountain down to Dooey or thereabouts. It would be my first long walk without a trail. It was trickier and wetter than I figured but it went into the wildest regions of Rosguill.
>
> Despite looking at a map in hand, it was not clear exactly in which direction to head, what would be in store for me. After a while climbing over what the map identified as Crockmore (an Anglicized word for CnocMor ("Big Hill"), a flat secluded valley between Crocknamona ("Hill

of the Bog") and Crockmore appeared. I later learned the valley was Clochar Dorcha. Kevin Ward, in his pamphlet on the peninsula, calls it "The Forbidden Place of Rosguill," and describes it as "a savage awesome valley."

From a distance some animals on the steep slope of Crocknamona became visible. To my astonishment, my binoculars brought me close to four wild goats. They were fantastic. Three white ones and a colored one. Two of the bearded white ones had no horns, apparently females, and one white one had long slightly curved-back grayish horns. The most intriguing sight was the other multicolored male with huge, dark gray horns. Primordial. His horns were magnificent, protruding far out and around his head, giving him a wide and fearsome presence. His colors were wild, as only the right side of his head had a wide stripe of black down through to his neck. It was as if it were painted on to make him look dangerous. Then he was white, then he was dark brown.

The Clochar Dorcha valley experience became a site of discovery of creatures never expected.

It was four years later that I remembered laughing at Clochar Dorcha about the spiritual web that Kay and other fairyfolk spread for me. When I had lived by the coast I was interacting with fairy avoiders. Now right in the valley above the village of Dooey I was interacting with fairy seekers! The enticement of Fairydom, the lure of the other world. Kay and others seemed to sense my affinity to her beyond the intellectual, beyond the social. She sensed the possibility of my coming to interpret the world in similar ways. Something was opening up.

A journal entry of 2004 reads:

> I just laughed out loud at myself. I laugh for, and with, the ridiculousness which is embedded in juxtaposing fairypeople's reality with those of people who think fairies do not exist or fairies are bad. The seemingly irreconcilable differences in humans' realities. Knowing that at some level that there is only one "reality" that is impossible to get to know fully, dogmatism about differing interpretations is in itself amusing.

When alone I would question and yearn about the people and perspectives I was encountering. Sometimes I would walk about in the natural areas surrounding my isolated cottage outside Baile an tSleibhe. Occasionally I would just sit down and admire the remote, beautiful scenery, especially at Clochar Dorcha, as my own journal relates:

> I sat out at this end of Clochar Dorcha earlier this afternoon. Initially my movement of my head and eyeglasses made it seem like the north side of

the valley was moving slightly in waves. I was trying to figure out if it could be that way independently of my glasses. I guess I concluded that it was just the lenses. In retrospect it is almost as if I wanted to be part of a physical reality outside my normal one, the scientific one I generally carry.

As I sat upon a rock in this compelling place, I realized that there is no good reason for me or man to assume that our three dimensional reality is the only one. Bees presumably don't know they make fruit and life possible. Electricity, radiation, magnetism, etc. are all invisible to the naked eye. Animals can see, smell, sense things humans can't. Ants are so small to us that we must be like behemoth gods to them.

My academic self gave some way to an added spiritual self or metaphysical orientation as the people I spoke with indirectly opened me up to myself. It wasn't that they convinced me of the reality of fairies or of reincarnation. Belief cannot be transferred, for it is a function of *experience*. Not through a rational process like active decision-making, I simply realized I had had an epistemic shift which allowed for the possibility of a personal understanding of fairyness.[4] Fairyfolk's own self-contained authenticities enabled me to let go of some of my own egoistic tendencies and more fully appreciate the wondrous.

This kind of experiential perspective of real encounters with other worlds has been discussed by other anthropologists (and psychologists). For example, see Ezzy's (2004:120-21) discussion of the hermeneutics of the ethnography of magical and mystical consciousness and of Greenwood (2000):

> By failing to attach sufficient importance to the otherworld, these [other methodologically atheist] analyses miss what pagans see as the essence of magic: otherworldly experience. (3)

Greenwood puts this most provocatively when she argues that:

> I suggest that magical identities are structured through a psycho-spiritual interaction with the otherworld, rather than constructed from social discourses of the ordinary world, as suggested by some recent works on identity formation in the social sciences. (18)

Magical experiences in the otherworld have real consequences in this world.

In my midsummer 2004 journal I quoted to myself Jeffrey Raff's (2000) book, *Jung and the Alchemical Imagination*:

> Patient waiting is often necessary for imaginal processes .... Of course an individual's desire for transformation and the experience of the self is necessary, too. That desire, coupled with attention and effort, provides the external heat necessary for change to take place. Beyond these factors, however, there is no way for an individual to control or "make" a process unfold. One cannot will the self to manifest. Working in the imaginal realm requires a willingness to follow, avoiding the temptation to control the processes. One must simply trust that the self knows what it needs to manifest. The inner alchemical processes emerge from the self and may not be directed by the ego. (161)

This all jived with my experience, and my informants' statements about not being too earnest, and about openness to lightness of heart and spirit. Another time I wrote:

> I just looked up from this keyboard to the wild fuchsia plants outside the window. I got an inkling of "that" headspace, of that invisible amorphous energy outside. But I didn't expect it.

One afternoon I expected Carol the artist for an interview at the Baile an tSleibhe cottage. While I was waiting for her, wind, rain, and occasional sun surrounded me, and I wrote in my journal:

> 2:40 p.m. I thought I heard a female voice(s) outside talking, but it turned out to be no humans, – maybe a fly? – I sat down again by the window to see if anyone was outside. It crossed my mind that the voices could be the voices of fairies. ... Not to be unfriendly or fearful, I said softly "Come on" to whatever creature(s) might have been by the cottage.

After Carol left I wrote:

> Carol had said on tape that the way to come to realize the presence of fairies was just to be, not to try. I really do not think I am trying. It just seems to come. Even now I almost feel like there is a mild buzz of activity around my head. I do not feel crazy or hallucinatory, or fearful, but it is a bit disorienting. An added occasional presence that gives me a little anxiety of a type I am unfamiliar with. It cannot be psychological imbalance in a conventional sense. I see in sylphy Kay and fairies-all-over-the-place Carol a real sanity, a real cogency, a real togetherness, a real functionality of mind that enhances orientation to all spheres. They might, like me, have a mild mania of sorts, but not an irrational, dysfunctional one. Rather one that lends itself to connection between people and fairies in the world. It adds a sense of belonging rather than withdrawal from the world. It feels like this section of Ireland, with its distinctive weather, landscape, and history, enables the mind to merge with spirit.

There are many different kinds of explanations for things. .... Once when I was on the phone in the U.S. with Kay in Ireland, I accidentally knocked the phone set and disconnected the call. After ringing her back Kay said that that is the kind of thing fairies do for mischief, for prompting our realization of their being about. You could just call it an accident, but then you are back to only scientific explanations of things.

How about this one? When in Kay's kitchen in Creeslough, Donegal one 2004 summer day, after jockeying to the local store to pick up a half dozen eggs for our brunch, Kay opened up the carton. She broke one into a bowl, not noticing what came out, and started to mix it in a bowl. Then she broke another one. It was a double yolk. Rare, but it happens occasionally. (I used to raise chickens and sell chicken eggs on my farm in upstate New York). The next one she broke was a double yolk. Quite unusual. The next one she broke was also a double yolk. And she noticed that the first one was a double yolk. Impossible? Now a miracle? We laughed, amused by what others might attribute to chance or even a different spiritual source, but what, in this worldview, is thought to be a consequence of fairy arrangements.

Later in the week Kay found that the two eggs left in the carton contained double yolks! I am not lying. Kay even went to the butcher who sold the eggs and he said that he had never seen or heard of double yolked eggs together before. Moreover, there is no way to tell ahead of time whether an egg has two yolks or not, unless you very carefully candle them, which he does not.... That was a "magical" carton of eggs. To this day Kay and I refer to those eggs as testimony to our shared experience of marvel.

Everything was influencing me without a conscious desire to have it effect me. After my visit to Minette's I wrote in my journal:

> The ability to talk now about my headspace, the energy field around my head, now is sometimes greater. My openness to the fairy world enables me to have discussions and share my own symbolic and energetic experiences with those three. As I sense more around me, it allows me further into the hole I slipped into in the winter. Had I not had those experiences in the cottage a week or two ago when I was writing, or not visited the Megalithic site in Minlara with Horst and Marta, and not been reading the Raff book, I might not have been able to converse well at Minette's, understood as much about my spiritual self, or join our journeys together. Each experience adds to the next in an organic way.

For me, and for fairyfolk and the fairyminded in general, fairies are part of an ongoing personal/spiritual process. My journal midsummer 2004 reads:

I could think of all of this stuff about personal process with a divine twist, as a pilgrimage to myself, to my soul. Life is a living mythological drama. "Drama" was the word that Val used more than once and Marc in his channeled stuff at the beginning of *One Heart*. I had used the word "stage" in my own journal above somewhere and then someone else used it a lot… It certainly appears that common threads and themes run through the talk and journies of all these folks, and me. And they all seem to reflect back to Jungian, alchemical, fairy, and spiritual psychology orientations.

A couple days later I wrote:

Yesterday was a fantastic day. Full of surprises. Jon, Kay and I drove in my rented Rover to Glencolumbkille. It just happened at Jon's suggestion and I was invited to go. There seemed to be a theme of directions on the trip. And directions in some metaphysical sense. The map did not tell us all we needed to know. We ended up going on roads we didn't know about. We also met some construction crew road managers who were disorganized in telling us to go. The light said green, but the cars were coming towards us on the one way driving stretch. After the cars passed one man waved us to stop, and one waved us to go, at the same time

At least two times we decided not to follow the road signs because we sensed they were wrong, and turned around to follow our sensibilities. A bit later we turned around again to discover that the signs were right. It also happened in Glencolumbkille on the way to St. Columba's chapel.

Later after we returned at dinner I said, regarding directions, that we should have known that something was amiss when the cars were coming towards us and the light was green. But Kay said it was perfect, meaning it was meant to be, and the divine plan is perfect. So I revised my statement to say things were "perfectly amiss."

Jon had described the three of us driving around Donegal as three fairies. Earlier in conversation while questioning him the evening before, he pointed out that I was assuming that I was not a fairy.

He talked to me about my journeying now, and being open to the road opening up to directions as they appear. That was the "way to live."

Up on the mountain road overlooking the ocean and Glencolumbkille Bay, at what Jon called the edge of the world, Jon had Kay and I hold each others' hands, close our eyes, and imagine that we were there in a time before human habitation. Bodyless. We imagined the wind blowing through our transparent bodies. I got a lot of it. Kay did too.

Jon and Kay's fairyness, their prehistory, seems encoded in their bones and DNA. All of us have our entire histories and prehistories, even prehumanness, encoded in us. If you think about it, it is quite true even in some scientific, cosmo-genetic sense.

And later:

Chapter Five

Sunday July 25, 2004

This journey of mine, this adventure-pilgrimage, helps me get out of myself, has me view myself as a character in a grand adventure-play. I am realizing that I need not take It quite so seriously. The playfulness of Fairydom, both in the sense of light-heartedness and in the sense of drama-full, liberates, within the generally plotted out spectacle. I can act, improvise, enact free will.

Friday afternoon on the beach I suddenly realized that I forgot my divinity. Then my hands spontaneously rose to the cloudy sky to let the sun shine into me. And then I broke out into the highest, smiley-est, most divine Tai Chi moments. Floating in the brisk wind at the beach, alone, but not even a thought of being alone. Not only did my open hands to the sky in the posture white-crane-spreads-its-wings enable me to feel a strong connection to the Source, but every step I took for several postures was euphoric. The sea was waving, and I was right out there, feeling as elated as ever before.

Then a few minutes later, a few confident steps along, I stopped again, turned straight into the wind, put my fingers together at my heart and asked for the winds of time to blow through me. Right here, in my heart, as I weep at touching the center. Joy, then a painful release.

I seem now, as in the car yesterday, to be able to spontaneously cry a bit, and smile a bit, weep and revel at the same time. In the past there was much more separation between sadness and joy. Now they seem to be converging.

July 27, 2004

At Kay's yesterday when she was talking about the difficulty of fitting into the human world and feeling different from others, having difficulty locating one's self in this realm, tears came to my eyes in empathy. The gentle, feeling way she spoke welled up in me my own feelings of alienation as a child, as an adult, the existential separateness coupled with being different. But in her sensitivity to that, and her connecting that to her divinity, her fairyness made me feel good for my differentness. My separateness is now more grounded in a feeling of difference, of being fairy-like in my sensitivities, my mischievousness, my jokingness, my turning things around, my desire to show the other side of things. It's actually connection, a belonging beyond the human community.

May, 2005

Despite my ability to make jokes, talk competently in the group here, and talk at length last night about fairy things with Ronald, there was an undercurrent of melancholy for me. But, just now, I automatically turned my head a bit to the left and felt a surge of spirit, of smile, of amusement at my life situation, of connectivity to the sky. The feeling was not intended, the movement was not intended. It was spontaneous, as if something else had automatically re-emerged. But I can count on it when I intentionally think of it, of the energy, of the elementals flying about, of God.

At the outset of summer 2005, when Kay first mentioned the possibility of no more fairypeople coming into the world for now, I felt heart-broken. My journal reads:

> May, 2005
>
> Yesterday, when Kay in the morning interview told me about possibly no more fairypeople coming into the world for now, I started to cry. This stuff means even more to me than I thought. It must be my identification with pain, Divinity and with Fairy.

(For a similar discussion of the development of "other" sensibilities to religious or mystical events and experiences, reflexivity of the ethnographer, and the academic and scholarly issues involved, see the introduction to Blain, Ezzy, and Harvey (2004) and especially the articles of Salomonsen, Griffin, and Ezzy. Ezzy argues that objectivity and subjectivity are enmeshed with each other and that spiritual experiences should be taken at face value: reported spiritual experiences should be treated as both real and socially constructed (7). For discussions of the complexity of the intersubjectivity of the ethnographer's position and the need to "shift personal positions in relation to one's subjects and other active discourses in the field that overlap one's own" see Marcus 1999:17. For other discussions of the existence of multiple realities and that "reality is experienced in different ways, depending upon cultural context and one's state of mind" (9) and of anthropologists "who have taken their informants' experiences seriously or who have had extraordinary experiences themselves" (12) see Young and Goulet's (1994) introduction and the articles within their edited volume *Being Changed: The Anthropology of Extraordinary Experience*.)

Chapter Six

Perspectives and Writings on Fairies

> Any profound view of the world is mysticism. It has, of course, to deal with life and the world, both of which are nonrational entities.
> —Albert Schweitzer

My work follows a few other explorers, academics, and mystics who have studied fairies or discussed fairyfolk, and have come to experience their reality. Others include William Blake, Charles Dickens, William Butler Yeats, Arthur Conan Doyle, and of course anthropologist W.Y. Evans-Wentz discussed in Chapter One. Evans-Wentz was a believer, although he believed that the Fairy Faith might be dangerous to explore, as in his mind the fairies do not want to know too much about humans. His research consisted mainly of talking to rural peasants and recording beliefs and stories concerning fairies. But he did not systematically talk with fairyfolk about their own inner workings. Accounts of the process, transformations, general worldviews, psychology, and personalities of those "running with the fairies" have been anecdotal and second or third hand.

The spiritual awakenings and evolution of consciousness which have emerged in the last forty or so years, primarily in psychology and metaphysical studies, represented by numerous authors like James Redfield, Ken Wilber, Eckhart Tolle – to name but a few, provide a supportive context for a contemporary transpersonal anthropology. And the Fairy Faith is now in a new shape and can be conceptualized as an authentic form of mysticism. But let us review some previous perspectives and literature.

In the last few centuries of Western religion, male-dominated institutions have generally frowned upon their publics having intuitive, mystical experience separate from the congregation. Church officials engendered a holier-than-thou attitude to the alleged superstitious beliefs of less sophisticated people. Spirituality became over-identified with form and dogma. Many scholars have discussed the decline of nature mysticism and of the so-called "paganism" of tribal peoples, pre-modern Christianity, Celtic Christianity, and of believers in nature spirits such as fairies.

The classic oral and written history of the origin of fairies in Ireland, as mentioned above, is that about two thousand years ago the Tuatha de Danaan, a race of humans substantially on the physical earth plane, had to retreat to behind the veil of visibility to avoid being conquered by the invading Milesians. All religions have origin and creation myths. (Jon said that the story of the Tuatha de Danann taking invisible refuge in the hills 2000 years ago should not be taken literally as the origin of fairies. Rather it points, he said, to the time and consciousness in which the issues of humans moving between the veils came to the fore.)

Elves also have been part of the history of fairy things. The word "elf" (*alfar*) comes from the Germanic and Scandinavian languages and mythology. The Scandinavians divided elves into two classes, light elves and dark elves. The light elves are (like) the light fairies, generally benevolent or harmless. In Scotland human-size fairies were called elves and Fairyland was Elfame. Elsewhere in the North Atlantic region elves and fairies are sometimes the same, sometimes with differences. William Shakespeare wrote of elves and fairies being the same.

The general consensus today among fairypeople and the fairyminded is that elves are not air fairies like sylphs, but are earth elementals. Thus elves tend to be more solid, more square, heavier in spirit, and more "grounded." They may look more serious, darker in color, and are more likely to look like wrinkled earth or be "gnarly" in some fashion. Elves, although still benevolent, may tend to be more grumpy than air fairies, more self-contained. Like fairies, they are intermediate deific beings, although it seems that their fairyness is less obvious and less obviously linked with the divine. The Norwegians call elves *huldrafolk* (A Norwegian word) and, as mentioned earlier, the Faeroese call them *huldufolk* (similar to West Norwegian), and were seen by many villagers I lived by on the Scandinavian Faeroe Islands. Like fairies of common lore, elves were not generally conceptualized as representatives/messengers of God nor as divine in the sense that they had sacred missions. Nor were they endowed with divine energy to be accessed by humans for spiritual awareness or transformation.

In the Faeroe Islands, as stated earlier, most people I spoke with said that the increasingly less seen *huldufolk,* the mischievous elves, no longer appeared much after electricity arrived in the 1950's. Elsewhere in the Western world similar beliefs and experiences support the notion that spirit beings diminished or disappeared with the advent of some form of modern times, and the invading appearance of non-believers. Whether you take these stories literally or metaphorically is not important. They all attest to "progress" overtaking direct relationships with nature and nature spirits. It is no coincidence that people today who experience fairyness are dismayed at the browning of environments, the destruction of natural places, and the materialism of development. Fairyfolk and others interested in spiritual transformation are more open to seek the myriad of Nature's kinds of energy.

Since the Middle Ages mainstream European culture often equated belief in fairies with madness or badness, and believed fairies to be residents of the dangerous wilds. In Scotland there was a demarcation between good and bad qualities of fairies, or good (light) and bad (dark) fairies. The rural folk divided the fairy world in two, the Seelie Court and the Unseelie Court. The Seelie Court were kindly beings of the spirit world (or Host) who engaged in benevolent acts such as providing food for needy humans. But they sometimes wrought revenge upon offenses to the fairy world, as by hurting human livestock or houses. The Unseelie Court, on the other hand, were fairy or fairy-like beings always to be avoided. They definitely engaged in injurious behavior to humans and were never considered advantageous. These fairies were thought to be the unsanctified, unforgiven dead who fly above the earth.

The Burning of Bridget Cleary: A True Story (Bourke 1999), a scholarly history, details the factual events surrounding the 1895 killing of an allegedly mad fairywoman. It is an account of the events and beliefs that led some Irishmen to persecute a woman thought to be running with the fairies. Fairyminded people, especially if female, were often considered to be (like) evil witches.

Countless beliefs in Ireland and elsewhere attest to the warning of people from going places where fairies were thought to live or hang out. Buildings were (and are) often constructed so as not to interfere with fairy paths, and, as we have seen, avoidance of fairy trees and places was commonplace. Many tales relate the dire consequences of contact with fairies. Many people used ritual precautions to guard themselves against fairies, while personal setbacks and disappointments were often attributed to fairies. Early folktales talked about humans being punished for intruding on the worlds of fairy creatures, and people often engaged in techniques for propitiation of potentially harmful fairies by various acts such as leaving milk out at night. These have been recorded and related elsewhere in numerous books on folklore. Only occasionally do two or three fairyfolk in this book leave offerings for fairies or think propitiary thoughts in attempts to contact fairies, as Minette did in the "FairyLands."

Generally fairies simply appear. Evans-Wentz (1935) describes how in the Tibetan context, elementals such as dakinis are part of a decidedly disciplined spiritual path. In contrast to traditional popular Western fairy belief and practice, Tibetans propitiate elementals on the road to transformative union with dakinis.[1]

Briggs (1976), the folklorist scholar of fairylore, (and a self-declared agnostic of fairies), has a long entry in her *A Dictionary of Fairies* entitled "Blights and illnesses attributed to the fairies," which strongly attests to the allegedly bad effects of fairies and elves. Parts of it read:

> The word "STROKE" for a sudden paralytic seizure comes directly from fairy belief. It is an abbreviation of 'fairy stroke' or 'elf stroke', and was supposed to come from an ELF-SHOT or an elf-blow, which struck down the victim, animal or human, who was then carried off invisibly, while a STOCK remained to take its place. Sometimes this was a transformed fairy, sometimes a lump of wood, transformed by GLAMOUR and meant to be taken for the corpse of the victim.... Many other ailments were supposed to be inflicted by the FAIRIES. Rheumatism, slipped discs, anything that twisted or deformed the body could be supposed to be due to fairy blows and wounds dealt invisibly but painfully.... For more temporary offences, people were often afflicted with cramps or with bruising supposed to be the marks of pinching fingers.... Wasting diseases, phthisis and tuberculosis were often blamed on the fairies, although they might also be ascribed to witchcraft. CONSUMPTION was chiefly ascribed to compulsive nightly visits to the fairy mounds, so that every morning the victim returned exhausted and unrefreshed.... IMPETIGO and many other skin diseases were a fairy infliction, and they could also be responsible for a plague of lice.
>
> Many animal diseases were thought to be inflicted by the fairies. Cattle taken suddenly ill were supposed to have been previously slaughtered and eaten by the fairies.
>
> INFANTILE PARALYSIS was not recognized as a disease by country people, but believed to show that a CHANGELING had been substituted for the true child. Incredibly harsh treatment was generally recommended as a cure. Indeed, if officious neighbors took a hand, it sometimes ended in the death of a child. (25-27)[2]

These beliefs and practices were generally most evident among the rural Irish, Scottish, English, and Scandinavians. Of course during the pre-industrial stage of Celtic lands most people lived in or by the countryside. As the nineteenth century progressed with industrialism, political movements, and communication with other cultures, economic forces led the population to live more and more in cities. There, away from fairy landscape and long-standing believers in the real existence of fairies, the Fairy Faith declined. Yet the nostalgia that educated urbanites, writers, and artists felt for the more unfettered, less mechanized ways of life led many of them, despite their disbelief in the reality of fairies, to romanticize them. Thus we get a genre of professional fairy painting (see Maas, et. al. 1997) and book illustration which tended to make fairies into caricatures and cartoon-like, with little sense of sanctity.

Human illustrations of fairies by believers and nonbelievers have varied considerably over the centuries. Several fairy painters of the nineteenth century portray fairies and elves in various sizes and with various characteristics. The fairy paintings of Amelia Jane in the early 1800's all portray fairies as more or less miniature humans with wings, about the size of insects, toadstools, or sometimes birds. Her portraits showed fairies as lovely Caucasian females with gossamer like clothing and angelic faces. Some later painters and illustrators also portrayed fairies as three foot high, sometimes as human size. The small ones were either solitary or "trooping" in groups, often dancing in circles or prancing through the countryside.

Many mid- and late nineteenth century artists depicted fairies as evil or devilish. But several exceptional paintings depicted fairy contact as friendly. Some even demonstrated how humans could actively draw fairies into their presence. This was often through music, (see Chapter Sixteen), as portrayed in the Edward Robert Hughes 1908 painting *Midsummer Eve*, in which a woman holds a flute in the midst of a fairy circle. There was also the celebrated, international bestselling 1914 painting, *The Piper of Dreams* by Estella Canziani, in which a boy against a tree, wearing a hat with a peacock feather (a symbol of immortality), plays fairy music on the flute, drawing woodland fairies to him. (See front cover.) This watercolor, heightened with body color, originally entitled *Where the Little Things of the Woodland Live Unseen*, was distributed to troops in the trenches during World War I and also became an inspiration for a piece of piano music. But still, these paintings were mostly "fun" for viewers, imbued with a fantasized life close to nature, a life then eroding in modern times. These paintings, although positive in outlook, were like later Walt Disney popular images, generally devoid of seriously spiritual imaginative content.

The miniaturizing and sexualizing of fairies is a trivialization of fairies. It is a sentimentality or cutesyness which desacralizes them. It does not conceptualize fairies as beings whose existence and occasional appearance attest to spiritual realms, or as God-created beings mystically useful in human wisdom. They are relegated, a la Tinkerbell, to an entertaining Walt Disney world of half-clad, sensuously female animal beings.

But the fairyfolk of a new ilk in Ireland today do not limit fairy size to miniature humans, and have seen or experienced fairies in one way or another as sometimes human size or larger, as Carol discussed earlier.

In the twentieth century, fairies, especially outside Ireland, generally came to be relegated to children and commercialized as children's fantasy objects. Fairytales came to be the province of children. Fairy beliefs in Ireland and elsewhere did continue during this period, but mostly for the rural commoner outside urban centers and mainstream culture. Fairytales also came to be fodder for folklorists and for scholarly and psychological interpretation, as in von Franz's (1970) Jungian *The Interpretation of Fairy Tales*.

The mass of literature that mentions fairies is in the realm of folklore, and there are many lay and scholarly collections. One of them is Keightley's (1978, originally 1880) collection *The World Guide to Gnomes, Fairies, Elves and Other Little People*, which as the title states, views fairies as one kind of "little people." (He does mention that some folk theories held, as with the *mazikeem* among Jews, that the little people had divine origins. But in general there was little use and conceptualization of fairies or fairy-like beings as vehicles for getting closer to God.) Fairytales would relay a person's experiences with fairies and/or relate stories about fairies that they heard from others. Unfortunately, in recent times, in light of widespread skepticism of the reality of fairies, a fairy tale has generally come to mean any unbelievable story or experience with fantasy or impossible beings or events, even if fairies per se are not part of the story. With the rise of science, and the relegation of fairies to superstition, most people are left with the idea that fairies are cute little beings for children to read about or dress up as. Indeed, Arthur Conan Doyle, of Sherlock Holmes fame, after being fabulously successful as a writer, lost public respect when his later writing, *The Coming of the Faeries* (1922), discussed the reality of fairies.

The extensive literature in comparative religion and the anthropology of religion essentially leaves fairies or other Western elementals/nature beings out altogether. This is despite the fact, as mentioned in the Introduction, that beings like the *dakini*s of Tibetan Buddhism, the *jinns* of the Arabs, the *manitou*s and nature spirits of Native Americans, the *Aziza* of Africans in Dahomey, and other cultures' similar, usually invisible, but sometimes contactable entities *are* treated in scholarly and theological literature. This alone well demonstrates how the power of Western, particularly mainstream Christian thinking, has ignored or repressed fairyness.

Virtually all the contemporary writings of the "New Age" which deal with fairies as real entities, rather than the stuff of folklore, are published by alternative, New Age presses. And they are placed either in the folklore or "Metaphysical" or "New Age" sections of bookstores rather than in the more serious sections on religion and mysticism.

But there *have* been a handful of scholars, theologians, or established writers over the last few centuries who have seriously and systematically treated fairy things as divine, rather than as malicious or nonsensical. Those who have seriously discussed and written about the Fairy Realm do not all agree on the details of the types of fairies, their origins, or their properties. This being the case, and as there are varying lay accounts and stories of fairy experience, there is no authoritative text or perspective other than that of an individual's own experience.

Below I discuss Paracelsus, Reverend Kirk, Evans-Wentz, Arthur Conan Doyle, Flower Newhouse, M. Pogacnick, and R.J. Stewart, even if they get little credit for their writings in scientific or theological circles. There are also a few artists and writers, particularly in Irish or Scottish work, who definitely stated their belief in the reality and sacredness of fairies. William Butler Yeats and A E. Russell are perhaps the two most prominent ones.

Originally, elementals were spiritual beings which Renaissance philosophers represented or associated with the four elements of life - earth, air, fire, and water - the basic substances and energies of the world. There was, and is, elemental science and medicine, which in European tradition is based on the same four elements of the ancient Greeks. This formed much of the basis for Western medicine. Ayurvedic (Indian) medicine (and philosophy) also remains in great part an elemental medicine, adding a fifth element, ether. Paracelsus (1494-1541), the famous Swiss alchemist and professor of physic and surgery, and others, associated different spiritual beings with the four elements. Gnomes were earth elementals, Sylphs [Fairies] were air elementals. Salamanders were fire elementals, and Nereids were water elementals.

While this four-part elemental classification is not held strictly today in popular "Metaphysical" literature or in the thinking of fairypeople or contemporary mystics, it is generally held that sylphs are the quintessential fairies. And, as we have seen, earth fairies include elves and leprechauns whose energy is heavier than the lighter, airy, sylph fairies. Although fairyfolk have different categories of inclusion or exclusion, they all agree on the reality of the spiritual beings and fairy energy in particular.

The minimum breakdown of the cosmos in the monotheistic West is two realms, one of God and one of humans. But usually there are more, and both the Old and New Testament speak of angels as real beings. (See theologian Garrett's (2008) history of Christian angels.) As far back as the fourth century A.D., in *De Mysteriis Egyptorum*, Iamblichus delineates and describes Otherworldly beings as gods and goddesses, archangels, daemones (demons), heroes, archons, and souls. In the twelfth century Geoffrey of Monmouth's cosmology of the order of spirits included angels, troops of spirits, and demons. Seventeenth century Reverend Kirk (1893, originally 1691) was specific in his understanding of the reality and traits of the fairy kingdom in his classic *The Secret Commonwealth of Elves, Fauns, & Fairies*. Kirk, a respected theologian, said that there was no conflict or contradiction between the existence of fairies and Christianity. This is still the case among fairyfolk in Ireland today, even if some officials of the Church see a problem or an unwanted "paganism" among adherents to the Fairy Faith.

But some Irish priests also believed in the reality of fairies. I talked to Kay:

D: I read that in the nineteenth century local priests knew about the fairy beliefs and practices but didn't see fairy belief as a big contradiction. Many accepted it as being able to exist simultaneously with the Christian tenets and practices.

K: Many of the priests weren't institutional types who had to get afraid of fairies. I interviewed one man who told me about this remote section of Ireland where there had been many fairy sightings. He said his priest would call somebody who also had a bicycle to escort him from one place to another if it had to do with some official task, so if he met a fairy he was protected. He told the story as a matter of fact.

Russell, Yeats, and other mystics of the famous "Golden Dawn" movement in Ireland believed in fairies. Russell, also known as AE, spoke and wrote of fairies (*sidhe*) not only for literature, but as a living faith. His book *The Candle of Vision* (1918) details some of his visions – real life experiences - of seeing these ancient beings. He writes:

> I saw, without being able to explain to myself their relation to that exalted humanity, beings such as the ancient poets described, a divine folk who I think were never human but were those spoken of as the Sidhe. I did not

see enough to enable me to speak with any certainty about their life, and I do not know that it would serve any useful purpose to detail visions which remain bewildering to myself. Into the lowest of these two spheres I saw with more frequency, but was able to understand but little of what I saw.... These forms inhabited Shelley's luminous cloudland, and they were the models in the Pheidian heart, and they will be with us until we grow into their beauty and learn from them how to fulfill human destiny, accomplishing our labour which is to make this world into the likeness of the Kingdom of Light. (165,169)

Since the Middle Ages a few laypersons connected to the fairy world were considered seers with special psychic and healing skills. Such people were often sought after for their skills. This shaman-like or medicine person harnessed spiritual connections - fairy energy and knowledge - to help in the human world. Such a person was both respected and feared, recognized as authoritative and skilled. (These people were sometimes thought to be changelings – humanoid fairy replacements for human beings kidnapped by fairies into the Fairy Realm.)

Much of Reverend Robert Kirk's *The Secret Commonwealth of Elves, Fauns, & Fairies* is about certain people in Scotland – usually male seers – who were blessed with the ability to see elemental beings and receive communication from them. He relates many specific examples of individuals' powers to foretell the future, e.g., that a person is about to become ill, attacked, or die. Kirk quotes both uneducated and educated persons' accounts of seership. The seer's power, according to Kirk, comes from fairies, although he is clear that not all spiritual or psychic healers are inspired by fairies:

Since the things seen by the seers are real entities, the presages and predictions found true, [though] but a few [are] endowed with this [second] sight, and those [are] not [people] of bad lives or addicted to malefices [wrong-doing], the true solution of the phenomenon seems rather to be [as follows]. [They are the result of] the courteous endeavours of our fellow creatures in the invisible world to convince us, in opposition to Sadducess, Socinians, and Atheists, of a Deity, [and] of Spirits, [and] of a possible and harmless method of correspondence betwixt men and them, even in this life. (47, Stewart's 1990 new edition)

And Dr. Evans-Wentz (1911) in *The Fairy-Faith in Celtic Countries* supports the idea of the fairy origins of some Celtic seers:

If, on the other hand, it be admitted that 'fairy' phenomena are, as we maintain, essentially the same as 'spirit' phenomena, then the belief in fairies ceases to be purely mythical, and 'fairy' visions by a Celtic seer who is physically and psychically sound do not seem to arise from that seer's suggestion acting on his own subconsciousness; but certain types of 'fairy' visions undoubtedly do arise from suggestion, coming from a 'fairy' or other intelligence, acting on the conscious or subconscious content of the percipient's mind. (476)

Human "fairy doctors" and "wise women," said to obtain their healing skills from fairies, and some musicians, artists, and dancers, said to have gained much of their talent from Fairy, were approached cautiously, especially if they were women.

Debbie, sculptor of the fairy doctor and birdman sitting in my house, wrote:

> Among the wise persons denounced by the religious authorities but respected in their communities was the famous Maurice Griffen., the faery doctor of Kerry. ... It was said he could cure a sick animal simply by looking at it. He had obtained his powers through drinking the milk of a cow which had eaten grass touched by a faery cloud. His name was well known even far beyond the borders of Kerry. The church however left him pretty much alone and reserved its most scathing condemnation for women.

As Mullin (1997) relates in *The Wondrous Land: Faery Faith in Ireland,* one of the most well-known wise women or *bean feasa* of the nineteenth century was Biddy Early. She had a widespread reputation as a healer and being "away with the fairies." Yeats and others recognized her as especially wise. Mullin discusses other notable fairy doctors in recent Irish history, folks such as Moll Anthony, Peggy Bhrocach, and Pether the Smith, all discussed by people she interviewed in the 1990's all over Ireland.

Other individuals and groups, including Rosicrucians and Theosophists, support the realities of Otherworldly beings, in addition to God and angels. And there have been in recent times two or three documentaries on people in Ireland and Iceland who believe in or see fairies or fairy-like beings. One is Jean-Michel Roux's (2002) *Investigation into the Invisible World,* which gives credence to the existence of invisible beings. But, like most other respectful accounts, it stops short of depicting fairies as divine intermediaries for mystics and of understanding fairies in the lives of fairypeople as meaningful to their spiritual make-up and to their psycho-spiritual evolution.

Perhaps the most notable Christian mystic in modern times who describes the angelic and elemental kingdoms in significant detail is Flower Newhouse (1909-1994). This is the woman Marita credits with her own (re)awakening to her fairy nature. Clairvoyant Flower Newhouse (1955, 1995 (Isaac, ed.)) wrote books, gave numerous lectures, founded the Christward Ministry, and in 1940 started Questhaven Retreat in Escondido, California. The latter is a spiritual retreat center for, among other esoteric Christians, believers in the existence of nature spirits/elementals/angels. It is still active today.

Newhouse detailed the cosmic order and hierarchy of many types of angels and elemental beings and devas which belong, according to her, to separate and different realms, although she taught that the evolution of elementals ultimately resulted in their ascendance to angels. Much of her work also centered around Christ and being a disciple. Here we are most concerned with her notions of fairies. Strictly speaking, in her cosmology, she called fairies "frakins," who are lower order members of the earth elementals. Their responsibilities, she claims, are for the flowering plants, grasses, and other smaller forms of vegetative life. She taught that Elementals – invisible spiritual beings of a Christian God's creation - are of the separate realms of earth, air, water, and fire, the same four elements of Greek tradition, and that each type has a caring responsibility for all the various aspects of life on earth, including the weather, the seas, vegetative life, animal life, etc.

In Newhouse's schemata elementals of the air include sylphs, which she said are the inspiration for children's notions of fairies - those light, winged diminutive beings of folklore. But technically, in her scheme of things, sylphs are not fairies, but earth elementals. Yet in common parlance in Ireland and among fairypeople, a sylph is an air fairy, a quintessential fairy. (Kay is an incarnated sylph(person), by self-admission, and is also recognized as such by fairyminded people who know her light-stepping, small-boned, ethereal traits.) Newhouse's organization of the invisible worlds and their beings is quite detailed in its delineation of a hierarchy of beings and their functions, from frakins to elves to gnomes to angels and many other beings. However, I must say it is difficult to comprehend that someone could understand in such exact detail the make-up of the generally invisible worlds.

Nature Spirits and Elemental Beings: Working with the Intelligence in Nature by M. Pogacnik (1996), a New Agey work coming out of Findhorn, Scotland, also details the workings of elementals, especially fairies. He discusses four (non-hierarchical) levels of fairy consciousness, meaning in this case the consciousness of fairies themselves. According to him fairies' realms of consciousness serve four different but interrelated functions: 1) harmony with the rhythm of stars and planets, "imprinting the cosmic time pulse"; 2) constant gliding in the air in areas and bathing the areas in love; 3) taking care of all different life processes in 'their' space by aligning earth life with universal rhythm and orchestrating nature kingdom's pattern of events into the "most harmonious" life atmosphere; and 4) connecting their work to underground spaces and grounding within the "being of Planet Earth."

The point here is not to try to discover whose understanding or categorical system is "correct," but rather that the understandings that mystics have of the invisible realms have existed over the centuries and have included nature beings. It is just the details and names which may vary from place to place or era to era. The variant interpretations and inklings of the Fairy and other worlds are akin to differing interpretations of other phenomena in mainstream theologies, such as is evident in different Christian sects' interpretations of the Bible. And just as Marianism, the appearance of visions and worshiping of the Virgin Mary, waxes and wanes in the history of Catholicism, there are sects of mystics which arise and decline within a particular religion. So it is with the evolution in human consciousness of fairies. These evolutions are part of the long-term co-evolution of human and spiritual beings on a grand level of cosmic order and consciousness.[3]

Now, in the late twentieth and early twenty-first centuries, belief and practices associated with fairies as divine, beneficial beings are similar to those of only a few mystics of the past. Thus today there are no well established groups or gathering places available to contemporary fairypeople or people with a fairy consciousness, no wide scale networks of believers who meet each other regularly. Those who have come to their awakening as fairypeople or fairyminded have generally done so as individuals on their own paths of spiritual unfolding. They have experiences which are not taught them, but are realized. What they experience is not a function of belief, but of knowledge. Yet many recent New Age books on the Fairy Faith (e.g., Roney-Dougal 2003) speak of the belief in fairies as just that, a belief or a "philosophy." That puts it in the realm of (an attempted) handed-down canon rather than personal mystical experience.) Even Brian Froud's popular books (e.g., 1979, 1998) on fairies, good and bad, seem to make them recreational, rather than sacred.

Some New Age fairy enthusiasts anthropomorphize fairies and desacralize divinity, even while approaching fairies as positive entities to contact. Some proponents seem to recreationalize fairies as a pastime for human play. For example, in the New Agey world of Wiccans and witches, in McCoy's (1994) *A Witch's Guide to Faery Folk: Reclaiming Our Working Relationships with Invisible Helpers*, the author says to the reader that we want to seek out fairies for "aid and fun" and emphasizes the belief in, not the experience of, these creatures who have "feelings and rights much like our own." She states that witches "have developed powers which many faeries also have" and that "you will always be in control of any faery encounters." She says fairies lack the "joys of human existence, such as romantic relationships, creative endeavors, a full spiritual dimension….." She says fairies are "jealous of the physical world" and "vicariously experience them" [the joys of human existence] by mimicking humans. The author attributes fairies with these and other characteristics that are psychological projections of humans, thus dispermitting divinity to stand alone as not in the image of man/woman. This extreme anthropomorphizing of divine creatures is akin to the Victorian and fashionable interest in fairies as cute, recreational, humanly controlled entities. That is not to say that such approaches preclude the opportunity for readers and followers of the dogma of such teachings to experience divinity. But such a heavily anthropocentric perspective seems to run counter to the words and experience of true fairyfolk and the mystic's perspective.

New Age writers of the "Fairy Faith" like McCoy and Roney-Dougal fall into the anthropocentric trap in talking about fairies, and use them as an entre to explaining all kinds of unrelated phenomena. Roney-Dougal classifies all kinds of beings, such as poltergeists and aliens from UFOs, as "faeries" or fairy creation, and tries to link all kinds of paranormal, psychic, and "magical" phenomena to fairies. She says "This belief in faeries, whatever form it takes, is a belief, a world view, a way of living in the world, a philosophy"(3) and that "the myths and legends of the fair folk are the oldest in Britain and need to be revived"(1). Her arguments are basically that parapsychology proves the existence of such phenomena as fairies, and that the "essence of faery is magic." Her arguments revert, intentionally or not, to the non-mystical. Fairy seems like a catch-all word for the occult for her. This approach, in my mind, reinforces non-believers' and non-experiencers' understandings of fairies as superstition.

Thus most New Age writing about fairies seems to replicate what Stella Beddoe (1998) says in her article "Fairy Writing and Writers" in *Victorian Fairy Painting*:

> In general, 19th-century writers used fairies for their own ends… Fairy stories could ease personal grief and psychological anxieties or provide a means of expressing hidden desires. Fairies could sound a clarion for Coleridge, Dickens or Ruskin in defence of the imagination against the forces of repression and censorship, for as Ruskin stated in his Slade

lecture 'Fairyland', of 1893, 'A man can't always *do* as he likes, but he can always *fancy* what he likes.'(31)

I do enjoy some of the fairy paintings of professional Victorian artists, especially John Anster Fitzgerald (1823-1906) and Richard Doyle (1824-1883), uncle of Arthur Conan Doyle, because they sometimes remind me to invoke my own perspective and experience. They remind me of the lightness and miraculousness of fairies, and bring a blissful smile and acknowledgement of the other dimension. But I try not to reify or externalize the paintings as of entities of my or others' fantasies. For me, they are simply reminders or signposts to go within. Perhaps that is why Marc and others don't mind too much the commercialization and fashionability of fairy items and talk, because for them the images invoke that lightness, that realization that they have already had from within.

R. J. Stewart (1995), who also eschews the trendiness of New Age fairy promoters describes "New Age" fairies as

> based on a mixture of modern fantasy and Victorian sentiment, laced with the confused notions of the Theosophical Society which permeate many areas of New Age thought and publication.

Stewart suggests, as I have earlier, that the authentic fairy tradition is not a faith.[4] The phrase "Fairy *Faith*" is a misnomer for the mystical fairyfolk because their understanding does not rest on faith, but on experience and knowledge.

Evans-Wentz's own urgings for acceptance of the reality of fairies and Fairy Faith went almost entirely unheeded in anthropological and popular circles. He wrote:

> Therefore, since the residuum or x-quantity of the Fairy-Faith, the folk-religion of the Celtic peoples, cannot be explained away by any known scientific laws, it must for the present stand, and the Psychological Theory of the Nature and Origin of the Belief in Fairies in Celtic Countries is to be considered as hypothetically established in the eyes of Science. Hence we must cease to look upon the term *fairy* as being always a synonym for something fanciful, non-real, absurd. We must also cease to think of the Fairy-Faith as being no more than a fabric of groundless beliefs. In short, the ordinary Celtic mind must readjust itself to a new set of phenomena which through ignorance on its part it has been content to disregard, and to treat with ridicule and contempt as so much outworn 'superstition'. (1911:491)

Let us proceed with this approach.

Chapter Seven

No Bad Fairies

In the "FairyLands" Minette, Marc, Val and I went *to find* the fairies or fairy energy, even embrace a fairy tree. This contrasts markedly with traditional villagers' common warnings to their children to avoid fairy trees and things, and the allegedly ill effects of fairy contact depicted in the previous chapter. The reputed fairy- and elf-induced ills listed in Chapter Six attest to the older conceptualization of many fairies as "bad". Other cultures also attribute misfortune to their fairy-like beings. The old Fairy Faith is akin, for example, to Moroccan understanding of *jnun*, as relayed by Tuhami in V. Crapanzano's (1980) work, that can strike, injure, or assault humans who offend or insult *jnun*.

The newer mystical seeking of Fairy is a result of an epistemic shift from the past, a change in the nature of knowledge.

I questioned Kay, Marita and Carol about "bad fairies." Kay had a long answer.

D: Some describe fairies as being fallen angels, created at God's Creation. One of the fallen angels is said to be Satan, and he fell below the earth. The fairies have been said to have fallen from the sky, but didn't fall as far or deep, and thus stayed around the earth. Are you familiar with these ideas?

Kay: According to some Christian doctrines, yes. But it doesn't follow logic. Real angels and real fairies could not be fallen because if they fell, they would be separated from God and divinity. And they are not. It was mankind who got separated from divinity. According to the *Course in Miracles* and New Age literature, *man separated himself* from God and from man. But the fairies never did that. They wouldn't be creatures of God if they had fallen, so that is just man's projection of what happened. Bad fairies are projections of human error.

According to Christianity there is an entity that exists that is called Satan and that he is the most separated, and if he chooses he will also one day return. ... The *Course in Miracles*, which is a pretty benign document, talks about the dark one, the dark forces. They are there, and we have a choice of lining up with them or not lining up with them. They do exist. But the fairies couldn't be fairies if they lost contact with divinity. It would be like your radio transmission wouldn't have a source anymore. So there is no validity in that, either with angels, or devas, or fairies.

Most people who have seen fairies have been frightened by them, even people who have had knowledge of the Fairy Kingdom and want to see fairies. When they actually do see them, they generally are afraid – the experience is out of context. But *the fairies only have positive energy*. They are our assistants. Fairies are content to be that way, and they don't know anything else but that. They are programmed to be helpers.... The fairies do not have free will. *They are simply instruments of the divine*.

The reason why fairypeople have such problems with handling negativity is because they haven't experienced it before. They haven't had the experience of free will [having in the previous or original incarnation been a fairy]. When you incarnate from the Fairy Kingdom into this world, you have to have both positive and negative energy to balance out, to have an independent mind that has free will.

But fairies have only positive energy. Humans don't know how to balance it when they become fairypeople in this world because it is new. They have trouble integrating it. It doesn't seem natural. So called "bad" fairies simply are not bad in themselves, they are simply following bad directions they got from humans. Because humans did not use them correctly they had to become invisible. But fairies themselves only have positive energies.

D: What about changelings?

K: Changelings denote people who have come from the Nature Kingdoms. Some of them look strange. Probably some of us [fairypeople] did look strange. Earlier on we may have been smaller in stature, and whatnot, so that there may have been a certain kind of deformity that was thought to be fairy. In the ancient literature, the reality, according to Jeremiah, is that the fairypeople actually did come from another dimension, did come to this dimension, and leave, without going through the birth process. So, over the centuries, alongside oral tales, stories have come to be translated and written down, like the story of the Tuatha de Danaan - the tales of fairies and how they disappeared. There may have been some reality to the changeling superstition. It just got waylaid and transferred into the negative. They are not always bad stories. There are some changeling stories that are marvelous. But the further along it went through the centuries, the more distorted it became. Some of the earliest tales I came across, when they were talking about changelings, some of them were magical little children, not the deformed ones that were substituted for good ones.

D: Do fairies have emotions?

K: Positive energy does not really even admit to sadness, but it could. That is as far as you could stretch positive. A loving being can be sad for his child, because the child isn't doing something, but that is still positive. I don't think fairies argue amongst each other. That seems to be putting a human characteristic on beings who probably do not have those kinds of characteristics. Cause that would imply free will. I don't think they are disputatious. It is more that they have sustained emotions of creativity and joy. And there would be sadness and confusion when things were disruptive, or if things did not go according to how they had hoped, or things were destroyed that they built. But I would think there would only be sadness or confusion. I cannot imagine fairy beings having negative emotions like hate, jealousy, envy, because it wouldn't make any sense. It would make them in the image of having an ego, and therefore independent. And they couldn't think of themselves being independent. So how could they have these emotions arising from a false notion of being a self-contained unit? Because they have access to each others' thoughts, constantly, so why would they harbor feelings brought about by the premise that they are encapsulated.

D: For a fairy what would sadness come from?

K: The way that the landscape is being blighted. Their job is to show beauty and yet beauty is being destroyed. Whether they actually feel joy and sadness I don't know. I would think so, but I can't remember [from my previous existence in the Fairy Realm].

I also asked Marita about "bad fairies":

D: There have been a lot of people around Ireland in the past, and still today, who are afraid of fairies and do things to avoid fairies. They think fairies are harmful in some ways. Do you think that some fairies are harmful?

Marita: Personally I have never had that fear or negativity. I have always been respectful of fairy forts and fairy rings, but I have met people who carry that fear.... About three months ago I was visiting where my father was born. It is very, very beautiful. I was with his nephew's children who are young. About nine-thirty at night we decided that we would all go out, the children and myself, into Mother Earth, Mother Nature, and they would show me fairy forts. We put on our Wellies [Wellington rubber boots].

It was incredible. When the children, in their innocence, are so connected to nature I just revel in it. And we were very much in nature in little places and the children were so connected. And they were telling a story about one fairy fort that people were afraid of. So we entered the fairy fort. It was very obvious the way it was built that it was a fairy fort. And I just said "Let's enter it respectfully and peacefully and prayerfully."... I got a beautiful letter afterwards from the seven year old son. It was really, really lovely. ... And yet I know others who are not so happy in those places and even one of the leading men in Ireland is afraid of some fairy places. He won't even enter them. I have heard him speak of his fear. But I don't understand that. I know fairies can be mischievous, but I don't see them as harmful.

I asked Carol if there are "bad" fairies:

Carol: Sometimes there are tricksters who sometimes appear. They trip things up.

D: But some people have said that some fairies are bad, while others say the badness is the projection of the fears and negativities of people.

C: That is correct because it really depends on your outlook.

Here Carol describes how she helped a local farmer who had sighted a horned fairy man at the top of a hill:

Carol: He was out farming with his daughter, tending sheep or something, and he was in the field by himself. He saw this thing at the top of the hill. He got quite scared... It is such a tragedy that people are so far removed from their culture and their history, that when they do come across that kind of thing that they get so freaked out... The farmer had been dying to talk to me about it for a long time, but when he would try to approach me other people would be there. He knew I was into the fairies and that kind of thing, so he said "look this might be your line of work" and he told me about the horned man, half man and half beast. He thought he had seen the devil. I said no, what he had seen was something more like Pan. He felt much better after I had explained to him what it was all about… That kind of connection is normal, and wonderful, but he and others had a kind of warped way of looking at it…. It has happened in history over and over again.

At another time I asked Kay about some of the traits of fairies.

D: Some people in the past and some people today leave food out for fairies to eat. Do you ever do that?

Kay: Not really. I would only do it in a playful sense. The fairies aren't physical and don't need to be sustained by physical food. So I wouldn't do that. But for the people who do that, the fairies might do something to amuse themselves or for whatever reason they do it. So it looks like the food might have been used.

D: So in a way it is the fairies playing a trick on and/or communicating with the person who leaves the food out?

K: Like a prank or something, so that the person will sustain their interest or connection. …

D: Do fairies have souls?

K: You would have to define soul. Fairies are divine creatures, like angels. The fairies are just a subcategory of angels. Again you have to define souls. I mean they *are* souls. They don't have souls, it is just what they are. Don't you think?

D: Yes. There seems to be a contradiction. If a soul is something that lives on past a human being's death, then it is an eternal something. And then if a fairy is an eternal something, then it is that….. There are both female and male fairies, is that correct?

K: Yes

D: Do they have sex?

K: I don't think so, I think I asked Jeremiah that and I think he said that they can shape change, and they can become male or female. But I doubt very much that it is as polarized as the human condition is. Do they have sex? I would think that they would have something more like a happening, that they can bring on their own bliss, and they would certainly do it with each other. But I think that it would be more to accelerate their energy together.

D: Are fairies immortal - have always been or will always be - or do some get born?

K: I don't know. That is beyond my ideas of conceptualizing. I think they are eternal, but they may evolve.

So, as we have seen, for fairypeople and those with this new fairy consciousness, fairies are divine beings who are good and do good. The past fear of fairies and fairy places comes from the perspective of humans, not as these contemporary fairyfolk see it, from the qualities of fairies themselves. Purported malicious or evil qualities were the result of misinterpretations or fear of the unknown. The widespread belief in evil changelings was, as Kay understands it, a fear of difference used as an explanatory tool for dramatic human differences. Such differences may be biological or psychological, or a result of the reality of a fairyperson born into this world who humans cannot accept in his or her strange looks. (Physical characteristics of fairypeople are discussed in Chapter Twelve.)

Even the very popular works of Brian Froud in illustrated books like *Faeries* and *Good Faeries, Bad Faeries* portray many kinds of fairies, often frivolous and, as mentioned above, bad and/or ugly. This essentially recapitulates the historical fear-based superstitions and fairy tales of the populace. With popularized fear and avoidance of fairies, a person may have little ability to transcend ego and mind in a way that permits spiritual unfolding or ascendence. In this context one does not perceive or experience fairy energy as uplifting.

Fairypeople do know that one has to be respectful towards fairies and that fairies can sometimes be tricksters. But fairy light-hearted trickery is not malicious. From a human perspective, some may think them as slightly mischievous, but their antics, as modern fairyfolk contend, are meant to draw attention to them or something for the benefit of humans and/or to awaken someone in a kind of Zen slap. It is for the positive purpose of helping people awaken to themselves, to Nature, and to God, even if one doesn't understand it at the time. Fairies are part of a process of self-realization, recognition and re-cognition of natural phenomena, of divine presence.

All the fairyfolk I met know that fairies are loving, caring servants of God. And nowadays, among fairyfolk and others seeking transformation (and in humanistic psychology in general) fear is recognized as unhealthy and antithetical to personal development. Alleged fairy badness was human transference, the placing onto fairies of qualities which humans feared in themselves and other humans. The spiritual and mystical paths of differing traditions often talk about overcoming fear. In truly mystical paths, as among these Fairy Faith people, the unknown is less feared, more embraced, part of opening up to Divinity. In this process one can confront one's fears as part of the path of spiritual purification and transformation.

Chapter Eight

The Unconceptual

Intuition, or a felt alliance, guides people. Kay had said

> You can't force a fairy experience. If you try and force it, it doesn't work.... I mean you have to forget about it, and it happens when you are not thinking about it. If you say 'Oh, I'm going to notice that,' then it doesn't happen, cause your brain is on it.

Kay had said that Tibetan concepts have a connection to the Fairy Realm.[1] I asked her how she knew Tibetans had a fairy consciousness. She responded:

Kay: It is more like a "been there at some time." I actually do not know. I can't answer that in a rational way. It is one of the few Eastern cultures that I have ever had any affinity towards. Some of it has to do with the pleasing color combinations and the way they put colors together. And in the same way I was drawn, without even knowing that I was being drawn, to the Celtic mythological designs, and anything that had to do with Celtic art.

Much has been written on the non-rational element in religion, spirituality, and mysticism by authors such as William James (1902), Rudolph Otto (1923), and recently by Hume (2007). The mystical religious experience is numinous (a la Otto) and at least partly non-rational. As Hume (2007:15) writes:

> Our beliefs are based on perceptual, behavioural and affective activities that lead to an existential world view from which we derive our sense of the 'real'. This world view does not necessarily have a cognitive component, that is, our emotions and beliefs are not necessarily informed by our reasoned thinking, which might explain why, for example, a scientist could believe in a particular religion or the existence of a spirit world (existential world view), while maintaining the rigours of an academic discipline (cognitive component).

Chapter Eight

Ultimately, as fairypeople attest, the mystical experience is incapable of being relayed directly or fully in linguistic form. It is ineffable, it is a sense, a *feeling*. From an empirical, experimental science perspective it cannot be verified. Yet, fairyfolk's words, actions, perspectives and experiences relayed for the researcher can provide anthropological data about the nature and process of spirituality\religiosity and a specific culture's individual interpretations thereof.

I commissioned Carol, the fairy artist, to paint a fairy portrait of me, whatever that meant to her. A few weeks later she gave me a watercolor in washed pastel greens, reds, and browns, of a large bird-like man with outspread arms, with what might be an apple in his hand, standing near what might be an apple tree. The figure almost merges with its environment, and one must look closely to distinguish body parts and feathers from the essential greenery surrounding it.

I asked her about her visionary experience of painting it. Like others, she describes the process of *not thinking* about what she draws or sculpts:

Carol: When I started I wasn't even conscious that I started. I was doing another painting, actually. And that's the way I normally do it. I was touring around Ireland and was kind of in the back of my head about your fairy portrait, saying to myself that it wouldn't materialize until I got back to Donegal. I thought I would have to sit it out and wait, so I was doing little bits and pieces of paintings for other people when I was down in Cork. And I was just sitting down outside, and Tanya the fairy being came out and she just said "Who is that?" and I said "I think it is Dennis." And that's what happened, just in a period of time when I was not thinking of anything. That's the way it goes with me.

D: What's the relationship between how I look now and the fairy portrait you made of me?

C: There isn't one. There is no actual physical relationship, I think. Maybe the eyes. Yes, definitely the eyes are similar... After that I don't think about a person's features. I don't think at all when I do those things. That's just what materialized. Even the colors are not what I would have thought of for you, and, knowing you, they are not something I would have picked for you.

I work on a kind of intuitive kind of thing. I have to be in a place where I am not being overly conscious of what I am doing in order to do that. I didn't even know that the painting would happen there and then when I did it. I just realized that that's what it was after I finished it. But I did know, once it was sort of more or less painted, that this was what it was about... That picture is not typical of what I would paint as a fairy face. It wouldn't be typical at all. I have only ever had one birdman before, so I never saw that birdman before.

D: Is this a shadow of me behind the veil, on the other side?

C: It's part of your spiritual person. That's the way I would describe it... There are different realms in the Fairy Kingdom. I don't know which one this was. It's not common anyway, and it's certainly not Irish. So I don't know.

D: So if I had the ability to enter those various realms, myself, or you entered, it is possible that I or you might see something like this that is connected to me in some fashion.

C: Yea. Yes.

D: So in your mind, are you pulling this through the dimensional worlds, through one dimension into another, or sensing my relationship with the other dimension?

C: It's not even as difficult as that. It is not hard work to do that. You just have to get into a kind of meditative state, and let whatever happens happen. The realization only comes after it is finished. It is actually not that difficult.... I don't try to understand what Realm it comes from. That's not my purpose, I don't think, on this plane, to do that. I think it is just to produce and be creative. For a long time I used to try and figure things out and that seemed just to get me nowhere. I don't bother doing that anymore... I just accept what I see now... I've seen a lot of different things. Different types of beings and things like that. I just don't worry about that anymore. I used to, but I would just get in a panic sometimes.

D: What do you mean?

C: Well, things sort of used to shift around my house. Sometimes shapes and lights or whatever, and I was going off my head completely. And then I just decided to accept it and then everything just settled down for me then. It was much better.

As well, a lot of people have told me different experiences that they have had with the fairies. Which is nice. And like I was saying to you before, a lot of the time I don't say to people that I believe in fairies or anything like that. The people just sort of turn up. That's the way it is.

Carol's experiences echo others in her letting go of her conscious mind to let the fairies into her life. It is not an intellectual or primarily cognitive phenomenon. She allows herself to connect, and does not even think about the functions of fairies, or intellectualize about the details of the other elemental realms. Her purpose, her function, she thinks, is simply to *be*, to translate from one dimension to another.

Debbie the doll maker and sculptor describes a similar spontaneity and lack of conscious intention when she works. Here is another excerpt from the letter Debbie wrote me.

> As is often the case, when I sat down to work I had no conscious intention to create a "faery doctor". When he was finished and sat before me resplendent in his green suit – even I still wondered who or what I had made that day. As I sat for a while in silent meditation with a cup of green tea (haha) I recall that an inner prompting urged me to make him the little clay bowl and bone pestle for the grinding of herbs, and simultaneously it came into my head that his name was the Faery Doctor.
>
> Later that evening, out of curiosity, I typed "faery doctor" into Google on the internet just to see what if anything it would throw up. Research is something that comes after with me, as I don't want my intellect to interfere with my Muse. I was really pleased to discover that Faery Doctors did in fact exist, being people with knowledge of herbs and the ability to heal both man and beast. It was believed that this ability was granted by an encounter with the Faery. ..... Faery Doctors existed and so belong to the consciousnesss of the land here. Working in the Fairy Faith, I often become attuned to this level of reality and so those experiences influence my art.

Here Minette, Marc, and Val describe in some detail their own inspirational processes, seeing their artistic methods as infused with fairy energy they intuitively connect with.

Minette: Let's put it this way. When I was writing the music of my album "The Fairy Tree," I had a pile of handwritten poems about the fairies besides me. These poems had been specially written for a friend, and I was composing the music at her request. I would always know which poem the fairies wanted me to work on next. I'd leaf through the pile and get quite excited when I found it. I'd say to myself "This is going to be the next one!" I could feel the energy of it.... I just *"knew"*.... And when I sat down to the keyboard, *they would give it to me. It is their music! Fairy music*! The words were definitely *theirs* as well! The poet told me himself that he had simply "written them down before breakfast." He didn't appear to have edited them in any way. These utterly delightful poems were written down just as they came!

I am not a particularly good pianist, but something happened under my hands. It just started, and then I recognized it in some way. Then it would begin to grow. There was a lot of work to be done. It's actually a science. But again I would have to tune in. I would have to know whether it was just right or not. I would absolutely *know*. And *I would know in great detail almost without thinking about it.* Like I would *know* the exact harmony, but I would just have to find it.

Val: It seems this artistic and fairy process is relatively new to me. It's the reverse of what I used to do. I used to be able to draw. I would spend ages drawing things in the company of people for years. Years of just drawing what was in front of me, picturing in my mind and then drawing. ...

And now what I am doing is using my skills and *feeling*, and I know when it's wrong. So I do a lot of rubbing out because as soon as I start thinking and overtaking in some sort of way, it's not coming too clear. So I do a lot of rubbing out. But the minute it's right, I know it's right, and quite often I don't know fully until the end. Especially when I have done a picture of an energy, I didn't know until the end quite how it worked. And then when I look back I thought yes, I got it. *I knew what was being explained to me and I was just letting it out.*

I was thinking of the last drawing I did, which was sitting in a fire, and the energy sort of then slows up. But this process, it's just so different, and it's so refreshing. I love it because I have a vague idea and I am playing with it, and I am seeing what comes out. It is a lovely surprise when I do, and that's the joy of it. It's coming from somewhere.

Marc: What we are really doing, we're allowing the light through, and that can be in any form. It's like drawing out, like you were saying. It's different from drawing as we would have been taught in art school. *But it is a drawing forth, and it is a drawing from another world and other realms.* Because you are, part of you, is attached to a realm. It's like having eyes in those realms. So you can draw around by connecting to them, like fairypeople have done drawing out from their [fairy] homeland. That's where they are drawing from. And they can actually draw from other realms. They are hearing the kind of music of their homeland going through them.

D: Minette, can you ever evoke or intend to receive a communication?

Minette: Well, I think you can if you practice it all the time. If you are interested in having guidance, then it's there for you.

Val: You don't have to go outward. But *what you are doing is opening to the possibility of.* At first you might have to do that quite consciously, but then it becomes more every day. So more is able to come through because you are actually opening up to the possibility. You're not rejecting it as much and you are not putting it in a situation where that is the only time you can do it… I think a lot of people are stuck there. They can do it, but it has to be a series of things that gets them there, and that's fine. But I think the beauty of it is when you can actually open up every day in walking around, walking somewhere. And you do get more open in places. Your whole system just relaxes more. If you're in the country or in a place where you just do open up more. I have a sense that I want to do a drawing a long time before it manifests. I have like a little build-up in me. I can feel it. I can feel it long before I get out the paper. Actually, in some sense that is very practical because I know that it is coming and I will arrange my day. I'll do what has to be done in practical terms, and then I will sit down and say, "Yes, now I am ready." So you do open up to it. I mean that's how it works with me.

D: Some of the fairy books have visualization techniques and other things. I'll call them gimmicks.

Marc: You can evoke something but you can't force something. That's where some people have crossed up, where they're literally forcing some things to happen and making and pushing things. It's a different approach. I think the approach we're all looking for is where we are opening something and allowing it to happen. We are present, but we are not forcing or controlling.

Clearly there is a relationship between sensibility to fairy things and creativity in painting, drawing, music, composition and other creative arts. The relationship between artistic and spiritual inspiration and Ireland is explored in more detail in Chapter Sixteen. For now it is important to keep in mind the intuitive aspect of envisioning and aligning with fairy energy.

Jon has direct experiences of the Fairy and elementals' world. He goes places to make connections with earth energies. As mentioned earlier, he and Kay sometimes go to a particular energy spot in the glade a few miles from Kay's house in Donegal. Sometimes he goes alone.

I asked him about his experience after he returned one day.

Jon: Fairies are what you might call angelic beings who are up there, and they kind of communicate through humans. Human and fairy beings are the bridge between heaven and earth.

D: When you call to those beings do you speak out loud?

J: Some people do. That would be the tradition in some people's way. I don't use any kind of explicit vocalization. The wordless songs are a direct expression of the heart, because it is not conceptual, or preconceptual. It is *unconceptual*. So this affects the expression and it also affects the reception. In ordinary conversation one tries to reconcile person A's and person B's and person C's information and logic together. But when you are in this clear space of the *unconceptual* - the truth of the heart - you don't have any of those logistical problems. Because it is a clear space. So all the frequencies can flow through. And insofar as there is clarity in you, they can all become part of your heart, and that is essentially the work. I think that is how vibrational feeling works.

There is no empirical order to this, the psycho-spiritual process of transformation.... In fact, I think you know that transformation is one of the things that we're in the process of doing: coming into the truth of one's heart. Life being expressed from the truth of one's heart.[2] Gradually I think we are piecing together that wisdom.

It actually works, the heart. Now I don't so much engage in ritual in the sense of a pre-structured series of actions, because the more frequently you look at your hands - remember what you've been tending to forget - the more you find that you don't slip out of that memory. The way reality is working for me at the moment, the flow takes me more or less where I need to be. The flow tells me more or less what needs to be done in the situations where I find myself. So I did not lose any sleep wondering what difficult questions Dennis is going to ask me today, or would I be able to come up with the answers. I didn't check out any books or anything. I just make it up as I go along.

D: Yes, of course.

J: I make it up as I go along, but I'm making it up as I go along not in the sense of a kind of accomplished ego, but just hearing this answer from the center of my heart. Whatever it needs to flow through in that location it would come through. I just trust that that will continue to be the case. I would see the elaboration of ritual consciousness as a perhaps necessary, certainly advisable, stage in the process of self-remembering. Remembering becomes creative, and there is nothing preset about that. That would be the essence of my experience. So sometimes at home I would *feel* a call to go to the mountains, sometimes I would *feel* a call to go to the valley, or the sacred river. Or I think, "I might do it by the water today." I won't think it, I will *know* it, and I'll do it. I tell you that it makes life a lot less complicated.

D: What does?

J: Not having a decision process.

D: Oh.

J: In fact I think it has something to do with the state of grace we were talking about last night. There is room for peculiar philosophical reflection there because for me that is the fulfillment of freedom. There is absolutely no active self-assertion involved in it.

D: So are you suggesting that at this level of awareness that free will is a non-issue. In other words, there is no active choice, no conscious choice. It just comes?

J: It just comes, yes. The creative expression of the life is just flowing through you, and it doesn't necessarily have to be something that would be publicly remarkable or anything. The simplest thing, the gift of the moment. But to talk too much of this stuff may be counterproductive, although it's fine to talk about it to evoke it.

    The beautiful thing about being in this condition is that *there are none of these tortuous knots of reflexivity involved. You don't spend time wondering what you should be doing*, because that's the going beyond good and evil.

    Kay had talked similarly about a knowingness about the presence of fairies:

> *The wisdom of the self is not intellectual knowledge, but a felt wisdom. The essence of things, of situations, and of people is directly assessed... It comes as an experience of knowing, and this knowledge is beyond question.*

This is the apodicticity of which Laughlin (1994a) speaks, the noesis, the gnosis, central to mystical experience. The knowledge and process of the development of fairy consciousness, as relayed above, mesh with others' depictions, perspectives, and practices in expanding consciousness. In a survey discussion of styles of "transpersonal knowing" the scholars Hart, Nelson, and Puhakka (2000) write:

> Instead of trying to grab hold of itself, knowing can hold its forms lightly and perhaps let go of them altogether, thus allowing the self-awareness of knowing to transform its own process. Glimpses of this occur frequently in everyday life. Many people have had the experience of a sudden insight, often preceded by an impasse in their thinking. Just before the "aha!" moment, the structures of thinking dissolve, out of which "knowing" then emerges afresh. Moments of insight illustrate the peculiar nature of knowing, namely that its self-awareness catalyzes change in its own process. This "self-awareness" should not be mistaken for "self-consciousness" (e.g., when a person's spontaneity is arrested by self-consciousness that reifies a "self"). Nor should it be mistaken for a conceptual analysis. Rather, the activity of knowing, such as a flash of intuition, knows itself in this very activity. *This transparency or self-knowing is at the same time a self-transcending process whereby knowing liberates itself from its own ground, eventually (often immediately) to create new grounds.* In this way, knowing that knows itself is a constantly changing activity. (2, italics mine)

These same authors write that there is a lack of first-hand investigations of the phenomena of knowing through "transrational" consciousness (Washburn 1995, Wilber 1983). These and other authors, especially transpersonal psychologists and scholars of consciousness studies, are beginning to discuss in detail the content and process of changes and experiences of "expanded consciousness." In anthropology Hume (2007) details the various sensory-based methods of changing consciousness into "alternate reality," what she calls the "sensory syntactics." Although fairy connection rituals and concerted, intentional practice are minimal for Fairy Faith mystics, there is a pre-existing or spontaneously created quality of mind, emotion, and attention for fairy connection in seeing or sensing Fairy.

Fairy encounter is, as Kay described, a "jump out of [mortal] time" experience with a timeless divinity that enters into the human transformative, in-time, spiritual and emotional evolution of a human. In addition to an expanded temporality or, better, non-temporality, the cosmos is also expanded in "geography", as one enters a realm not normally entered. This mystical experience through the "unconceptual" at first shifts one's paradigm of linear time and solidifies the ontological shift periodically when one enters the expansion of time and space of divine encounter. This ontological shift and experience give a strongly different "flavor" to the life experience. Like religious or spiritual ecstasy or alternate states of consciousness in general, such experiences and uses of the heart, rather than cognition, can be part of a larger world and a longer-in-time ontological position on the planet. Among other things, it can enable a person to accept mortality more easily with the knowledge that one's own life is connected to a much larger world of time and space. Moreover, with the belief in or knowledge of reincarnation, (see Chapter Eleven), there is also a greater sense of time (and space), which also enables the individual to feel that s/he belongs, in a very fundamental way.

Fairy connection contrasts with some other spiritual practices such as in Zen Buddhism which attempt to empty the mind through concerted, defined, discipline. Human connection to non-human fairy entities outside the self is a different kind of spiritual or mental connection. In Zen meditation, the goal is quite purposively and regularly to sit and empty thoughts to purify and unclutter the confused mind, emotions, and soul. This is not an intuitive, spontaneous process and connection to a being or energy which is substantially outside the self. Zen meditation attempts to reduce or lose the ego and distracted self by emptying the mind of thoughts, the Fairy Faith through enhancing the self by joining an "Other," an intermediate semi-deity. Perhaps fairy connection and fairy consciousness are better described as filling the self with external energy, (which also helps to dissolve the ego). In Zen there need be no conceptualized or experienced God. This contrasts with Western prayer or communion which is an active, mindful, often rational attempt to reach up and let in. (For example, *Contemplatio* is a traditional Western, Christian style of meditating on a particular picture of a heavenly scene.) Fairy-sensing empties the self as a result of merging, through a "pull" from or open door to the sacred realm of fairies, not through a conceptualized practice of emptying the mind by sitting to empty thoughts or by active, rational prayer. Nonetheless, fairy attunement is not unlike other Western forms of alliance which seek communion with divinity.[3]

Chapter Nine

Realization

Here Kay talks about how some of her friends from the US, and others, weren't interested in her fairy side.

D: They didn't want to touch the subject of fairies, you mean.

Kay: No, they didn't want to touch it.

D: Is that a common event between believers and non-believers, that they don't want to touch it?

K: Yes, they don't want to know what I know about it. They don't want my opinions on it, although they respect my opinions on politics and cooking. It's like they are thinking "we're not going to talk about this, maybe Kay has gotten over that. Since she doesn't talk about it maybe she has gotten over it."

D: And how do you conceive of their lack of interest in talking about these things? What is it about people who don't want to go there? What is it about them?

K: I understand it. I understand why they couldn't understand what I understand. There is nothing in them that has awoken an interest in the mystical. I mean they are so caught up believing that they're separate, real people living in one lifetime. The mystical stuff just doesn't attract them. You know some people are just like that.
   It always attracted me. Whenever anybody was talking about anything mystical I wanted to hear that, even as a kid. It was always there, even when I was an atheist. (I mean I wasn't an atheist for very long.) I was still looking around if I could find my right church, and was interested in anything that had to do with the mystical. There was always in me a sense of awe of the magical and the mysterious and a sense of being in touch with the divine. You know it's very much a part of the Celtic nature.....

But many closed it off, it's not popular. You know some people are just like that.

D: Is that because of a certain kind of trait that people have? The mystical has been so much a dimension of human experience in all cultures, through all time. I mean even mainstream Christianity can be quite mystical, if people want to conceptualize or experience it that way. But nowadays, a lot of people might think you are crazy or something like that. So what is it that leads most people to be uninterested?

K: I never thought of it that way because I was always in the minority.

D: So I think you're evoking what maybe I was evoking, that they are following something. They are following the mass images of mainstream culture, in thinking that fairies are cute, but unreal. Or are not participating in religion, or not questing for a journey.

Psychologist Ana had asked Kay if someone who is more psychologically individuated (a la Jung) has more connection or more potential connection with fairies.[1]

Kay: Not necessarily. A lot of people are so right-brained, that they are just way out there, not integrated, not living well in this world. But they can be very much in touch with the fairies. There are people who are just flighty, but their involvement with the fairies may be real. But in one sense it is not: they think they know what they are doing, or they think they are getting in touch, but sometimes they are just getting in touch with their own imagination. It doesn't really have any value, like the Jungian "undeveloped intuitive."

But people who are evolved on a spiritual plane, they certainly would have a connection with fairies that would be more sound. But some of them are too serious, too much into ritual to be free enough to listen.

Ana: Yes, that is a danger in Western styles of spiritual life, people getting very caught in ritual and practice, being too earnest, being caught in a rigid approach like "I've done my three hours of meditation."

K: Earnestness is a good word for it. They get too earnest. They lose their sense of humor and capriciousness, and if you lose that you lose your contact with the fairies.

A: It has to do with one's judgment function. If it is light, you are not judging with ego. Your own discriminating and your mind get softer, when things can come in.

Awareness of Fairy

Kay differentiates between fairypeople who are conscious of their fairy backgrounds, those who aren't conscious of their own fairyness, and those who have some fairy energy but are not reincarnated fairies.

> I was talking to Billie about a friend of mine, and her absolutely not wanting to get anywhere close to recognizing or admitting to, on a conscious level, her fairyness at age 15. Billie says for her it is like trying to hide the fact that she has black blood. That is how it feels to her. . . . And that is how it felt to me in the beginning.

Here Kay talks about her experience with some fairypersons who don't want to admit or deal with their fairyness:

> When I was writing my book Jeremiah told me of two people whom I knew were fairypersons. One of them was very willing to talk to me when I was just formulating my ideas. But the other lady would have nothing to do with it. She didn't want to admit it, she didn't want to talk to me. She didn't want to admit that she came from the fairies - but she had a sense that she did. She just didn't want to go any further with it than that. And a friend of mine, Benita, also a fairyperson, didn't want anything to do with my project. She didn't really want to help me.

As hinted earlier, there are also some people who falsely claim to be fairy. Kay, again, relates:

> If somebody is deliberately trying to claim to be fairy, and knows that they are not, then perhaps it is because of the mystery, intrigue, or celebrity quality to it. ... It's part of the Celtic nature to be interested in the mysteries and the mythic world. I mean it wasn't anything I wanted, and it was a long time before I would even admit that this was going on to me. So for me it is still embarrassing in some circles, but for some you would have a certain status if you were from the Fairy Kingdom. So some people claim fairyness even though they know that they really aren't fairy. But then there are other people who seek it unconsciously and they don't know that they don't have the credentials – but they hope that that is the case.
>
> On the other hand, some people have so much fairy energy to them that it is not in dispute.

126   Chapter Nine

Some with strong fairy connections may also be fairypeople who don't know it:

Near the end of my summer 2005 residence three people of new acquaintance came to visit at Kay's house. They had heard of her as "Queen of the Fairies." Lorraine was a shortish, gentle woman who had a sparkly gleam in her eye. She had a constant twinkle of knowing, of being. She only spoke occasionally, and softly. Her quiet, patient comportment seemed almost meditative. Her husband Bob, a man of soothing demeanor and soul, spoke freely of other beings. He had for some time been giving workshops on connecting with beings. Their friend Denis was an energy healer. He was big boned, heavy, earthy, and energetic, and exuded a comforting joviality.

The guests clearly recognized Kay's fairyness, and she spoke openly to all of us about her experience as a fairyperson. They spoke of a few of their own acquaintances and friends whom they knew were fairypeople. I directly asked Bob if he was a fairyperson. He said no. Lorraine looked fairyish to me[2], but when I asked her whether she thought she was a fairyperson, she said she was more of a treeperson. But all three were heavily fairyminded, and well attuned to the concerns and issues of fairies and fairypeople. After they left, Kay said that maybe they were not just fairyminded, but fairypeople who hadn't (yet) realized they were actually descended from the Fairy Realm. Kay said Lorraine looked a fairyperson to her, Denis was probably a leprechaun [person], and Bob might be a fairyperson.

***

During the tour around Donegal Carol had talked with Kay and me about some local people in the rural countryside whose places we were going by:

Carol: ... Now we're entering real fairy country. This is the main part down here and it was heavily inhabited years ago, like a hundred years ago. There's an awful lot of ruins of old houses all over the place... Recently a little boy lived in this house, he was "with the fairies." He is now a teenager and he would probably talk about it. They are lovely people, really lovely people.... Along this road all the people are very content, and they are all very kind of fey as well. ....There is now only one family that lives down here, the rest of them are all individuals living alone, and all extremely happy people. To me they are like a leftover of some kind of fairy group or something. There is a lovely fairywoman who lives up here. Emma is her name.

D: Does she know she is fairy-connected or a fairyperson?

Carol: I doubt it. I never mentioned it to her. Like I was saying to you before, I have always been very careful... I don't know how old she is. She thinks she is nearly a hundred, but I don't know, she looks young to me. Her skin is perfect. Everything about her is really light and kind of airy. She is really lovely.

Kay: You were saying that you are cautious.

Carol: I am cautious with people, yes, because I don't want to invade people's privacy as to whatever their beliefs are. It doesn't really matter to me. When I meet those people I feel the fairyness of them. I don't feel the need that I have to talk about fairies. I just get a nice energy about them and I kind of just leave it like that.

Here Carol answers a few questions about the elusiveness of fairy consciousness for some people:

D: If somebody is fairy, but doesn't know it, you don't tell them because you want them to come to their own realization?

Carol: Yes.

D: But if there is someone who is seeking to find or become their fairyness, I guess they are in their fairyness.

C: In their beings.

D: They are in their beings, they have the traits of it from the other realm, but they don't know it?

C: Yes.

D: So if somebody is looking for that, what do you do?

C: *The first thing that you do is you don't look.* That is the first thing you have to do.

Marc, and Val and Minette here speak about the variety of elemental beings and coming to understand and recognize elemental aspects of the self. I asked if the fairypeople they know believe that they were incarnated from a previous lifetime as a fairy. They responded:

Minette: *It's not about belief.* They have had direct experience, and the memory of it. It may have been very sudden, and they may have been quite shocked, but they actually have a knowledge or a memory of it. They cannot deny it.

D: But some fairypeople don't know that, or don't have the knowledge of the connection, but are they nonetheless fairypeople?

Val: They have the knowledge, they just don't remember yet.

Minette: They, we, are all playing parts in the play. But not all of us know that we are playing a part.... For those who don't know that they are fairypeople, their fairyness is at an unconscious level.

Marc: We're in a place where people are from many, many realms.

Minette: You need to understand from beyond the human geographic end of things. You are talking about people from different "places." You know there are completely different systems, and they are coming and traveling and visiting, and they are quite different.

Marc: And then within each person you come across, people are quite diverse in their own energies within them. It is so with fairypeople, and other people, who are very much a blend. There are people all along the spectrum and others who are maybe from one end of the spectrum. But I believe it is derived from habit, training, and by force of will to stay in that limited area of the spectrum, to grow used to being a certain kind of person. But they have learned to survive by using a very limited spectrum of their abilities. That's unfortunate.

Val: It is much nicer to see someone using a wide scale or set of frequencies, because everybody has this huge range within. As people wake up, you might go here or there: you don't know which way people have gone. After a while you have this huge stretch where you can recognize those frequencies because you have been there. You're claiming back that part to be. It is easier to see it in another person than yourself, or it is certainly easier for me to recognize it in a person who is just waking up to it. Just to be one step ahead. That's all I am, one-step ahead. And I say yeah, great, you are doing it, you are getting there.

Sometimes it's just being with someone, and what appears to be a little chitchat actually clears a lot for them. And you know you are just having what appears to be a fairly normal conversation and that helps turn little things to fall into place. I have had it done to me. I am so amazed that it was done. It's sort of like pieces of the puzzle in twenty minutes. Like I had all the pieces if you like, and I didn't see how they fitted in, and I just talked to someone for twenty minutes and suddenly everything went in, and I got it. You don't know how it is done, and suddenly you got your pieces back together again and it is a fantastic feeling. Interaction is the whole key, and the realization that the interaction is never one level. I keep using this word, but it feels like a *dance* the whole time and it's not ever anybody ever trying to be in a position of authority or power or anything like that. It's a dance, it's an invitation to find out who you are, who I am, and how things are at the time, at the moment. It can be quite intense for a short period of time, and that can lead to a lot of trouble too.

Marc: A lot of these beings – whatever you want to call them - are coming from realms where they don't communicate in any kind of way that humans would. So it is quite a leap for them to be here, and it is quite a leap for us to actually communicate with them.

D: You talk as if there are many, many of them.

Val: There are. I know some people put a number on them, like a thousand, or something very limited. But I think that as we are awakened, all of us, we are seeing more and more of them and our connections to them. And that is opening them up as well. And I think that we will see more and more of everybody else too. It has become more obvious. I mean it has become more obvious to us as we recognize the fairy or elemental in our selves.

D: What do you think about the number of fairypeople or other being people who exist?

Marc: Oh how many there are and all that kind of stuff. I never honestly think that way. I never try to quantify things so. In the circles we move in we meet a lot of people. We have a skewed opinion of the preponderance of fairypeople. Often fairypeople think that everyone is a fairyperson - it could be like any other group thinking that there are more than there are. The other thing is, historically, I think that we are going full circle. It's like in the FairyLands [not far from Minette's house] which we are in. In earlier times they were sort of fully functioning and fully intact.

I had the experience of meeting someone who was open to, but unclear about her origins. Marita told me about a woman who she thought was definitely a fairyperson, and said I should go and observe her:

> She wears short miniskirts, even in the winter. She is in her fifties, and you look at her, and wonder what is this being. It is just unreal, but she's from the Fairy World, and she is very close to them.

I went alone to visit this woman to talk to her. She worked at an angel and fairy shop where there were a lot of books about fairies. I told her that I knew Marita. She said that when Marita first came into her shop, when it opened earlier in the year, that she sensed something magical about Marita. I asked the shop woman if she thought that she herself was a fairy[person]. She said she didn't know what kind of incarnated being she was, but that she was going to try to find out. She did have a "fairy garden" by her house, and certainly knew about fairies, but she just wasn't sure what kind of being she came from.

Like Marc and Val, and Minette, this shop owner was very interested in the Fairy Realm, perhaps was even fairyminded. But she was unknowing of her own specific alliances, ancestry, or previous incarnation(s). She was not clear about her origins, unlike how Kay, Jon, Marita, and Carol were clear about theirs. But there are many fairyminded folk who, as Kay says, are not fairypeople themselves but who have a strong sense of connection.

Ana and I later talked to Kay about one's realization or not of one's fairyness.

Ana: You talked about awake fairypeople and non-awake fairypeople.

Kay: I guess you could have three categories. You could have an unawake fairy[person], who would be more like a regular person. Then you could have another person who is awake spiritually, but who is not awake to their fairyness. And then you could have a spiritually aware person who is aware of their fairyness.

A: In yoga there are endless practices one can do to purify oneself and connect with spirit. In fairy life are there things that one actively does, to connect to one's fairyness?

K: If the fairies inspire us in the ways they do, they would inspire us to do those kinds of things, whatever it is, yoga, meditation, Tai Chi. Whatever spiritual path befitting a personality.

A: Let's say the fairy path is the spiritual path. Are there things specific to Fairydom that are practices. Maybe there is not a sense of progression.

K: Well, not now. There might be something in the future on the fairy path that would be wise to do as practices. But what these practices are, are not outlined, at least not to me. I think Jon, with his workshops explores just that, with air, water, fire, earth workshops and his attunement to myth and dance and body movement and meditation. Jon's workshops are to awaken people to their spiritual paths, not necessarily fairyness.

A: Not all spiritual traditions, and not all spiritual awakening, works on progression. Sometimes you do it in the hope that something happens. You can progress by just being awake or noticing things or "seeing." And even if someone is awake, she or he can also get covered over by other aspects of living.

Jung's understanding of the individuation process, a natural, inherent process in human beings, is that it cannot be stimulated by something external. But Jungian individuation, which includes accessing the collective unconscious, does not involve the existence of independent divine entities. For fairyfolk, realization of fairyness and/or personal fairy history in another past life time, goes beyond Jung's delineation of the realms of reality to include bringing to consciousness the *fairy unconscious* in humans with fairy backgrounds or sensibilities.

Thus the contemporary Fairy Faith model of the structure of the universe and of the process of transformational growth, part of a transpersonal anthropology relayed here, goes beyond Jung's understanding. In the following chapters we will briefly explore some post-Jungian models which could incorporate the fairyfolk orientation.

CHAPTER TEN

INCARNATION AND REINCARNATION

Incarnate: invested with a bodily, especially, a human form
Incarnation: assumption of human form or nature, as by a divine being

Reincarnate: to give another body to, incarnate again
Reincarnation: the belief that the soul, upon death of the body, moves to another body or form

The knowledge that a fairyperson is the human embodiment of a previously divine being from another dimension is central to many fairyfolk's understanding of themselves and others. It is possible that a fairyperson a) is without previous human incarnations – the fairyperson is the *first* bodily incarnation of (the soul of) a fairy **or** b) has a (soul) history which includes previous incarnation(s) as a human being before or after being incarnated as a fairy and then *re*incarnated as a fairyperson. In the latter case the memory of the Fairy Realm may be more distant.

Reincarnation in the West usually refers to continuation of the soul or essence of a human being after one's biological death. Westerners usually think of reincarnation as Hindu or Buddhist re-incarnations of humans or non-divine beings from one human lifetime to another. The difference between incarnation and reincarnation in (a) and (b) above may be moot to Westerners, as they probably don't believe in any form of incarnation or reincarnation from human to human form, from human to divine to human, or from divine to human form. Yet in Christian cosmology human beings like Jesus Christ and Saints are often considered incarnations of God. They are not really considered *re*incarnations. Western notions about reincarnation often overlook the fact that in Hindu, Buddhist and other systems, as well as in Theosophy, humans can incarnate as divine beings, and/or divine beings can incarnate as humans.

In Tibetan Buddhism there are human dakinis, *jetsunma*, people who are incarnate, embodied dakinis. Simmer-Brown (2002) states that, like buddhas, the motivation for dakinis to be born as humans is "to tame beings and support them in their spiritual development" (193) and to aid others. The author quotes G. Chang's translations of writing by Milarepa, a famous 12th century Tibetan, about spiritual realization and how female human dakinis possess spiritual qualities beyond ordinary humans (232-3). Like Tibetan dakinis, fairies, as spiritual beings, and like *jetsunma*, fairypersons as incarnated fairies are messengers and intermediaries to help humans on paths of realization and enlightenment.[1]

Some Christian, Jewish, and Islamic authorities and texts do refer to the existence of reincarnation, despite Westerners' generally eschewing of the concept. Most of these reincarnationists have come to be considered esoteric and mystical, and not reflective of the central tenets of the religion. But we do find references to and claims about reincarnation among Jewish Kabbalists, Islamic Sufis, and some Christian mystics. Thus, all told, there is disagreement about, or avoidance of the issue of, reincarnation among members and subgroups of these religions. This is not a small issue: a belief in or knowledge of reincarnation can provide an important personal ontology that can dramatically affect one's daily outlook and a sense of belonging in the Universe, as it does, for example, in Hindu understanding and acceptance of caste status.

For members of some subgroups of these religions, it is possible that someone can be a "good" Christian, Jew, or Muslim and believe that reincarnation exists. And that could include reincarnation as the origin of a fairyperson. Some fairypeople and others who believe/know in fairypeople as reincarnations of other previous forms are practicing Catholics or Protestants who see no great conflict between their understanding of what a fairyperson is and their own participation in mainstream religious affairs. As we have seen, Flower Newhouse (1955, in Isaac 1995) wrote of Jesus and elemental beings, and Marita often invokes Jesus in her dialogue.

Some Christians with extraordinary experiences have been elevated to saints or prophets for having seen or communicated with God, Mary, or Jesus and have taken on semi-divine qualities. This contradicts the generally held Church notions that humans are humans, and divine beings are divine beings, and they don't generally mix. Yet in Hinduism, avatars are humans who manifest divine traits or powers.

Marita knows about reincarnation:

D: As a reincarnated fairy it is clear that you know, (correct me if I am wrong), that in previous lifetimes you were a fairy on the "other side." You were also raised as a Christian, as you said, and you are still devout. But traditional Christianity hasn't evoked reincarnation as a major concept. I am wondering how that fits with you. Does Christianity involve the notion of reincarnation?

Marita: To me it does. So it is not a contradiction for me. It's a knowing, and when I read *Insights into Reality* [by Flower Newhouse] it confirms it to me, again. Some years earlier I had been toying with reincarnation. Reading the book answered a lot of questions that didn't fit right with me in my upbringing. It made life flow more easily for me, being a Christian. I have followed for many, many years the esoteric Christianity of Flower Newhouse. She has written books on reincarnation.

D: Earlier we talked about how you thought that your own incarnations, your own history, went back maybe two or three thousand years. During that period of time do you know when you were a fairy, or were you a fairy during all that time?

M: No. I feel that I haven't been a fairy for at least two thousand years, perhaps longer. That's my span and it goes back a long way to pre-Christian times. I have a sense of that, very much so. I think I go back to the essence of the land, very much in nature beings. I think that I lost touch with that through my human incarnations. I think being born back in this lifetime has given me the gift of reconnection. I feel old as a human soul, but I also feel new. I feel a newness of the nature being and the energy inside myself that I had lost touch with for many lifetimes. I am very open now.

My sense of it is that I've been fairy-like. It's very difficult to put in more words than that. I feel I have had recollections of that part of myself. Very ancient. And yet I feel that I have incarnated in that veil which human eyes mostly cannot see. I *feel* that in myself. I *know* that in myself.

I think that I have been in human incarnation for quite some time. I really experienced my sense of being part of the Tuatha de Danaan in the last few years, particularly in the wilderness in particular parts of Ireland, and when I went to study to be a Jungian psychotherapist. I also studied Irish mythology for three years. That ancient part of myself I went back to, in the aloneness, into the wilderness of that, as I was also facing my shadow, the darker aspects of myself which were really full on. I was strong enough to embrace many, many incarnational aspects of dark, shadow parts of myself. But at the same time I was able to transcend and go back.

And it was in the heart of winter, and I was alone, with Wellies on, where no one would go. People would think I was crazy. I went to retreat centers, to bed and breakfast places. I just got blessed. And I came home and went to one of the sacred places that I know, so that I could look at the shadow of myself and many aspects of human incarnation. And know that there was something also very beautiful in me, and light, full of light. Through the mountains and through the lakes even in winter time, covered in frost and ice. I could go in and out of those dimensions of myself, again, without thinking that I was insane. And yet I was in the darkest part of myself at that time.

D: So realizing that you were once a fairy, and other human beings or other beings, also brought up the realization of the darker parts of yourself?

M: I don't think the darker parts were fairy. But I think it is my reincarnation as a human in so many lifetimes that made for the darker parts. Cause I feel very human, as well. I know great pain. I also know great joy. I think I am very sensitive, and sensitive to pain, because I have been reincarnating many, many, many lifetimes as a human. I have been in and out of all those places of pain and tragedy, and I have hurt, and been hurt. The evolution inside myself, and feeling, feeling, feeling the pain in this lifetime, as I have gone through it, has reflected back to me numerous times and moments that I have done some pain to others. Finding compassion for myself in those places. I haven't got myself off the hurt because I have felt a sadness. I have become more compassionate and passionate through suffering, through feeling it.

When you come in from that [Fairy] Kingdom, first you have to take on the emotional body. I know in myself, I have gone through all kinds of bad stuff, emotionally and mentally. That will continue. But there is a kinder side, a kinder human. But also the fairy and nature being of myself has matured and grown, and also known that light. *You have to get down there, you have to get down into the earth, you have to get down and work hard at every level, at every dimension.* And not be afraid of that dark side. So you know in my eyes, through your eyes, looking into them now, *I feel the safety I can provide in the gap, in the gap for others now in those two different dimensions of human and fairy.*

Marita's continuous spiritual path involves having the essentially good and light nature being, the fairy part of her, help transform the darker parts of her humanness experienced over the centuries. When the light shines, the darkness dissolves. The raising of light on darkness means facing, incorporating, and transforming the shadow revealed in the light.

I asked Kay about reincarnation:

D: Several people including yourself have use the word "incarnate" or "incarnated fairy" to describe yourself or other fairypeople.

Kay: Yes.

D: I'm not sure what that means.

K: Well this is Jeremiah's story, but the literature seems to back it up. If you study early Irish mythology and history and listen to fairypeople, they were crossovers. They could go from one dimension to the other. It's considered mythology, but Jeremiah said that they actually could. It's actually history. When the fairypeople first came over they could do the dimensional switch, although they could have some problems. If you have people around who suddenly disappear you're very uncomfortable. You might probably hang them or burn them. So somewhere it was decided that that didn't work and so the fairies had to be born in the normal human way, rather than just showing up. Throughout history there is so much mystical literature, including fairy, about saints and others showing up, and then disappearing. It is certainly very much there in the Celtic religion. We had to be born in the natural human way.

D: Is there either an evolutionary genetic line, or a spiritual line, through time that makes some people incarnated and others not. What is it, other than your openness to that [fairy] dimension, that makes it that you or Jon or some other person is incarnated?

K: You mean "why us?" Why of all the fairies that there are did we get chosen to be in human form? I don't know that. I guess because we wanted to, or because they thought that we could stick it out. I don't know how they selected us to do that. But they chose us to some extent because we wanted the job. I can't get any further than that. And it's not that all fairies eventually become human, that's not it at all. There are only some selected to come over.

I don't know much about the relationship between the Fairy World and the human world of people who look like fairies. I don't know how many times I have incarnated or what my first incarnation was, or even if there is such a process as we currently define it.

Here Kay answers some of Ana's and my similar questions:
Ana: In a previous lifetime you were a full fairy on the other side? Is that what fairypeople are?

Kay: Yes, that is what I mean by the term. Other people might mean other things by that term. A fairyperson has fairy qualities, or they have had journeys into the fairy world. Both Raj and Jeremiah were specific that I used to be this 12 inch fairy, you know. It doesn't particularly excite me. … No, actually I find it amazing. I can't quite assimilate it. He even gave me a description of me.

A: Before you became more overtly involved in this kind of life, did you have a strong belief in reincarnation over the course of your life?

K: I started to become consciously aware of it, probably when I was in my twenties. And then the Bridy Murphy thing came out. She was a woman who, under hypnosis, recalled her life as an Irish woman and American woman. I read the book and was fascinated by it. That was in my thirties. But before that, my friends in Idaho were always reincarnation buffs. We were not so articulate about it as teenagers. During the time of Bridy Murphy I had psychic friends where I lived. And one woman in particular would tell me about her experiences, and her former life that she would remember. She went to Tibet and went into some temple and she knew exactly the outline of it. Something used to be there, a door or something, and there was a door there in 1500. She remembered the whole thing.

A: Have you had experiences like that?

K: I have had regressions…. but of the two lives that I remember, I died in my early twenties. In one lifetime, (this was before I was getting fairy information), I was definitely a fairy type, living in the woods, and was a poet. And in my regressions I had an adopted mother and father, which is a way of me telling myself that I didn't belong.

When I was very young I told my kindergarten teacher that my brother and I were adopted. We weren't really. My mother was very embarrassed when the kindergarten teacher told her. They finally got it out of me that that was what I thought. The reason I felt that, the reason I gave myself anyway, was that we had red hair and green eyes, and freckles. My parents had black hair and blue eyes. So that was the reason. [2]

But in both of these regression lifetimes I was also a young woman living in a very rural area. The other lifetime when I was in the woods I can remember the house, and I could remember the arbor that I built and things like that. When I was 21, this lifetime, I had pneumonia, and I almost died: I was in a coma for three days. But I decided to stick around, to get this "assignment" [fairy work] done.

When I died in my previous lives, I always died of the same thing. When I died as a poetess I died of consumption. And when I died as the other young woman, there was a forest fire. And I complained consistently that my throat chakra was blocked. A couple people recently have told me when I had bodywork done that my throat chakra is blocked. It is getting unblocked through various things that I am now doing to unblock it. So that all fits.

A: From a fairy perspective, what happens after death for a human?

K: Well, what would happen after death would be reincarnation. It wouldn't make any sense in the fairy world for anything else to happen, because the soul has to evolve back home. The soul isn't finished yet. At least my soul isn't finished yet. *And so what other choice is there besides to finish the job. The fairies are eternal, so they don't know death. But we are eternal too, we just don't know it.*

D: So in your case, or our cases, if we in part or fully came from the Fairy Realm, in our passing from this lifetime, would we potentially become fairies again? Or is it possible for non-fairypeople humans after death to become fairies, to then enter the Realm of Fairies.

K: I don't know. The fairies who have come over as fairypeople have made some kind of contract to stick around as humans to help the evolvement. But they can also decide to go home, whatever that means. If they go home, do they come back again as humans, I don't know… One of five fairypeople who came over to help with the transition may make it. There were originally 5,000 that came over. There are only a thousand or two thousand of us left. I mean, I don't know how the others didn't make it. I mean whether they died or left, like I did in my other incarnation. I presume that they died early. I don't think they committed suicide…. The three thousand who decided to go back may have gone back as children, for all I know. I do not know how they went back.

A: What does that mean, died or passed over?

K: According to Jeremiah, when you come over from the Fairy Kingdom, you go back to the Fairy Kingdom after you die. And he also said that you have a choice to either keep both life forms or to go back to the Fairy Realm. Since the fairies don't have free will, it would be a difficult transition, I would think. I don't know if that is true or not.

What happens to us when we presumably die? Do we get reincarnated or go back to the Fairy Kingdom? Billie said we fairypeople have a choice. [3] Apparently in between lives we make that choice. I do not know what I would do. The longer I live the less I think I can come back, reincarnate here. But since I do not know what it means to be pure fairy, I do not know whether a human being, with free will, would want to go back to not having it again.... Another time Jeremiah said I could be both. That I have earned the right to both life forms, simultaneously.

[Laughter].

D: That would be very handy! [Laughter]

K: The fairypeople who are checking out early, they may be coming back again. You know, what Billie said, there may be a temporary moratorium on fairies coming into humanhood. It's not like they are just here once. Again, I don't know, except that Billie did say that there was a group coming over for the transformation of the earth at this time. Every spiritual discipline is talking about this time being a time of great change. So it isn't like the fairies just kept going and going and going. We have no idea how many times we had to come into incarnation in this plane of consciousness to be able to volunteer to be here now.

Some of these fairypeople who are aware may be what are called "old souls," those who are closer to finishing their reincarnations. They are wiser, they are more settled, they are more spiritual, more aware than the average person.... The fairypeople who are aware are maybe old souls in the fact that they have been in the reincarnation cycle for a long time. I would guess that that is true.

Marc and Val also said that the individuals who are reborn for the first time from the Fairy Kingdom into the human realm are the ones who have the hardest time adjusting to this world:

Marc: Let's say you are a fairy incarnation into this realm for the first time. That would be the toughest challenge you have.

Val: They are the ones who find it really, really difficult. But then it happens to any realm that is incarnating for the first time. It is the most difficult, and they are the most obvious.

Marc: Well, it's funny. In a sense they are the most obvious in that they might be the clumsyest, or the most ill at ease in the world. But they can be the most disguised because of their being early in their evolution. For instance, if you are coming into a body for the first time you may be bringing the most fairy with you. So you can see the fairy in the person. You meet someone who seems like the most grounded person in the world, yet suddenly you watch them and they aren't really anywhere as grounded as you thought they were. And so if you imagine you coming into a human body for the first time, you are entering a family line, an evolutionary line of that family. It may be a very heavy family or may be a kind of family that would look not in the least like a fairy to the observer. But you are in that body so that's when you get these enormous problems with self-identity, and get confused over what you are, who you are, and why you are here.

Val: And you may have no one to relate to you either. But there are certain families, like fairy families in which it's much easier for them because their gifts are accepted. But for the first time it is going to be a real shock, isn't it. You have all this and yet you have no one to relate it to.

Marc: Often you can see a subtle thread in the family. It has come from somewhere. These people have chosen this incarnation, to come into a family, in a seemingly hostile environment. It's quite a challenge to do so.... The same issue comes up with people who feel they are starving in their body, or for a man who would be in a woman's body or a woman in a man's body. It's the same issue really because your form is partly different from who you really are, your sense of yourself. And that's a challenge that you have chosen to deal with, if that's the body you have chosen.

I also think that you can also express yourself in a way that is very fairy-like as people would see it. Even if you have a body that doesn't seem like it.

Val: Because that is how you recognize them. It can be that extreme. It's sort of like inflection, in a sense I have to know what I am looking for and recognize it, and know that that's in there.

D: You have invoked a Hindu or Buddhist concept of reincarnation in that people karmically chose their incarnations, even though they are not conscious of it. I wonder if fairypeople in general would look at it that way.

Marc: Most people nowadays who believe in reincarnation believe that it is a choice. It is not just a thing that you are on a wheel and it's like a lottery. Most people don't believe that it is a lottery, not in the West anyway. Most people believe it's actually a conscious choice… It's almost like a cosmic lottery. It's become almost a standard, especially for people who are angelic or fairypeople. Most of them believe that it is a choice. So then why did you choose this body? In a sense you could always blame somebody else if I say "Oh I just happen to be in this body, that's just the way the cookie crumbled." But if you realize that you have chosen this form, this family, this life - especially for a fairy being - and you are in a place that seems very hostile, it's like a….

D: A double whammeee.

Marc: Yeah, yeah. "What am I doing here? Why did I do this to myself? I must have wanted punishment or something."

Val: But usually, I mean in the best cases, at some point, the person realizes why s/he is here. Something actually clicks. It might take a long time, though. You do have to undo the damage of this life, let alone any other. But there is this late recognition why you have done it.

Again, with Kay:

D: So for the people who become more conscious of who they are, it makes sense that they become healthier and healthier. But if you have, what I will call for the moment, a disability that doesn't allow you to cope, and you don't know about it, then it can destroy you. But once you realize it, like what you were saying before about sensitivity, once you realize your servitude or sensitivity, then you can work with it and get beyond it. But if you can't recognize it, then it can destroy you.

K: Right. Well, "destroy you" is not the right word. Checking out and going back to the Fairy Kingdom is not considered a failure or destructive. It is just an experiment that had a certain validity to it, but not as much as one hoped. I mean, you climbed a mountain, but you only got an eighth of the way up, but at least you climbed the mountain. *And it did some good - some kind of fairy energy was brought through*, and therefore the experiment was not a failure.

Marita and Kay, fairypeople, and Marc and Val, fairy-conscious, all know of reincarnation and its relationship to fairypeople and to fairies on the other side of the veil. They refer to how incarnation and reincarnation from human to human, and from fairy to human, can affect how conscious a human might be of his/her previous lifetimes as a human and/or fairy.

This degree of one's knowledge or awareness of previous lives can affect the degree to which one conceptualizes his/her roles and purpose in this lifetime. And depending on one's awareness and personality - one's notion of the Self – it can affect the degree of psychological integration and one's sense of belonging in this earthly world, as well as abilities to cope with everyday life.

Jung's model of the psyche is based on the central notion of the necessity to become one's self. In Jungian terms, awareness of the unconscious (past) arrives because of the *transcendent function*, the psychological mechanism that unifies the conscious and unconscious, bringing the "manifest self." As Raff (2000:10) describes it:

> As a result of the work of individuation, the self gains the position of the dominant spiritual force within the psyche. When images manifest, they manifest as the self, and though they cannot be controlled or even predicted, they can be trusted.

In these terms, fairypeople who know of their fairy past on the other side have, through individuation, brought their latent, unconscious part of self to awareness and thus the self is more manifest and integrated.

The ego needs to be willing to consider the possibility that it is not complete, that there are viewpoints other than conscious ones. This can be difficult and may be Jungian reasoning for the inability of some fairypeople not to know, or admit, their fairy backgrounds. This is especially true in light of the awkwardness and lack of widespread supportive spiritual environs for fairy consciousness and reincarnation in the West.

The multiple lives background of fairypeople with fairy consciousness and the unknown past of those with unnoticed fairy connection are linked to divine entities who, according to fairyfolk, exist independently of the human. And realization of past fairyness is in part dependent on any previous (cultural) exposure to the idea of fairies. The aware, essentially "hybrid" fairyperson is not simply enacting the conventional Jungian process of individuation, but is going beyond it to link, not with archetypes or images, or even the collective unconscious, but with, in their experience and ontology, real nature spirits.

In anthropological circles, Feinberg (1996) has discussed how in the Polynesian Solomon Islands there are "permeable boundaries" between human and spirit, and between self and other, a generally non-Western concept of selfhood. Lambek (1996: 243) describes this approach:

> The departure from naturalized Western models of highly bounded individuals and species has been admirably conceptualized by Leenhardt [1947] in his depictions of a "cosmomorphic" world and "relational personhood." ... comparisons of selfhood themselves should not be delineated in simplistic binary terms ("ours" versus "theirs')....

The penetration or existence of fairy qualities in human beings and of a human being who has fairy traits from a past lifetime, a Fairy cosmomorphology, breaks through standard Western dichotomies, and reverberates of some indigenous cultural understandings..

Chapter Eleven

Mission, Purpose, Responsibility

D: You and others have said that the fairies' function is to take care of the earth. Is it through individual contact with humans?

Kay: No. I think what the fairies behind the veil want to do, the elementals if we are talking about all of them, is to take care of the earth. And humans could help them. And the fairies could help the humans. Humankind is supposed to be in charge of taking care of the earth, but the fairies carry out the means to do that. They can work with energy in a way that we don't know anything about yet. If we would help them, if we could work in concert with them, we would really have a planet the way it is supposed to be. It would be a green paradise. The climate would be perfect. There would be no polarization, no south pole, no north pole, no deserts. So they would be working with their energy to make that happen. And we (humans) are supposed to be caretakers of this planet, and we are sure not, are we.

Here, Ana asks Kay some poignant questions.

Ana: Could you say more about the mission of fairypeople?

Kay: We are like bridges: we stand between the human world and the Fairy World. We come over here, and literally, just by being here, we are bringing some kind of energetic form. But I don't understand how that works. But it makes it easier for humans to make contact with the fairies, by us being here... And the more we talk about it, the more the word spreads And Dennis writing his book and Jon doing his workshops. And that workshop in Glastonbury, and what not. So just by speaking out, we strike a chord in anybody who is receptive enough to hear. And so the word spreads.

A: What is it that the Fairy World wishes to spread?

K: It is their sense of attuning to the beauty of the earth, and taking care of the planet in the way the planet is supposed to be taken care of. And that involves literature, poetry, music, architecture. Everything that the fairypeople are doing is integrating beauty with the earth, with the planet. In that sense it is a very specific kind of thing. Inspiration to inspire beauty, and to inspire joy. Other people can do that too, it is not exclusive with fairies.

When I see the work of [the architect] James Hubbell, for example, then I understand more clearly what the mission is. I mean his work just speaks. Gaudi is most likely a fairy[person] and, the kinds of things that he does are the kinds of things that James Hubbell does. If you ever go to Barcelona, you'll see that he [Gaudi] sprang from the earth... And William Yeats, in his early poetry, for instance, had very much of a fairy connection, and so did A. E., George Russell. And James Stephens is just a born fairy. You know anything you read of his, you know absolutely that he is a fairy[person]. DeBussy, for instance, was a great composer of Fairy.

A: Is it a sense that the earth is too serious, that it needs this beauty and joy for balance? Or is it beauty for its own sake?

K: The planet is supposed to be a garden paradise. It was originally designed that way and the original design was that humans would work with fairies and the fairies would assist humanity in making it. The fairies have fairy dust, for instance, to balance negativity. That it is one of their functions.... People's destinies are different... The fairies are waiting. It has to be the human who makes the step.

As I understand it we came over to help with the transition. The Nature Kingdoms hope that the transition will take place. The transition for people to wake up to their spiritual reality. So that they will take responsibility for the planet. Or for each other. Or for the cosmos. The transition is to become awake. Synchronicities happen, just happen, and sometimes they are very funny, synchronicities that awaken people.

D: Do you attribute them to fairies or the Fairy World?

K: Yes, sometimes. Or other dimensional aspects of yourself, your higher self, or whatever words you want to use. In my case, and in the case of the fairypeople, we have a special energy to bring across. Jon does a real good job of talking about this. So our jobs, our guidance is specific to that. But anybody's guidance is specific to whatever their mission is, or their higher self. So it's not special, but it's specific.

Not all the fairypeople think of having an explicit mission, or a task at hand to accomplish. Carol, as we have seen, does not actively speak out in that way. I asked Kay about Carol and others.

Kay: Some of the fairypeople may not even know that there is a project. They are just called on or not called on.

D: That strikes me as Carol's perspective. From Carol I do not get a sense that her fairyness is part of a larger mission.

K: Not mission, but *representative*. Yes. She is just an isness….. My granddaughter is just an isness too. She is not aware of her mission. According to Jeremiah she has one, but she is probably fulfilling it to some degree unconsciously by the way she is relating to the world, and the gifts she is giving.

One day a woman, who read about Kay in the newspaper and who had recently discovered her connections with the Fairy World, visited Kay and stayed for a long time. Kay eagerly spoke with her at length, showed her books from her shelves, and loaned the woman several books. When leaving, the woman apologized for taking up Kay's time. Kay's response was "It's my job."

Jon said his mission, and he used the word "mission," is to *bring in nature awareness*. He does occasionally see fairies, more as light beings rather than as forms. At one point he said he did not need to see fairies because he has a fairy sensibility of experiencing nature as alive, as spiritual. He said he "sees as a fairy" does. He defines himself as a "double agent," as a go-between the two worlds of human and fairy. He is most definitive, without being arrogant, about his being a "go-between."

Here is what Jon has to say about the mission, and the task at hand working with fairy and nature being consciousness:

> Human beings are the bridge between heaven and earth…. That's the maintenance, the elaboration of the balance of that initial beautiful design, which is dependent on our ability to hold a correct course at the same time as we are learning about good and evil and choice and all those kinds of things. ... So we did some work yesterday in the glen calling these orders of being together, so we had a very harmonious greeting or blessing today.

Jon is also clear about human and fairypersons' relationships to the divine:

Jon: *Human beings are the rainbow people, made in the image and likeness of God.*[1] You can understand that as an abstract symbolism, if you like. Fairies would be an expression of the creative power of the universe, associated with this creative principle that we call God. So, human beings, as I understand it, have the capacity to incorporate fairy gifts in a way that fairies do not have to incorporate a full spectrum and possible range of human experience.

D: Earlier you mentioned the word "Fairy," and it sounded as if it were a capital letter F. I was wondering if the word Fairy with a capital F is different from fairies?

Jon: Yeah. I guess *Fairy with a capital F would refer to one of these lines of articulation, that the mission of which is to assist in the building of the natural world as a manifestation of Spirit.* So I like to use the word Fairy with a capital F because it defamiliarizes it from the banal, post-industrial version of fairies. So Fairy is something to look at and something to be respected... The process is not closed. *That's the whole point of it.*

So the way I would see it as a human being with fairy consciousness is that I have a range of awareness and a set of gifts available to me that are extremely helpful in a way of living creatively, magically, consciously, in the world. These gifts are available to my human consciousness. My human consciousness has the freedom to avail of them fully, partially, or to ignore them.

So the whole point of fairies, as far as I am concerned, is to build, to build, to build. To transform, to participate in the process of evolution. You can't just put it down in books, and walk away from it. It is a creative process. That is the primary role of the fairy dimension.

D: Is achieving peace on earth, as you mentioned earlier, the mission or one of the missions of these different frequencies? Is there a plan or design for the existence of those various frequencies?

J: Mind you, we're talking in terms of a yet unwritten New Age mythology here. The idea would be that each of these frequencies represents a different line of articulation of *the adventure of God*. And creating a world, and getting lost in the world, and coming back. So all of these separate frequencies, separate lines of articulation, alter my relationship...You go beyond innocence or naivete, you go through the lessons of experience, and then on the other side of those experiences you remember. You remember what was dismembered. Apparently the goal of this whole process is an increase in the quality of consciousness or awareness, and you experience what it actually is to love. Because beforehand, if your nature was just to love, you don't have the option of not loving.

I had mentioned to Marita that Kay and other people's knowledge of their fairyness is in part to spread the word to other people about the need to respect the earth. I asked her about it.

Marita: I don't feel the need to actively spread the word, or something like that. But in myself if I can, and if through my connectedness with that part of myself others can feel that part and experience the joy and the lightness, that's enough for me. If people are interested, you know, I open. I have been helped by others, like Flower Newhouse. It is wonderful if others can be helped and I can help them. But I don't think I have a mission or anything. I think that by just being more and more present to who I am, that joy and lightness comes.

Carol said that she has a sense of what fairies are trying to say to her or what they are trying to direct. That generally includes her relationships with other people. The fairies help her be acceptant of other people, to allow the best of a person to come out, because one is not blocked by some of the negative energy or bad aspects of a person. "That's my understanding of what they are trying to tell me."

Jon, like Flower Newhouse, Conan Doyle, and a few other mystics of the past, said that fairies weave material substance from the etheric world, literally making the earth come into existence. He said the New Age is not just one with the potential for renewal, for nature to come alive again, for bringing back nature consciousness and nature spirits like fairies, but also for something more creative than renewal. God made the possibility for free will for humans, part of the duality of creation itself, in which something comes out of nothing – with good and bad. Now the emerging consciousness has the possibility of creating a unity through re-uniting. Jon calls it "One Heart." It rises above duality, above the original creative process. This is one way to talk about the thrust of positive energy of fairies as intermediate deific beings which embody the goodness of divinity. Humans have the opportunity to interact with these divine entities and therefore bring more divinity into the human realm, improve individuals' lives and the earth, as well as repair the separation of man from God.

Other religions point to the role that humans have in encouraging and shaping divine forces. In Kabbalah and Jewish philosophy doing good deeds and paying attention to the sacred in myriad ways "repairs the world" of humans and God (*tikkun*). In Yoga and Buddhist philosophy and practice, compassion helps not only individuals, but the cosmos. In Mexican Huichol Indian cosmology, human pilgrimages enable the gods and the world to continue to exist. These are but a few examples of the interplay and mutual enhancement of humans, intermediate spirit beings, and God(s), and how they can work together for the benefit of all.

Here Kay speaks of her friend Michael, and his relationship to the mission of fairies:

D: If Michael is an unrealized leprechaun, a kind of earth fairy, does he have a mission, but doesn't recognize it as a mission?

Kay: I would say that would be a way of saying it. But I wouldn't say that he had failed completely in his mission. His mission might not have been the same as mine. He may have had something completely different to do, and he is not in his isness. But in his soul, he is not against any of this. He believes, for instance, that I am a fairy[person]. He doesn't have a problem with that.

Ana, Kay, and I were discussing the purpose of being in the world, and of fairies, fairypeople, and the general state of contemporary consciousness.

Ana: That whole thing of being in the world and also having things that one is charged with doing here. And that sense of how difficult that might be, because the world is how it is. In a sense it is harder because one is not just here to be here, but also to do certain things … It is not easy to be here anyway, and it sounds like responsibilities to fulfill.

Kay: I think the fairies themselves can work independently of the fairypeople. Let us put fairypeople aside for a minute, because I think the fairies, whomever they can work with, would want to work with everybody with the tasks that they are given. Anything they can do to work with people, to work with improving the quality of the planet, or to inspire through music.

(There are not so many stories of fairies helping humans till the soil, or at least they didn't give the fairies credit for that. That credit to fairies is more so in places like Findhorn, where people claim to have seen the fairies. There the fairies were quite specific in what they were doing to help the people grow better vegetables and flowers, how to compost and get the most out of the soil, what a good gardener would tell someone to do.)

The fairies know what work specifically is for each specific person. *The fairies are helpers for whatever one is. The fairies know your essence, and so they know how to help you.*

Thus fairies' purposes are to help humans as individuals in their spiritual development, realization of the closeness of God, personal tasks, and to inspire humans to respect and treat nature well. Fairypersons' purposes are to bring in more closely that energy and purpose to represent and/or spread it, to enhance and foster an understanding that Nature is precious, divine, and to be heartily looked after. To repair the separation of man from God.

Chapter Twelve

Fairypeople Traits

Kay, as mentioned above, is quite fey looking and is very light on her feet. Sometimes when she gets talking she uses her arms, hands and fingers in tweetling gestures, moving her fingers gently about her face, as if she is primping the air around her skin and hair. Sometimes she draws her index finger across, above, her mouth. It is a distinctive set of gestures which highlight what she is saying, as if she is speaking as a representative. It looks like she is preening her fairyness with a gentle, vapory bounciness. Or rather her fairyness, a state of soul-stirring enchantment, the "shine" as Val puts it, comes into her.

Kay: There are differences between the fairypeople, but there are more similarities in the whole group of fairypeople than there is outside of the circle. There is a quality of being artistic and expressive in a distinctive way. Most of the fairypeople are quite psychic, or would have the ability to be psychic if they recognized the ability in themselves. All of the fairypeople I know without exception are very spiritually oriented and pretty right-brained. Most of the fairypeople I know have degrees, are formally educated, have high IQ's, and are excellent students. Perhaps that is not universally true, it just so happens to be the case with the ones I know. There is often an interest in learning, with a psychological emphasis, as a good number of them are psychologists, therapists, Jungians, and/or spiritual psychologists. All the psychologists that I was ever interested in were humanistic psychologists, not Freudians. And quite a few of the fairypeople who I know are sevens in the Enneagram.[1]

James Hubbell expresses his nature through architecture and poetry. Jon is a philosopher, and he expresses it through nature. Interests in gems, homeopathy, etc., are more of interests for the gnomes and elves than for the sylphs. My own music is a fairy expression. The kinds of music that I liked and still like, even when I didn't know what I was selecting, have been fairy.... In some cases fairypersons' artistic qualities might be repressed.

But with these kinds of characteristics, there is a downside to this type of personality. It is difficult to stay here, in the world. I don't fit. I never fit in with the general way of thinking. In earlier days I wasn't particularly aware that I was different, unworldly, fey. I thought maybe that everybody was that different, but I found this world to be a very cruel place. I came to realize that I was hurt more easily than others. Fairypeople have a very high sensitivity to everything. To rhythm, to color. Almost too sensitive to stick around.

D: You said earlier that fairies have no ego. Since fairypeople are part fairy, does that mean that fairypeople have less ego than non-fairypeople?

K: I think that their ego structure may be different. We agreed, when we came over [into the human realm], that we would take on this negative energy, and take on the forgetfulness of a separation. So in that sense our ego was born. So we certainly have egos. They may be less integrated and certainly less tough and more sensitive, but the ego structure is just the same. We are not pure spirits, or anything like that.

Physical Traits

I came across a number of people in Ireland, sometimes friends of Kay's, or friends of friends, whose faces, bodies, and/or behaviors seemed in one way or another to be fey, star-struck, fairy-like.

Val reported similarly:

Val: A lot of people will very clearly recognize a fairy[person]. That has happened with a friend of ours. Everybody was seeing him very much as fairy. He did have a very light body and he was very light.

You can recognize layers in people. Some of them are so fairy there is no doubt. They are so light and fairy-like. They are the obvious ones. But to me there are lots of different kinds of fairies [fairypersons]. You are probably talking about sylphs. I know most people have seen them. They are very light, very bright, very slender: what most people would think of fairy[people]. I have met some, but I have also met others that I would still call fairies, but who have different qualities about them. Like you could almost identify a tree or a plant, more than just bright energy. You could actually see a plant in them; see an acorn in them, if you see what I mean.

I think the other thing is what Minette said, that when you recognize the fairy in them they just shine immediately. You don't have to say it, you just recognize it in them. They know. Somehow it is that you recognize it in them and suddenly they brighten up, and even though their lives might be in a mess, they become this bright, bright fairy again and absolutely shine....

Kay and I also talked about the physical and behavioral traits of fairypeople:

Kay: Some people look so much like fairies that their fairyness is obvious. My friend Benita is one of the fairypeople who lives in the States. Her ears are kind of pointed. I mean they are not grossly pointed. If there were a thousand women her age in a group and you were to pick out the one who would look most like a fairy[person], it would be her.

There are all kinds of people in Ireland just walking around, musicians and whatnot, who look fairy. If you find out that the person is a musician or storyteller or artist, or if they talk about Fairy in conversation, then that is a likely indication that they are fairy. It is not for sure, because there are a lot of small people here in Ireland because of the famine and the diets.

Marita is very striking looking. She is in her fifties and very fairy looking. And James Hubbell, everybody says, looks like an elf... It is not that all the people who look like fairies are from the Fairy Kingdom, but it is a good possibility that they are.... Kirsten is definitely an earth fairy. I think she is definitely a gnome or an elf. She is not a sylph. She's got the rectangular body. Slyphs are different.

I would say as a guess that those who look most like fairies, strikingly, were fairies on the other side and are in their first incarnation as human beings.

I asked Kay how she could tell by looking at them if a person is a reincarnated fairy:

K: I have heard that the eyes jump around a lot, or that they have a different way of expressing themselves. Marita told me that, and that was one of the ways that she decided who was a fairyperson. For me it's more like looks and the way people move their bodies..... You know if you see Jon in motion when he is talking about fairies it is almost like he changes. You can actually see something different than a solid person, although I don't mean that literally. It is an elusiveness in their demeanor.

Of course some people just look fairy. Regarding the whole Fairy Kingdom and different types of fairies, I can pretty much guess who is a sylph[person], and who comes under the gnomes[people] and the fire people. The sylphs are the smallest and lightest of the fairypeople, the most delicate. They are lighter and thinner boned. In their human form sylphs are most fragile and find it the most difficult to be here. Elfpeople are much more solidly grounded, and stockier.

D: Is Jon a sylph?

K: I would say Jon is, but he can be kind of both. I mean there are people who are kind of both. He has a lot of grounded quality to him.

To me it's amazing how some people actually resemble drawings and paintings artists make of fairies, elves, gnomes, and other (mythical) humanish nature beings. Whether the artists receive inspiration from what they think are fairies or from fairy-looking people they have seen, is perhaps moot. In any case it appears that those familiar with fairyness can pretty easily see that there's *something* fairy going on that resonates with the physical aspects of some humans.

I asked Jon one time if it was true that some people actually look like fairies, that fairypeople are physically different. For example, with short stature, delicate bone structure, certain qualities of eyes, etc. He said he thought that it was true.

D: What is your understanding of how humans take on fairyish physical and behavioral features, in some loosely defined evolutionary sense? I don't mean evolution necessarily in a strict Darwinian sense, but with respect to some kind of passing on of physical traits or even of kinds of consciousness. How does that come to be?

Jon: I don't know how to formulate an answer in scientific terms. In my own case it has nothing to do with direct lines of genetic transmission. No other people in my family would have these characteristics that I notice in myself. I do note these characteristics in myself, and, indeed, in other people. Sometimes it happens on particular occasions, on occasions which are conducive to the evocation of the fairy dimension of the soul of the person in question. In such cases it seems that his or her fairy traits become a mirror expression of soul dimensions which are being called forth in a situation. Those are the circumstances under which it becomes clearest to me.

You can see it, this kind of thing happening very clearly with musicians as they begin to play. The more they are carried by the wave that passes through them the more their physical form adapts itself to the requirements of the energy of which they are accommodating at that point. It is the closest I can come to an explanation of it. I don't understand it except to say that our DNA is a lot more mysterious than we currently understand, and that under certain circumstances the depths of our souls become apparent in the quality of our physical appearance.

D: From day one in a person's life in some cases?

J: From day one in some cases, yes. From day one you sometimes see potentials in little beings. The physical body is obviously conditioned by the experiences to which one is exposed. While I take your point that there are sometimes quite striking distinctive physical characteristics, I also think that there is some kind of mysterious dimension to it which has to do with the mystery of the essence of the person shining forth through the vehicle of the physical being.

Perhaps a new science could provide a more adequate explanation. *But in the beginning, and in the end, the purpose of fairy is not to be scientifically explainable.*

I also asked fairyminded Marc and Val about the physical traits of fairypeople.

Marc: There is a huge spectrum of fairies. As a useful parallel, in a sense it is like any ethnic group or nationality. It's like looking at all Irish, or whatever group in general, when actually there are many, many types. Actually there are no types, it is a spectrum.

Val: I have no idea how the manifestation of fairypeople's bodies are so that some have very obvious physical traits. But I do know lots of them who are fairies who haven't got the typical fairy body.

Marita also had ideas. She says that she can see fairyness in other people's eyes and behavior, especially in their bright-eyedness, whether or not they might be reincarnated fairies. Her own eyes can change a lot, and at one point her light hazelish eyes had almost a pin prick of a pupil. She, at times, has a fairy look in her own eyes, light and comforting. She says her own eyes have been getting brighter, more alive, more inviting, as she opens herself up to herself and others.

Marita: I think that people's traits and physical features come in from the Fairy Kingdom. James Galway, for instance, who came in from the Fairy

Nature Kingdom, came in specifically to bring the flute into the orchestra. And he is Irish. And his eyes are just going dance, dance, dance, with his flute. And he is only a couple of lifetimes, I believe, in from the Nature Kingdom. ... I think that such people either move their heads a lot, or their eyes are sparkling. Or they have light bodies. Or their ears can be pointed. Yea, I think that there are fairy features that manifest in the genetic physicality of the human. Now, I do not know if the soul is giving that to the physical identity of the body, I don't know what that is. The DNA? But it comes through in the nature beings. Genetically you carry the magic. There is a magic in some of the human physical characteristics. Playfulness. Lightness.... *I think God is a wonderful scientist.*

One day I was with Kay and a local woman who had read about Kay in a newspaper article. The woman had tracked Kay down to talk about fairies. We sat in Kay's kitchen, mostly the two of them talking. The 35ish woman said she came by because she is interested in fairies and writing happy, not fearful, children's stories. She had recently received a healing as part of her getting fed up with her workaholic life as a nurse, feeling busy all the time. As part of her healing she was told she could be a writer and she became interested in recapturing a light-hearted, childish fairyness. She said she became interested in reading about and experiencing more fairy things. She said she had not seen fairies, but had felt them. After she left, Kay said to me: "She has a lot of fairy energy about her, the way she moves about and whatnot."

Carol had said that one of her neighbors looked like a leprechaun. Carol says she can tell when somebody is a fairyperson, mostly by the energy that she senses or sees. She states that definitely the eyes make a big difference. I asked her if fairypeople are born with fairyish physical features, or if they come to take on starry looks as they live. She said that they can do both. "I think you can definitely see children who are born with features of fairy."

Sensitivities and Personality

Jon, Marc, Minette, Val, Kay, and others all say that fairypeople tend to be very tender, and that makes them vulnerable to hurt. At the same time they are capable of making connections with the divine, which can allow one to get beyond hurt.

Kay says fairypeople may be more conscious of their own dualities:

Kay: We as fairypeople may be more self-aware than many others, most others actually. But we are not necessarily more aware than others who are self-aware. We are less self-aware than avatars.

We could say that we are more in touch with our higher self, and more aware of our lower self. More aware that we have a lower self, and also aware that we have a higher self. (Neither Freud nor Jung quite got in touch with the fact that we are not separate minds. I think Jung maintained that until he died. Jung, although startling in his time, never quite connected the collective unconscious to divinity in a direct way. He didn't quite know what to do with it. If he were living now, he would certainly have a different concept.)

Fairypeople's sensitivity to a range of human distress can cause them to socially withdraw. Kay is well informed on these issues:

Kay: In the Fairy World the fairies don't have free will, they are simply servants or instruments of the divine. Only when you cross over [into the human realm] do you acquire free will. That is why fairypeople have problems with negativity, because they haven't had it before. They don't know what to do with the negative energy because it is new. The life force here has positive and negative poles, plus and minus, just like a battery, because that is the nature of energy here. Originally, as servants of God in previous lifetimes, fairypeople have a problem standing up for themselves, and being independent. Getting out of "well I have to do that because she said so."

We have to learn to stand up for our own needs. I had assumed earlier in my life that everybody had this problem. I know that Susan and I talked about this when we first found out we were fairies [fairypeople]. We were programmed to take care of other people's needs, to respond to the needs of other people. It has to do with service and with serving people. You want to know what they are like or how they work so you can serve them better. Susan said that was the biggest problem in her life, to the detriment of her life. Marita and I talked about that as well, about how sensitive we are about not hurting other people. You can also get weirdness around that too. You can get some dark energy around that, about defending yourself and not being able to do it well. And you can get covert in some of your operations. So don't think by any means that the fairypeople are wonderful without faults. They have as many faults as anybody.

The other day when we were over at Carol's house for dinner she was talking about her desire to please and assist the man who was living at her house. That is very much a fairy[person] trait. Couldn't you just see her, like a servant, like a mother, or a Jewish mother. She wasn't considering herself at all. Was he considering anything about her needs? Her whole conversation, her whole interest, was in serving him.

Being programmed in some way to work to help the world is another kind of unconscious thing that I had. It later became conscious that I was doing that. Later I found out that that is a problem with the fairypeople, to go from involuntary to voluntary service… But even when I talk to my childhood friends, the people who knew, and know me, they say that I do do that, that I was and am on the lookout for them rather than for myself.

I can feel the energy of fairypeople and they have different energy. Ira, who works with people's energies, said that my energy pattern is the lightest that he has ever come across. He thought that there was something wrong with me when he first gave me an energy treatment. He said there was something imperceptible. … I am so delicate [as a sylphperson]. The truth is that we sylphs are very delicate.

Whatever the fairypeople are bringing through is so, so joyful. And so full of life and creativity, that I am happy, proud, to be associated with that. But I also realize that it is very hard to survive as a fairyperson in this world. And if Jeremiah is correct in what he said, then it is really only one in five who can make it effectively.

Fairypeople are intuitive. And there certainly is a changeability about fairypeople. They change. They change locations. They change partners. They are not tedious.

Jon echoes:

> Fairypeople tend to be very sensitive, and dealing with humans can cause them to withdraw. So the sensitivity which potentially makes you very vulnerable to hurt also makes you sensitive to resources, particularly the sense of divine connection. But I do not want to portray this kind of sensitivity, this kind of capacity to overcome the past, as distinctive to fairypersons, as opposed to any other kind of person.

Marc, and Minnette, and Val had also spoken of fairypeople's sensitivities:

Marc: Many fairypeople feel like they are exiles because, in a sense, they are like exiles from their homeland. And they are bridging back to that realm for us. They are hearing the kind of music of their homeland going through them.

There is a big difference between those who are fulfilled and those who are unfulfilled, and those who are happy and those who are unhappy.

Some of us feel distinct and separate from our society. Some of us feel connected. Some people in general find life to be incredibly unjust, and find it impossible to break freely into life. They feel like they are from a different place, and they just can't figure how they got here. And they are not too sure if they want to be here all the time. Sometimes they feel when they are with fairypeople who are close to them, or people who have a sympathy for them, that they can be happy. But other times they may feel incredibly unhappy when they feel they are in a situation where they feel like they are exiles again…..It would interesting to see how many fairypeople get drawn into themselves by addictions and stuff. How others keep alive is usually by keeping the musical flow going or the creative flow going, by helping others. They become giving and very open.

Some of the happiest people, and some of the most unhappy people, are fairypeople.

Minette: You know the fairypeople are servants of the Gods, the Goddesses. They come here in service. So unfortunately what happens to them is, if they are not very careful, they can be taken over. Their lovely, delicate fairy nature can actually be taken over by very heavy people making requirements. Fairypeople are often desperately trying to look after everybody, and do things for other people that their own energies are not being nourished. But that's because that's what fairies do. They are always trying to help the situation. They are light bringers.

Val: Some fairypeople seem to have personal problems that seem unresolvable to them. They have put themselves into these situations usually for altruistic reasons, but they don't understand the rules of the game. They got really enmeshed in it. So I really don't think that fairypeople get enough contact with each other. If they could support each other they might get themselves released from some of the difficulties.

There are some who really want to be helpful, and have so much love in them, but they get depleted. In doing that they are actually not solving the problem, they are creating a huge problem for themselves to get out of. They don't understand what they have got themselves into, or what they have to get out of. A lot of it is naivete. They don't know the game.

Marc: Their problem is with getting out in the world and achieving things. The frustration is that most fairypeople don't get any of that work out there. They mostly don't get it out of themselves because they don't have the environment for them to do it. When they do achieve something, in most cases it doesn't reach the end of the street. So many fairypeople get caught in the loop. The loop goes around and around and around.

You can hear the same stories from many different fairies[people]. It's the same story of the negative and positive elements in their lives.

Val: The themes are the same. It is as if they need someone really solid besides them who they feel really safe with so that things can come out. So that that person can ground them and help them stop falling. It's not that they don't want to do things on their own, but they do need this bridge person.

Marc: But also the problem is that they are also kind of very lonely because of the background that they have been brought up in. They have always had to express themselves in secret or in the wild. It is a very difficult thing to work with other people.

Fairywomen tend to go for men who are definite pillars of strength, like trees that can kind of hold them in the world. But they don't get to be fully themselves. Often it can be quite abusive to the fairyperson, I think. The male feels that he has to control her in different ways. I mean the women might not actually be physically abused, but emotionally they certainly are. They kind of trade in their fairyness for security.

D: Are there more fairywomen than fairymen in your experience?

Val: Yes. But having said that my immediate reaction is yes, but no. Not really. There is something in a woman that is shown in me that I didn't expect to see in men, especially the men that I have found it in, you know. That was the surprise. There are more fairymen than you would expect, and that must put them in a dreadful position, because women express more than men. The female's role is now expanding and the men now are wondering what on earth that is. I have great sympathy for men because of all this stuff. I mean the men have been deprived also. It's a balance that we have to come to, and we all have to find our own balance. I do a lot of the female stuff, but there is a balance with the male, and I think that males really need an awful lot of help now in finding their own roles. So it is difficult for fairymen. Women have expressed themselves to a certain extent, but I think the men find it even more difficult, and suppress it more.

Numerous discussions and (comparative) perspectives on the self, or the Self, have been put forth by scholars of religion. (See, for example,

Rouner 1992.) Psychologists and psychoanalysts, (e.g. Kohut 1985, in Ornstein 1978), and especially Jungians, and post-Jungians, (e.g., Wilber 1985 [1979]), as well as theologians, are interested in notions of the self. I will only briefly take up the issue of the self as it relates to traits of fairypeople which in part derive from their feelings of connection to, and historical descent from, other-than-human persons.

In their introduction to an edited collection of works in *Self and Self-Transformation in the History of Religions*, reviewing the articles, the general subject matter, and the history of ideas about the self, Shulman and Stroumsa (2002) emphasize that religions have not only specific views of the divine and the cosmos, but also of the person and the self: "The conditions and circumstances under which this person can be transformed are different in each religious context."(7). Summarizing Shaked's (2002) work in that volume they suggest that

> people seem to live simultaneously with many distinct and competing conceptions of self (functional, magical, astrological, demonic), even as today we seem to move easily among various "selves" (scientific, astrological, psychoanalytic, expressive, and so on); which self comes to the fore at any given moment is determined by context. Moreover, many of these selves are highly ambiguous and difficult to distinguish; they can be benevolent or malevolent, threatening or propitious. In the Sasarian [Babylonian] case - as in others studied here – self-transformation thus speaks to the reconfigurations of any such multivocal person, inhabited by personae of indeterminate provenance. (11)

Shaked (2002: 129) says:

The person seems to be definable, among other things, as an individual component in a conglomerate of individuals, both visible and invisible. While relations with other persons in the visible society can be friendly or hostile, they differ radically from relations with members of the invisible section of society in one important respect. The former type of relations (those with our neighbours and fellow humans) are external; the latter (those with the invisible beings) are internal, part of the constitution of the person itself – the dialogue with them is an internal dialogue. *The sum of one's associations with invisible beings is in a profound manner a way of defining and characterizing oneself.* (my emphasis)

Suffice it to say that the notions of the self in the consciousness of fairypeople are different from most Western concepts, as the self for fairypersons is partially comprised of timeless, mostly invisible beings of the past and present. Among fairyfolk, the self is in part inherited (as in Eastern reincarnationist religions), and capable to varying degrees of being realized and activated in this lifetime. The self – which is in part the soul of the past fairy background of the person on another plane of existence – is divine.

Thus the current self is subject to having traits that have been transferred from a divine nature spirit. This is a more particular and specific form of what many in some religions consider a human (partly) made in the image of God, as mentioned above. The self then, for fairypeople, is, in part, kin to nature spirits. This is similar to, as Bird-David (2002) describes a la Hallowell (1960), "kinship" among the south Indian Nayaka. There, *devaru* spirits are constituted as "persons" with whom the Nayaka share and relate:

> ...devaru are relatives in the literal sense of being 'that or whom one interrelates with' (not in the reduced modern English sense of '*humans* connected with others by blood or affinity')... They are superrelatives who both need and can help Nayaka in extraordinary ways. (88)

Fairyfolk's interaction with fairies in visions, intuitions, and contemplations is an animistic epistemology, and, as Bird-David (2002: 96-7) summarizes, a relational issue:

> If the object of modernist epistemology is a totalizing scheme of separated essences, approached ideally from a separated viewpoint, the object of this animistic knowledge is understanding relatedness from a related point of view within the shifting horizons of the related viewer. Knowledge in the first case is having, acquiring, applying, and improving representations of things in-the-world (see Rorty 1980). Knowledge in the second case is developing the skills of being in-the-world with other things, making one's awareness of one's environment and one's self finer, broader, deeper, richer, etc. Knowing, in the second case, grows from and *is* maintaining relatedness with neighboring others. It involves dividuating [interrelating to] the environment rather than dichotomizing it and turning attention to 'we-ness,' which absorbs differences, rather than to 'otherness,' which highlights differences and eclipses commonalities. Against 'I think, therefore I am' stand 'I relate, therefore I am' and 'I know as I relate." Against materialistic framing of the environment as discrete things stands relationally framing the environment as nested relatednesses.

With regard to spirits granting abilities to humans - fairies giving humans musical talents or healing skills - fairies are similar to one type of spirit entity of the Yarralin Australian Aborigine, the *mungamunga*. Rose (2000:96) writes:

> *Mungamunga* make friends with humans and teach them songs, dances, and designs.... In making friends with ordinary people *mungamunga* provide an entrée across boundaries, making ordinary people clever, or giving them corroborees.

Fairyfolk's sense of identity and self is deeply embedded in their ideas of being a human part of the community of nature spirits, and thus their selves, their identities, their personhoods, are relational. This relationality is in a closer sense than the conventional (Christian) theological notions about closeness to God or Jesus, who are so grand that inter-"personal" divine contact is not as personal or as earth-oriented as it can be with a fairy or fairy energy. The monotheistic God's responsibility encompasses everyone, and thus relationships between an individual and the God are less personal, less "kin"-based. Smaller, potentially more physically formed and observable, fairies are divine friends and companions.

Chapter Thirteen

Healing and Well-Being

As we have heard, for fairyfolk, for fairypeople especially, there are often heightened emotional sensitivities and feelings of being out of place. Yet for those who have consciously worked on their psycho-spiritual, mystical development, the Fairy Faith can contribute to health and well-being.

D: Once you realized that you were a fairyperson did you have more joy in your life?

Kay: More joy and more appreciation of the Mystery. More appreciation of the mystical. More sureness of the invisible world. More tranquility. More sureness of spiritual realities.

D: And that provides joy itself.

K: Joy, but it is more of an even joy. *It is kind of joy mixed with tranquility. A running joy. An upliftedness...* More contented and less interested in the material world. There is more tranquility in that sense. There is a lack of interest in competition, if I had had any anyway.

D: Would you say among the people that you know who are fairypeople, and those who aren't, that fairypeople are more content in general than the ones who aren't?

K: Well they could be, but I do not know that they are, because of their extreme sensitivity. The world is a difficult place for many fairypeople. If the world were truly spiritually advanced then all the fairypeople could be quite content. But many of them are in kind of a hell hole at the moment.

All the fairypeople and fairy-conscious persons I met understood their connectedness to the Fairy Realm not only as spiritual realization and as repairing separation from Divinity, but also as central to their own emotional, psychological well-being. Their sensitivities to fairyness, their heartfelt and joyful understandings of the Divine, enabled them to become more cognizant of their human psychological traits, problems, strengths, and weaknesses. The individuation process proceeds by getting out of one's own human ego to one degree or another, and connecting to one's transcendent self. This is the path of not only spiritual growth, but mental health. By transcending rational consciousness one begins to shed negative emotional and mental patterns.

Several scholars have indicated the mentally integrative nature of mystical experiences and approaches to life. As anthropologist Grossinger (1980) suggests in *Planet Medicine*, mysticism itself is a healing science. Psychoanalyst Kakar (1991) summarizes:

> Some of the more recent work in psychoanalysis recognizes that mystical states lead to more rather than less integration of the person. The mystic's insight into the workings of his or her self is more rather than less acute. Although consciousness during the mystical trance may be characterized by "de-differentiation" (to use Anton Ehrenzweig's concept), that is, by the suspension of many kinds of boundaries and distinctions in both the inner and outer worlds, its final outcome is often an increase in the mystic's ability to make ever-finer perceptual differentiations. In other words, the point is not the chaotic nature of the mystical experience, if it is indeed chaotic, but the mystic's ability to create supreme *order* out of the apparent chaos. (3-4) (author's emphasis)

And transpersonal anthropologists Laughlin, et. al. (1983) assert that those individuals who can "cross phases of consciousness," that is, can integrate experiences derived from two or more alternative (other than normal waking consciousness) phases, do well. They argue that in traditional societies "cross-phasing" is the norm, but that in relatively monophasic societies like our own, the labels and "negative valences" associated with alternative consciousness, as in dreams, trances, mystical states, etc., inhibit the integration of such experiences.[1]

But psycho-spiritual development can be a painful process - coming to realize and confront fears and guilts created by one's own mind and by cultural forces. And others' skepticism or scorn of personal mystical practice can add to difficulties. It takes confidence and security in one's self, and one's own path, to take steps into the unknown, especially if they are not supported by friends, family, community. Jon spoke about this earlier. In general, the path of fairyness is informal and ad hoc. It is thought, felt, and experienced on an individual basis in a sort of self-help manner. Thus some fairyfolk sometimes want to be with one another to have support on the journey.

Here we will examine how fairy connectedness is described as part of mental health improvement.

As Kay mentioned above, one of the interesting aspects of the new Fairy Faith is that a good number of the adherents I met are psychologists or help-givers, some with PhD's. I met several people who were either currently, or previously, professional counselors and therapists. It is not just coincidence. Those who were or are attracted to helping others are seekers of an ever-developing personal (spiritual) psychology and well-being. Their own professional studies of the human mind, and of emotion work, are likely, consciously or unconsciously, partially a projection of their own desires and part and parcel of their own spiritual path.

Here Kay, Ana, and I continue to talk about the process:

Ana: Is it important to the fairy tradition that people be psychologically integrated in the world? Is it seen as being important to fairy[person] life?

Kay: I don't know who would "give" the determination. The fairies wouldn't give it a value, because it wouldn't have a meaning. Mainstream psychology can't deal with it.

The fairies would be more likely to contact children than they would adults. Children would be more receptive, more open. When I have talked to children about any of these ideas, which I did a lot, children just sit around listening, just waiting to get more.

A: Because that is where they live anyway.

K: Yes. The fairypeople themselves are not yet, and may never be, a group apart, a fraternity within themselves, to make up these ideas. My guess is that it is such a specialized job, so to speak, that it wouldn't necessarily fall on people who were integrated. It is kind of living on the fringe. Most of us don't want to be integrated. It still depends to some extent on societal values. So I think the fairypeople are more inclined to wonder how they can survive as aliens in an alien world. But on the other hand, if you are going to stick around, you have be integrated.

D: Are the fairypeople who make it healthier?

K: I think so. That still depends. You are still putting a societal value on "making it." We are talking about a plan that we don't really have a clue about or even what the plan is.

D: Perhaps a task could be to try to convince some people that getting more aware or awakened to spiritual entities such as fairies or elemental beings is good for the person as a mental health practice.

K: Absolutely. But I am just saying that it is difficult, because there is nobody ahead of us. It would stand to reason that if you are born into this world in a certain way, that you should try to get there. I am saying *it is difficult for people because there are no guidelines, no plans, no clues.*

Although well versed in clinical psychology, Jungian and spiritual psychology, and mysticism, Kay, a former clinical psychologist, suggests that fairy consciousness, especially for fairypeople, is in great part unknown territory in contemporary thinking. It is a unique form of consciousness and practice yet to be recognized and accepted. As I have argued earlier, most New Agey books on fairies and angels are not really mystical, more simplistic and gimmicky, relating only the "happy" side of psycho-spiritual development. They tend to be "fluffy," without the recognition of the complexity and depth of personal work necessary for addressing psychic pain and for truly mystically communing with fairies in a transformative way. This can often entail emotional lows and feelings of alienation that can attend to periods between divine connection.

Marita describes her clinical use of fairyness.

Marita: I have a client at the moment who has been with me for about a year. In fact last Wednesday in our session we sat down, and we were really two nature beings together. We were like children. I was a child and she definitely was a child. In that way we talk, and then we can have very deep sessions, with profound emotional or psychological work. We are able to transcend the difficulties of our humanness, which is a journey for her. She transcends that, and comes back to me. She surprises me in that way because she gives me the gift. We share little fairy cards or she brings fairy objects.

D: When you say fairy objects you mean things that look like fairies?

M: Yes. That's because she is young, and it gives her something to work with. She is an intellectual, a very bright intellectual.

D: So at times you invoke or use your fairyness or fairy connection as a way to help other people in their own human psychological life.

M: Absolutely.

D: We could call you a fairy psychotherapist if we wanted to. That probably wouldn't go very far out there if you had it on your business card.

[Laughter]

Here Marita speaks of her own emotional and mental maturation:

Marita: The Fairy Faith keeps alive the mystery to humans of another World that they don't perceive or see. It's a doorway into something.

D: So when you were a teenager or later, before you read these books and realized you were a fairy[person], was there a dimension of pain to you in that your whole self couldn't come out?

M: There was a joy immediately upon discovering those books and my fairyness. I could reconnect back to something beyond the pain that I had experienced. That part of myself has always brought me through the pain, and continues to. That's the gift. I think that even on your journey that you share with the fairypeople you will find the gift.

D: How would you describe your journey?

M: It's been a hard journey. In a sense I have been a victim for a long number of years and circumstances of life. I was in that category of victim, and then waking up and knowing that you can come out of that world, and really walk away from it. And stepping out of that world. It's like a miracle.

D: Was the pain or struggle along the way a consequence of difficulties in social relationships, husbands, children, friends or lovers?

M: There was so much frozen that couldn't get out of me. So there was a meeting of the pain, genuinely meeting it and holding it, loving it. And learning to love myself and appreciate and forgive and be more tolerant. And it continues. I guess basically it was around relationship difficulties. Not so with my children – they kept my heart open and growing. But definitely with relationships because there is a part of yourself closed and protected through pain and feelings of inadequacy, blah, blah, blah… I'm now not afraid to share myself at all.

D: So it sounds that the fairy connections helped you become and stay more grounded, healthy, stable. I am not sure what words you as a psychotherapist would use. Would it be that your unconscious or latent functions have become more manifest, or your unconscious has risen to consciousness, or that your soul or spirit has risen to meet your ego?

M: My dreams show me the steps. Places inside myself where I drift away, maybe not drift away now, because I really try to be conscious. But they show me steps or areas of challenge. I have choices in how I adapt and integrate. *Nature is a place that renews and gives presence for insight and tenderness.* Blessings for me, to help the nature being in the psychological sense of our self.

D: It helps the nature being in you, and the nature being in you helps your human self?

M: Yes, it is very much integrated.

D: The fairies lighten you up?

M: Oh my God, yes. They lighten me up.

D: It sounds like lightening up is health, healthy. So the fairies are an aide in coping, in growing and enjoying.

M: Yet in those nature being places there are no worries. You can't talk sometimes, because there is such a silence, such a communion.

Unlike Marita, when Kay herself was a working therapist she hadn't fully realized her fairyness, nor did she do "fairy work" with clients. Ana, herself a clinical and Buddhist psychologist, and I discuss these issues with Kay:

D: You got your fairy stuff more dramatically after you were practicing psychotherapy?

Kay: Oh, yes. For a while there I was still doing both. I never integrated the fairy ways. At that time I was kind of winding down my therapy practice. But there were some of the people who were seeing me on a long term basis who were absorbing some of this new material from me. I was talking about it with people I could trust with this information – only a very few.

D: Were they receptive?

K: Well, they were receptive to everything that was preceeding my fullness as a fairyperson.

D: Do you have a sense that there are more people in California in the mental health fields who are integrating spiritual stuff.

K: There is more of it there. Many psychology graduate students now have a spiritual practice in California, depending on what school they go to. Or at least they are aware of it. All of my interns, for example, had a very definite spiritual practice.

D: Did you feel more competent or effective when you started to integrate more of your spirituality into your client work? Did it help you get better with your clients or with yourself?

K: No. Because at the time it was not integrated within myself. I almost isolated myself from trying to integrate it. I did very structured things like psychological testing. I couldn't handle both worlds. It did not make any sense to me at the time. I could do it now, but I couldn't do it then. *I needed the transition to my full realization of my fairy connection to understand what all this new material was about.*

Ana: Doing psychological testing outside a spiritual path helped you maintain a clear boundary. This is this world, and this is that world. A clear space to develop and expand.

K. Yes. And I could represent myself as the same effective person. Because you know my colleagues were getting wind of it.

[Laughter]

Supportive or unsupportive social environments clearly affect one's level of well-being in general and full integration of fairyness into oneself. The sharing of spiritual understandings or the fairy path, or not, is potentially important for some.

We continued to talk:

Ana: Well, I think that is a whole issue, of how others see us. And then how can one come out, to be full, with all of those parts. That is a huge part of our lives, how others look at us. How much room there is for ourselves in our world. From what I understand that was part of your coming here to Ireland, that you could open up.

K: When my friends visited me here in Ireland they did notice the difference in me, how much more happy I was. More integrated. More creative. They noticed that, which brought them to decide that I wasn't insane.

Some of it is acknowledging to myself how I am different. That it is OK to be different. That I shouldn't attempt to conform, because I really can't.

It is easier for me now than it was, of course. I mean when I first received that information about my being a reincarnated fairy I was extremely dubious and upset. But I wouldn't call it depression. Not in any clinical sense of depression. It was more like angst. But why did this terrible thing happen to me? How can I do it? I am the first. I am alone. There is no one ahead of me. Which was true at the time.... But now it seems much more natural. It is just what I'm doing, the best way I can do it. And it is much more interesting than anything else I would be doing. It is much more fun. I am meeting such creative people.

A: Bringing people in. That whole idea that the more you show yourself, the more you draw in those of like mind. I know this for myself. If nobody sees my kind of true essence, than I say I am lonely. If I am lonely, how can I be fully connected to people.

K: Yes.

A: How can I be in my world if I am not showing who I am.

Another time I asked Kay about how her fairyness helped her:

D: Since you realized that you are a fairyperson, do you think that you are more tolerant, or more or less judgmental of human beings than you were before?

Kay: I never really thought of it in those terms. You know it is not separate from the spiritual work I am trying to live up to. It has to be less judgmental. I certainly now lack an unnecessarily strong sense of seriousness, or a need to judge someone else's path.

D: How about anger? Compared to before you realized that you were a fairyperson and now as you have grown older have you become more or less angry, or angerable?

K: I would say that I am much less angry.

D: Do you think it is the fairies that have helped you with that?

K: Certainly they have helped. They have gotten me closer to working with the beauty of nature and to working with the beauty with anything that I am doing. And also to appreciate the humor in so many things that I wouldn't necessarily have appreciated before that. I also have no interest in status now, and that of course makes life easier.

D: It is interesting the ways in which fairyness helps or hinders a person's mental health. To what degree or in what ways does one's consciousness of and connections to fairies, relate to one's mental health. …. They say that prayer itself is therapeutic, psychologically speaking. That contact in some way with a divine source is therapeutic. I am just wondering how that works…. I have found that over the last two, three years that my increasing spiritual connection grounds me in a way that I belong more in the World, in a way that makes me feel healthy. I can lift my hands to the sky now and feel the energy that is out there, which I didn't or couldn't do years ago. It makes me happy, although many would think it crazy. Maybe the question is, do you become healthier psychologically as your fairy consciousness grows?

K: Yes. For one thing, it kind of answers my unknown query that I am a stranger in a strange land. And why am I so different, and not even knowing that I am different. Why can't I relate mental health to non-mental health. Mental health means that you are a survivor in this world and I don't want to be. So it is very helpful to me to understand that this fragility is nothing to be ashamed of, or to try to change. And the way that I can't relate to the materialistic world has a lot of positive mental health as far as I am concerned, not the opposite... And my shyness and lack of assertiveness has a quality that is better understood. My definition of myself is a lot clearer. And why I am interested in what I am interested in is a lot clearer. And the closer that I work to my spiritual center, the happier I am. So all that is connected....

But, on the other hand, all fairypeople are strangers here. How can you necessarily measure their mental health. What are you going to use as a standard? [Laughter] Is adjustment to the material world a standard that applies to the fairies? No. The more adjusted they are to the material world, the more they are away from contact with themselves. So mental health to them would be integrating who they are with where they are.

D: We have said that fairyness is a spiritual path on the way to happiness. Yet most reincarnated fairypeople are hypersensitive, and many of them, as you said, don't make it because this world is too tough for their sensibilities. If fairy sensibility is often hypersensitivity, then it is possible that the more that somebody realizes their fairyness and their sensitivities, the less they will be able to cope with the demands of everyday life.

K: I am not following that logic. But for me I would say the opposite was true, in the sense that fairypeople are more sensitive than the average. Supersensitive. I would not know in what range you would put them. I do not know, because one doesn't know how sensitive one is compared to other people. You can't get inside somebody else's head. Except in counseling you get an idea of what people are like. And you can observe your life in retrospect as to how careful you are not to hurt other people.

D: In other words, you might go out of your way not to hurt somebody else.

K: Yes, because I would assume that the other person would be hurt like I would be hurt, when it is quite possible that they wouldn't be hurt. Or that they like the fight. Or they like things to be clear, or not glossed over. But once I understood my sensitivity to be part of the fairy nature, it was easier for me to protect it, rather than the other way around. It was easier for me to acknowledge that that's the way I am. And that I am much more sensitive than most people, almost anybody. It is a consolation to recognize the reason for that. Does that make sense?.... For me it is a consolation that that's the reason I am more sensitive, and get hurt more easily by life. That that is OK. To recognize that, to recognize that that is the way I am. It brings it up on the surface. It's been hard, and it is the reason it has been hard. It is almost like you have something physically wrong with you, but it has never been identified. When it gets to be identified, then it has some shape and form to it, and you can do something about protecting it. OK. Before, if you didn't know anything about it, you didn't have any way of putting it anywhere in a protective sense.

D: So there is more anxiety about something that is not known, or locatable.... So for people who are trying to recognize their fairyness you would say it is a healthy path. It is always a healthy path?

K: Yes.

D: Earlier on you were saying that doing this stuff consciously was a struggle for you.

K: Oh, yes.

D: You said it was difficult and a struggle, but it didn't make you unhappy, did it?

K: No, but with my being a psychologist, it didn't make it any easier. If I had been a harpist or an artist as a career, maybe it would have been easier. But if I am in charge of evaluating cuckoos as a psychologist, it was anxiety producing. In California it might have been helpful in the sense that California is a far out place. *But still, nobody in their right mind has ever told a psychologist that they used to be a fairy, and get away with it. There is nothing in clinical psychology that has a place for that. Nothing.* Not evenly slightly. Not even in the Pathwork [A system of psycho-spiritual understanding and growth]. Pathwork does not have an opening for that.

Marita sometimes uses her fairyness as a therapeutic tool. I am sure I have done that without realizing that I have done that, to help people become more light-hearted. Certainly when I was a therapist I didn't do it consciously. But Marita has worked as a therapist also knowing she is a fairy. I didn't do that.

D: You are not giving yourself a hard time about what you are doing or who you are. That's great.

K: Pathwork calls that the "forcing current." I have an absence of the forcing current as far as this project is concerned. And that is good.

D: Cause forcing is a negative thing?

K: In the forcing current in Pathwork, you are pushing. You have a need for a certain outcome. You can feel the forcing current in your body when you have a project that has got to turn out the way you want it to.

D: Maybe it is similar to the Buddhist notion of attachment, attachment to results. Strong desire gets in the way of clarity or consciousness.

K: Pathwork deals just with that. Desirelessness is impossible for us in this realm of consciousness. We have to make differences between healthy and unhealthy desires and wishes.

Marc and Val talk about people becoming comfortable with a fairy or elemental background:

Marc: When fairypeople realize that there are a lot of other strange people here they are certainly not going to feel so strange. We are all strange, we are all here from other places. We are all on the earth and we are all from the earth. But we are also from other places. I think that's what one has to live out, reminding everyone that we come from many, many origins. And that there is nobody here who is more deserving to be than anyone else. We are a very complex weaving of the evolutionary threads. It's accepting it, and enjoying it, that's important.

Val: I think that's what it is really. When we come to accept that in ourselves, then we will really feel at home with our selves, and on earth, and with everybody else, even though everybody is going to look diverse. You don't have to be socially acceptable in that way. You just have to *be*, [as Carol declared] and that's fine, and the next person can be very different from you. You can sit at peace with the next person knowing that you are incredibly the same at the core. You are just expressing it in a different way. So it's going to be quite exciting, I think, and people are going to feel far more at home and far more relaxed. As soon as people start showing bits of themselves, you become far more exciting.

Fairyman Jon is most articulate about the mystical process and its relationship to personal and interpersonal growth and well-being. He answers my questions at length:

D: How has your growing consciousness affected your relationships with family or others. How has that been going?

Jon: Well, as consciousness develops you are no longer living in the same place, and of course that poses a challenge for people around you. But it may be welcomed. It may be one of the reasons why they are with you in the first place. So then they have the option, not of becoming more like you, but maybe becoming more like themselves. Let's say that you know I had agreed to live with you within a certain kind of informally established set of parameters, and this is the framework of our interactions, and we can manage nicely within this. And then all of a sudden you are not "there" in the same way, so that the old strategies don't work anymore. OK, so then I can't use them in the same way. So I have to come into a new balance within myself. I can blame you for letting me down, and retrench and stay where I was. In that case, assuming you continue to flow, you will move further and further away from me. Or I might come into my new balance and find that this allows me to appreciate you all the more, in which case we travel together. So insofar as I am an element in the context of other people's lives, and I begin to move and flow, they might respond positively to that in their own terms. Or they might accuse me of having changed on them or something like that, in which case, of course, I can't assume responsibility for their reaction.

What tends to happen is that frequencies that are previously in accord are no longer in accord. So just as a magic can govern the process of coming into new relationships, it can also govern the process of moving lightly, gently, not acrimoniously, away from relationships. So I've learned not to hold on, not to resent, not to cling. Actually these partings can happen quite gently, and quite easily, and there are frequently elements of human poignancy involved in this. But more consciousness is introduced into the situation. This breaks through into an awareness of the deep beauty of the sacrificial universe, where ultimately we are all on the same side, promoting each other's good and awareness the best we can, sometimes wittingly, sometimes not.

D: Sometimes?

J: Sometimes wittingly, sometimes not. As soon as you begin to appreciate that then that, too, is fed back into the heart of compassion. You might have enemies or adversaries, but you know what it means to love them rather than think that they are the pits.

D: So it sounds like it is a positive experience for you, in terms of relationships with lovers, children, parents, etc.?

J: Certainly there is a developmental process involved in letting go.... A hypothetical scenario close to most people's experience is "I'm the one who has changed, so I used to be different," and the other person says "where are you now." Then behind that there are insecurities, like "Do you still love me? Am I okay for you?" That's automatically raising doubt for the other person, because insofar as the two are living together, and one moves in consciousness, you have crisis. Or at least are threatened with that, depending on the insecurity or disability of their balance. Certainly in the early stages my confidence and imagination are not so strong, but I have been through this a number of times and I know the cycle very well now. But I didn't know the cycle very well at first. When I went through it the first time, it was a catastrophic shattering. One day there was a framework and another day there wasn't. But that was in the early days of low awareness....

With hindsight one becomes aware of apparent dysfunctional tactics that began to creep in, efforts to prevent changing such as "Can't you understand me? Can't you stay awake with me?" So you're still hooked, you're still reacting. Ultimately that's an expression of your own reluctance to move beyond, or to be alone in, this new place. So it takes some time for the appropriate insight to come. But with it comes clarity and grace. *You have to kind of suffer the cracking of the shell before you can come aware*, and find some positive way of going with what it was inside you that could be. There has to be a big shake up before this liability can be integrated. *You have to suffer in some sense, whatever that might mean. It could be a mild process or it could be a quite severe one.*

D: Did you have a cracking of the shell, as you call it, at any point in your life?

J: Repeatedly, repeatedly. But I was prepared to go into it. So it happens this morning. *I wasn't exaggerating when I spoke about each day having an extravagant framework*. You need to orient yourself in the midst of this apparent chaos. That's not a reflection of a specifically fairyperson. All kinds of bits come knocking on the door. So it has happened many times. Beyond a certain point it becomes easier and easier because you have a coach. I notice that I have been there so that after a while these elements that were formerly novel are no longer threatening.

D: You have known all your life? You've had this continuous reconstituting of the shell throughout your whole life?

J: *That stuff is happening to people all the time, but we don't know about it.* I really only became conscious of this process about fifteen years ago, and it was a catastrophic experience. That was when I kind of literally was propelled out of one version of myself, or one identity, into something that wasn't what it used to be. How could I make sense of it? It was a huge opening, looking around. And it created a lot of uncertainty in the people around me.

D: Taking the divine conscious out of it for a moment, it sounds like you're discussing a psychological process, a maturing process about living life in the world, about relationships, about letting go of the past and one's ego. Or transforming into a more whole, true self. People talk about those kinds of psychological processes or maturings without the invocation of divinity or without the invocation of fairyness. It sounds like you find that Fairy with a capital F helps or enables that psychological process to manifest itself. Or even to accelerate maturation in a way.

J: Yes it does, but it needs to become part of one's active sphere of awareness.

D: Active sphere?

J: Active sphere of awareness. When you align consciousness with this potential then those changes become easy. I mean you can actually welcome them because you know it's leading you into a richer, fuller life. *As for the divine connection, that is certainly not irrelevant because there is something, not just something to let go of, but something to let go into, that makes the whole process interesting and much easier. And apart from that, there is the adventure of this. And the adventure element wouldn't be there if there wasn't a mystery element.* I'm certainly not being fully precise, talking about this divine connection, because it is very difficult for me to say anything to you about it, to characterize the essence of it. It has to be discovered, it has to be experienced. Perhaps hearing a number of people talk about it would stimulate your own imagination and daring. And yes, of course, that's how we serve each other.

I think you can go back off the cycle as you are opening, and ask what's driving it. I think invariably you arrive at a spiritual phenomenon. Namely something in the life that is seeking to be, something in the potential of life that is seeking to be expressed, realized in the life, and that will not be content, no matter how comfortable, in the trappings or heavily fortified defenses that have been set up. One hears "Let me out, let me out, let me out." So it's as if the comfort zone is being subverted from within. This is a creative process. So insofar as you identify with the comfort zone, or you want to cling to the comfort zone, then you are heading towards a catastrophic opening. There really isn't the wisdom in the culture to anticipate this, or to facilitate it, so it tends to feel like life falling apart. If that happens then the identity seems to be blown apart. And it's frequently associated with the experience of betrayal, or something like that. The life that you counted on existing in perpetuity isn't there. "Where are you, where are you?" You are back wondering "Where am I? What is my story?" But the process is creative.

The imperative to unfold the spiritual essence within the person is part of the psychological process. It certainly cannot be charted in terms of developmental stages.

The path of fairy consciousness that these people describe and, as Kay emphasizes, its uniqueness, are difficult to integrate into conventional or even transpersonal psychology. Yet Jungian analyst Bernstein's (2005) notion of "borderland consciousness" of Western individuals who have evolved into a heightened sensitivity to Nature capable of "participation mystique" could be relevant here. And the "dark green" religious orientation which Taylor (2010) attributes to Eco-Pagans and some radical environmentalists might also be linked here. But fairy consciousness's unique psycho-spiritual communion with externally existing fairy beings or energy is not really recognized by Western others as a "sane" or mystical course. In broad anthropological terms, one could, as I do in Chapter One, liken contact with fairies to indigenous peoples' contact with spirits (Mageo and Howard 1996), guardian-spirits (Benedict 1923), or vision quests (Lowie 1954), although these and other discussions are more sociological than psycho-spiritual, and about non-Western cultural groups.

The fairy path can, however, be likened to a Western mystical approach and process described in Christian and Kabbalistic communion with angels, and with psychologists Raff and Vocatura's (2002) new spiritual paradigm, an approach to the use of an "ally," an "ethereal visitor," a personal spiritual guide.

Judaism/Kabbalism recognizes the reality of angels. Rabbi Steinsaltz (1992) explains:

> The domain of angels, the world of formation, is a general system of nonphysical essences, most of them quite simple and consistent in their being. Each angel has a well-defined character which is manifested in the way it functions in our world. This is why it is said that an angel can carry out only one mission, for the essence of an angel is beyond the existing many-sidedness of man. The particular essence of an angel can be evinced in terms of different things and separate forms, but it remains a single thing in itself, like a simple force of nature. Because even though the angel is a being that possesses divine consciousness, its specific essence and function are not altered by it, just as physical forces in the world are specific and single in their mode of functioning and do not keep changing their essences.

Christianity does also, as Garrett's (2008) recent history attests:

> Across the expanse of Scripture, angels are supporting players and bit characters, who seldom steal the limelight. Yet, they are often essential to the unfolding story. Because angels can appear in visible guise and converse with human beings, they assist in the portrayal of an invisible, ineffable deity (237) ...... The angels teach receptive humans that the divine is suffused throughout creation, and therefore that all things, including humans, are in some measure divine. (239)

But these Western theological understandings of the reality of angels do not detail the potentially transformative or healing dimensions of aligning with angels, and, of course, do not talk about fairies. As well, fairies are more earth-centered than heaven or God-centered and thus the purview of angels is wider, and less about Nature on earth.

Raff and Vocatura (2002) address, but also go beyond, attunement with angels, in what they call a "new mysticism in which the human being is an equal partner with the Divinity."(188) Their approach seems closer to the experience of fairyfolk. They expand on the concept of the "psychoid," Jung's term for the "bounded area where gods and goddesses reside" in myth, also called the collective unconscious, into which, for Jung, humans do not have real entry. Raff and Vocatura extend the idea of the psychoid to include the

> life energy which truly exists beyond our closed universe which may account for the concerted efforts by many to discover life beyond our own world.(8).

The ability to commune with that extra-human life energy, they suggest, is through an ally. That ally is contactable through active imagination, and is the third entity which forms a triune with human divinity and the divinity of God:

> It is the ally as memory that guides the human Self to its manifestation, awakens the Self of God to its dysfunctional state, and binds these two halves together. Moreover, it is with the addition of the ally to the union of human-Divine and God-Divine that the final awesome state is reached, when a new being, a new God emerges." (xiv)

Raff and Vocatura review previous conceptions of the angel as an ally in medieval theology by John Dee (1527- ca. 1609) as discussed by Corbin (1994, 2000), in the work of Rudolph Steiner (1996), and in Sufi mysticism. These orientations all see the angel as a separate spiritual entity that can align itself and communicate with humans for human spiritual understanding and transformation. The main difference in Raff's and Vocatura's "ally theory" is that, in uniting, there is a transformation of both the human individual and the ally, and thus the overarching Divinity of which the angel represents. Their model, which accords with what Kay, Marita, Jon, and other fairyfolk say, is different from the general New Age model of angels which posits that angels bring happiness and do not deal with suffering. Raff and Vocatura, and the fairyfolk, understand that psychological advancement and well-being entails suffering and is part of life and thus that ally work, as in Jungian work in general, entails also facing the dark side of human things, and bringing light onto the dark. That often entails emotional/spiritual pain, on the path to healthier psychological integration.[2]

Raff and Vocatura say that Sufi mystic work with angels is most like their ally work in that not only do angels exist as independent divine beings but also that in Sufism angels have the power, in working with humans, to initiate and move along the human's path of transformation. Although Sufism speaks mostly of angels which are personal guardians (as do some New Age writers), fairyfolk are not always clear whether or not each person is associated with a particular fairy. It seems mostly that different fairies appear to, or are sensed by, humans at different times. Nonetheless, fairy alignment, as in Sufism and Raff and Vocatura's ally work, is also a process in which the perception of fairies or fairy energy can spark and then facilitate ongoing spiritual realization and personal transformation.

In their book, Raff and Vocatura (2002), in a chapter "Working with the Ally, delineate the process of transformation in consistently working with an ally. Space limitations here disallow a full discussion of their ally work, but its kinship with the fairy process, however tentative, is not to be overlooked, even though for Raff and Vocatura the ally is one constant companion akin to a guardian angel, whereas different fairies are often felt or seen by fairyfolk. Suffice it to say for now that it is quite relevant, particularly as it breaks away from most transpersonal psychology and from rationalist science. Their work relies on the fact that even though at first the ally – an animal, a being of some sort, (in this case, a fairy) is possibly just an image and might not be distinguishable from a personal imaginal world within the head of the seeker, such psychoidal entities, beings, can be felt and/or seen in visions. And ultimately they are separate entities.

Raff explains:

> Many individuals with whom I have consulted recount that psychoidal entities – in particular the ally when experienced in the psychoid realm – seem to have a type of form that is subject to change rather than fixed. They have rudimentary personalities that are underdeveloped in a human sense, and there is tremendous energy or power about them. Some describe this energy as "looking like air above a radiator", a kind of visual vibration with a rippling flow. Sometimes there is a form connected to the energy and sometimes not, but it has a great deal of power and impact. When this energy appears, it is connected with a felt sense of the "personality" of one's ally. So the ally seems to be an entity with something of a personality, sometimes with a form and other times simply appearing as "energy," and, when brought into relationship with its human partner, containing great power. (176-7)

Ultimately the authors think that the alchemical notion of the "genius" is most like their conception of the ally:

> The genius communicates not only with words, but also in direct transmission of knowledge. In whatever way it communicates, however, the experience is often accompanied with a certainty of knowing. It is this certainty that most characterizes the encounter with the genius. (125)
>
> The genius becomes not only a guide or source of information, but an inner friend and companion. Walking and talking with this friend in the imaginal world is a great joy, informative, and stimulating. One does not always engage the ally or genius in deep spiritual work, for at times the active imagination connection is light and playful. (124)

The "light and playful" connection, as I have argued in Chapter Four, is particularly characteristic of fairy energy and is healthy for self-realization, openness, and getting out of one's ego.

Raff and Vocatura's model of "ally work," however, differs from "fairy work" in that communing with fairies is often not as self-conscious of a process as this decidedly intentional ally work. Fairy experience can be more spontaneous. Fairies appear, are heard, or are felt at moments often when one is thinking about other things, or in the course of mundane things. The Fairy Realm seems to sometimes act on its own to awaken people, as in the case of Carol's spontaneous realization upon jumping into the lake. Moreover, fairy mission and purpose, as we have seen, seems specifically about Nature and the natural world, (even if placed in the larger context of spiritual transformation for the individual), rather than about all divine and human concerns, as angels are thought to encompass. Angels seem to have more to do with heaven than with earth, and fairies concern with Nature, while Divine, is for earthly concerns, for preserving the well-being of the natural world and enhancing alignment between humans, Nature, and God.

Raff and Vocatura's notion is that the ally and God are wounded – the title of their book is *Healing the Wounded God* - and are helped toward healing in merging with the human. All three entities – an individual, the ally, and God – are transformed in the process of communicating together. This is akin to the Fairy Faith idea that Nature and God are partly repaired by humans interacting with fairies, increasing human consciousness about the Divinity in nature, and in working for the preservation of the natural world. Again, in Judaic/Hebrew terms this is *tikkun* – repairing the world. (In Kabbalism, especially Lurianic Kabbalism, devotional prayer and good deeds heal the cosmos.[3)]

Their description of the ally's role resonates with how the fairyfolk experience and are helped by Fairy over time.

> The ally teaches by creating experiences such as taking you to the imaginal world to encounter other types of beings or wisdom figures, or simply to sit in a meadow and hold you in its love. It can dialogue about all the problems facing you in your individuation, or lift you out of a negative mood and into a peaceful state. *The power of these visions and ecstatic encounters can convince you of the absolute reality of the ally.* Once you accept this reality and learn to trust the ally as a dear friend, the work moves from the initial stage of creating a relationship to the manifestation of the Self and union between the ally and the Self. (170) (my emphasis)

In the terms of transpersonal psychologist Hillman (1971), the variety of figures of the imagination which are perceived as existing beyond the imagination, as fairies do, are part of a healthy "polytheistic psyche", a psychological polytheism, where the soul has many sources of meaning. (Although this is reminiscent of polytheistic Paganism (Harvey 1997) mentioned in Chapter One, the Fairy Faith is essentially monotheistic.) Hillman (in Moore 1989) speaks eloquently to polytheism, monotheism, and daimones:

> Polytheism is not necessarily half of a philosophical pair, requiring monotheism for its other side. In itself polytheism is a style of consciousness – and this style should not even be called polytheistic, for strictly, historically, when polytheism reigns there is no such word. Where the daimones are alive *polytheism, pantheism, animism*, and even *religion* do not appear. The Greeks had *daimones* but not these terms, so we ought to hold from using monotheistic rhetoric when entering that imaginative field and style we have been forced to call *polytheistic*.
>
> Then we might better discover this other psychological eye by imagistic, mythic, and poetic means, releasing intuitive insights from sensate particular events. The psyche, and the world's psyche too, would show its patterns in tales and images and the physiognomic qualities of things. The whole show would be different…
>
> When William James described *A Pluralistic Universe*, he set this sentence in italics: *"Reality MAY exist in distributive form, in the shape not of an all but of a set of eaches, just as it seems to be."* Then he added: "There is this in favor of eaches, that they are at any rate real enough to have made themselves at least appear to everyone, whereas the absolute [wholeness, unity, the one] has as yet appeared immediately to only a few mystics, and indeed to them very ambiguously."(42-43) (my underlining)

This depiction of a "style of consciousness" contributes to our understanding that the Fairy Realm is an "each," one interpreted portion of the whole. Fairy experience, fairy consciousness, is a respectable, authentic Western mode, potentially enhancing of psychological healing and well-being.

Chapter Fourteen

Individual Transformation

Consciousness of divinity within, of one form or another, comes to some, not to others. Some have inklings of their divinity. Religious, mystical, or spiritual-minded humans all more or less agree that awakening, or discovering and developing, the oneness of one's self with God, divinity, Nature, elemental beings, Jesus Christ, Allah, etc, is part of a life-long path. Alchemists work on the physical and mental planes to uncover the essence of things, the physical and metaphysical gold behind the non-precious metals of everyday existence. Buddhists say that we start and are always one with the divine, but that knowledge gets lost in doing the daily physical, emotional, and social tasks of survival and in being distracted by cultural and material forces. Thich Nhat Hanh, the bestselling Vietnamese Buddhist author, says that we are all part of "interbeing," being one with everything. As fairy conscious Marc proclaims: *"we are not human beings with spiritual experiences, but spiritual beings with human experiences."*

In general, mystical perspectives and practices of various kinds invoke a connection with, an identity with, divinity that is already potentially there, already within. All point, to one degree or another, in one format or another, using one term or another, to meeting the divine as it manifests within. *Knowing* the reality of fairies or other divine elemental beings and coming to realize that you are a reincarnated fairy, are variations of the gnosis and experience of mysticism found in many traditions. These or other allies are aides on the path of personal transformation, the ongoing development of divine consciousness. Jon had said that the gifts of consciousness give people the "freedom to avail of them fully, partially, or to ignore them."

Here Jon and Marita, on separate occasions, speak of the struggle of transformation:

Jon: My human consciousness may be even driven to despair by the gifts of consciousness because of the sensitivity aspect. … That's a chance we take… we can be crushed, just like anybody can be crushed, depending on the circumstances in our lives. We can hold on. We can hold onto the point that we forget what it is to have the option of freedom, to be other than what we are, - that's an option that presents itself to our human free will, the freedom to recognize and go with the Wave. Or we have the freedom to pretend that it is really not happening. In this struggle we have to let go, and letting go is more of a trust.[1] That is how the path is charted.

There tends to be emotion involved in the early stages of that personal awakening because of the element of recognition. It's as if aspects of our potential for glory or bliss have become numbed out, or frozen, perhaps atrophied. So superficially it is like the process of developing physical fitness...The more you manage the more you are able to manage.

Marita declares:

Marita: I don't feel much difference between the angelic and the fairy realm. I never have. I think that as a fairy, a nature being, that one serves the divine. God. And we aspire as a little fairy or nature being to be angelic....

I think that a fairyperson is a little child of God who is free. A love, uncontaminated in that part of themselves with nature. And unafraid of nature. And very, very safe with nature. A sense of belonging, a sense of lightness. There's a lightness. With others who are fairypeople I can dance in that lightness with them, again inside myself. If there is a lightness of their connection to Mother Earth. And it's childlike, very, very childlike. But the struggle that goes on between the two, you know, the human side and the fairy side, is always there. In order to be earthbound I think that I personally am learning and continue to learn ... to be kinder and softer with humans, and with myself.

Nora, the Irish filmmaker discussed earlier, said, as you may recall, that she had strong connections with fairies as a child. She said she had lost most of it. A number of years previous to her moving to Dublin for some years, a psychic told Nora that she was on the verge of coming into a great awareness of her fairy past and connections. Nora didn't pursue that avenue, as we have seen, but she kept a tape recording of her session. I transcribed part of the psychic's talk to Nora where the psychic is trying to stir Nora into a transformation of fully taking on her fairyhood.

> There is this fairy that I can't describe, but it's a fairy. But I am beyond words to describe it. It's more like an illumination that looks like a shadow of a person. And these are your guides since you were a child. But they

had to move out of your awakened state probably into your dream state. And then probably out of all states, because if you ever didn't believe in them they could be destroyed, because *they live in their connection to you*. So when I walked in this room with you, it was very hard for me not to start playing in all that energy. But the thing that I know is that the more you, the more we, make it part of our total reality, and the more we speak it, like we're guardians of it and authorities in the world about it, the more it happens. That is what you are going to do over time - more and more. More and more what's happening to you is that you're sort of losing touch with one world and you are being engulfed by another. And at first that's a little scary because you kind of wander through. But as you lose touch with that self you'll get in touch with the self that you actually are. It's very exciting. It's like they want you to get with their music, and they want you to go listen to their sounds, and they want you to go places where you can see them, and they want you to start talking to them, and they want you to know that they are there, and they want you not to be scared, and they want you to know you are fine, and they want you to know that you will be happy, that you'll be happy when you open all that up to yourself. ... It's like you are being engulfed, it's like you're being taken back to your world. ...You don't live in growing up, you live in eternal spirit and that is really who you are.

The psychic, like other fairyminded people, describes the possibilities and actualities of connecting to the Fairy World, using similar perspectives and terms as others above. The psychic was important in Nora's life for a while. Nora was on the cusp of a transformative process, in her acceptance of the legitimacy of the perspective, but didn't really enter a fairyminded state. The spiritual path and personal evolution of consciousness are not always on a straight path, nor is it always actively decided upon or "actively imagined" (as Jung discusses). And some of us, even if we have glimpses of the divine, without ongoing active imagination, or a disciplined spiritual practice, remain on the lower branches growing away from the main trunk of spiritual growth.

Some who may come to realize their fairy background or connections may feel unprepared or uninterested in incorporating it into their lives, their consciousness. Some people, as Kay mentioned above, are outright opposed to fairy experience or consciousness. An Irish friend told me that a woman she met had told her that the woman's husband had said he saw a group of fairies one day. But the wife forbade the husband to ever talk again about the fairies to anyone, including her. The man died a few years later: now the wife regrets having forbid him from talking about the fairies.

Kay herself admitted how in the beginning she felt uncomfortable about her own transformation and how it is painful confronting one's fears, difficulties, and feelings, and giving up "images and false impressions. Ego stuff." It is not uncommon for people to become disoriented by journeys into the divine. The containment or integration of such experiences can be difficult, as we have heard from these fairyfolk, as Jon and Marita spoke of in their own evolutions, and as the literature in spirituality and transformation amply relates.[2] Kay reiterates:

> I know how I felt about it in the beginning. It was just too weird, and I didn't want to be weird. You know I was a responsible psychologist. It just seemed like a lot. "What does it mean?" "Why are you picking on me?" "Why can't I have a normal kind of heritage?"

Here Kay continues, with me, talking about how even as one may be going through transformation, one may not be well aware of it.

Kay: Yes. And those of us, looking back in retrospect, would think "How in the world did I know how to do that?" This very thing may be happening right now, and we are not aware of it, because we are in the middle of it. I may be doing things of which I am not aware that are under guidance.

D: It is funny. Increasingly in the last two/three years, my life has changed dramatically, and I have done many things I've never done before. As I lead my life, or choose things to do, I have asked myself - *almost above myself* - How did this happen? How did I get here? How did I even have the ability to put all these things together? Where did that intelligence and motivation come from? …Sometimes I just say to myself, I could just be sleeping or depressed all day, or hiding in a hole, or watching television. What enables me, or anybody, to organize their lives productively, particularly in crisis situations? It is like I said to you, sometimes I walk into the classroom not really knowing what I am going to talk about, even though there is an hour in front of me. But it just comes.

Some people manage to evolve from an unawareness to a partial awareness to fuller and fuller awareness. Mystical understanding and experience are progressive and multi-leveled.[3] Many Western and Eastern religious orientations historically have promoted and systematized spiritual growth as degrees of increasing psychological and spiritual awareness/consciousness.

As Shulman and Strousa (2002) relate:

In late antiquity, or rather during the first five centuries of the common era in the Near East and the Mediterranean, various religious movements offered salvation to individuals. Each had a different perception of who and what was in need of salvation, of the nature of this salvation, and of the means to achieve it. But all agreed that the self, if it were to survive, mature, be enriched and completed, was in need of radical transformation, either "interior" or "spatial" – in need, that is, of reform, return, repentance, or exiting the body or the material world. Stoics, Pythagoreans, followers of Isis and tenants of various other Oriental religions, Jews, Gnostics of all stripes, Manicheans, Mandeans, Zoroastrians – all searched passionately for ways and means to work this alchemical mutation of self.(8)

Wilber's (1977) "spectrum of consciousness" has seventeen levels of individual consciousness, which increasingly "nest," integrate, with higher and higher levels of consciousness.[4] Yogic and Hindu approaches have long had specific terms for kinds/degrees of spiritual awareness on the path to enlightenment or pure consciousness. The Mahamudra tradition of Tibetan Buddhism has eighteen stages of transpersonal/ spiritual growth. And pure consciousness itself, as the perennial psychologists (e.g., Forman 1998) suggest, exists as a cultural universal which exists independently of any specific cultural, religious, or mystical orientation. Fairy consciousness, like other consciousnesses, is one personal path towards a pure consciousness.

Jon, Kay, and I discuss experiences of the transformative path:

Jon: I have some latent gifts or potentials that I discover in the course of making my own journey. And then, if these frequencies become available to me, my world can change.... *The magical people, I think, are the fairypeople who would have this gift, a gift of a kind of magical transformation of being able to turn things around on the earth.* So I find that I have within myself, without ever having gone on a training course, an ability to develop this attitude, and the confidence and imagination to combine worlds together. It takes you beyond the horizons of limitation.

So the moment of betrayal of coming out of innocence and being assaulted by the world is actually necessary for the fulfillment of that mission. We kind of have to be betrayed out of innocence, in the sense of naivete, to learn what the world is like. Then we respond creatively to the challenges that it presents. That's why we are here, and that's why we are always in the middle, because there aren't just one, two, or three challenges.

Kay: Yes, and when you get out it's OK. So you get out, and you know that you're out. But with some people I have been betrayed. Their human condition is different than mine, and I do whatever I need to do about that.

J: Yes, OK. So those circumstances exist, but the truth about circumstances is relative to the level of consciousness of which these folks are operating. If we simply react to that level, we are drawn into that level, unless we respond creatively to it out of the deeper awareness and from the divine resources within. Sure, it's meant to be. At least until we can come sufficiently clear, and have consistent contact with the creative resources within us. So we always act out of that, and that is when the magic comes alive. But it can't be until you have mastered the struggle.

Jon, Kay, and I continued to talk about transformation and realization of connections. It came up that some people "fall flat on their faces" in the process of coming to realize themselves.

Jon: People must have a sense of their connection independent of their condition, and one needs initiative to move beyond yesterday. Saying "I'll do it again," living the same way as previously, you can't do that.

D: Jon was talking earlier about how dramatic or tragic events can open up a world of possibilities. I guess it is about incorporating divine consciousness, because if you have a sense of that connection it can provide a well spring of energy to get beyond one's personal or social conditioning.

Kay: For me that sense of divine connection has never been erased, even when I didn't know it existed. Even in the despair of my life, there was always a center, that "this" wasn't all of it. I didn't know about it, and I didn't know that it existed. *But there was never a time in my life that it wasn't there; there were only times in my life when I was unaware that it was there.* It was like a center that could not die, that could not be defiled.

J: Yes, couldn't be defiled. So if you act out from that your actions will be successful. I think you're most likely to have the experience of feeling that you're falling flat on your face if you're trying to hold on in the situations where your life is trying to become open. There is more than your personal intelligence involved, just as there has been proven to be these synchronicities, as we sit together and talk about this. So catastrophic moments are moments of emergence. They're moments of stepping forth into a great order of awareness. You have the impression of falling flat on your face if you try to deny this potential, and just try to hold on to what was. If you are aware of the way out, aware of the center that's beyond defilement, and that that's always there, you can act out of that.

You can step forward confidently into the new order that's attempting to be expressed through your mind. Then you won't fall flat. You can't fall flat. That's back to trusting that knowledge that you are connected beyond what x, y, and z may have told you.

The fairy path can provide a confidence, a grounding in the divine, that enables a sense of belonging in Nature and Divinity, and a ground plan for further growth.

D: So, on the one hand, fairy consciousness and sensitivity made Kay unprepared for the betrayal of human trust. Yet, on the other hand, that consciousness provides the energy to forgive the betrayal of mistrust. I don't know what the question is, but I'm pointing out the paradox.

Kay: Responsibility. I'm responsible for the reparation. I'm responsible for the healing. I've taken on in my consciousness to be like I am. And even in this consciousness I'm happy to have that because I have the strengths to do it. I don't doubt that I do have that strength and power to do this. I think even when I didn't know what I was doing, when I was unconscious about my connections, that I had the strength. But it wasn't then apparent that I had enormous personal strength. That's hard to say. But it's always been part of me and it's a part of me being connected to divinity that knew my power was infinite. It was constant, it couldn't be erased. It can be unconscious. What I am trying to say is that it is there. You come in with this, that it is there. And so it's there.

J: Can I say something about that? Because I think you hit on something that you may continue to find very frustrating about the human condition. You have access to this divine consciousness, and therefore this divine power. And you have the integrity to use it correctly. But even that divine power doesn't have the capacity to override the free will of a human being. So although you may feel responsible for any relationships within which you find yourself, you don't have the power to override or indeed take responsibility for other people's responses to the gestures that you might make towards them. The expression of your divine consciousness is simply too devout. So, as you were saying this morning, a part of fairy consciousness is not to be governed by this free will. "I do good, I do try to do what I must do, and if I can't do it because I am having a battle on my turf or something, I move away." *But when fairy consciousness comes into the human situation, the challenge then is running up against the limitations of human awareness, and to overcome that sense of limitation within oneself.* But you can't do it for another person. You can't chart the path that they can take.

D: How many times of falling on your face does it take to not even recognize the possibility of falling on your face?

J: I think it's a question of just taking small jumps and finding your support all the time. These locations arise in your life, I think - correct me if you don't recognize this - and you are hurt, and you can spin stories around that. But it's best just to go the way that your heart knows, because your heart is responding not just to the situation as you define it, but to the way that it is carrying that situation, and trying to project you beyond that situation into a richer, more encompassing life. So if you allow that way to carry you in a small way, small way, bigger way, a bigger way, a bigger way, and then this huge way, I'm not going to fall on my face. The only way that I could fall on my face is if I create the conditions in which what will happen comes from having the expectation. But I no longer have that expectation because I've jumped a few good times. And I'm sure everybody has in small ways. When I was quitting my professorship, there was nobody in the office, and I said "do I really want to get this notice of my resignation out today? Do I want to commit myself." So it came down to "do I really want this? By God I do." And then *that* was a great feeling. *That* exhilaration *is the criterion of correctness.* [5]

And that's the thing about fairypeople. That's the way we should live, isn't it? Jolly in ecstasy and exhilaration.

D: Sometimes when you're in confusion you can't feel a way that's carrying you out of it.

J: Well then, that's what we were talking about this morning. When you're in confusion, you remember. You try to remember not to act out of that, but to go into stillness. This is the center that Kay was talking about, that is always there. It only appears not to be there when something is blocking your access to it. It's like the sun is always there even if it is cloudy today. So just remember to go into that. That's why human beings for thousands of years have meditated. "OK I can go here," and then I can act according to my heart center. And if you do that, you won't do harm to anybody, because you're coming into your right place in the world, and then as people adjust to you in your right place in the world, they're coming into the right relationship with you and close to whatever their right place is. So, don't identify with the confusion.

D: Some people suggest that with fairypeople or fairy consciousness, the sensitivity to not fully belonging in the world as a human allows them to get crushed by the cruelty, disloyalty, or insensitivity of other people and the world. And so they hide at some level.

J: I would be inclined to revise that a little bit. I would say that some fairypeople, and indeed people in general, have the capacity to live more in a sense of their divine connection in the world. If you have a sense of that divine connection it allows you to do what you do, to go into the center. You go back into that sense of divine connection, so you are less dependent on what other people are saying about you, and you connect out from that awareness. You create your own magic.

Jon and I discussed this more when we were alone:

D: But does it strike you as a shame that the process, the mapping of the path has to entail such difficulties, with people surrounded with manipulation, fear, and aggression.

Jon: Well, sometimes our individual lives, or our collective lives, can go so off course that it takes an extreme expression of our alienation to turn us around.

D: I don't understand the premise that there is the need.

J: There is not the need, there is the freedom.

D: Then why is there the necessity for some people to choose to use the freedom not to love.

J: Because we're born out of unity consciousness into duality consciousness. So the experiment is set in motion, and all of these lines of diversity, these different frequencies, are set running. ... It's gonna take quite a while to look across the borders of prejudice and geographical boundary and say we are One.

D: So you're suggesting that creation is premised on duality because it is something that comes forth out of something else, and therefore by that process alone it is two things.

J: The self alienation of God in the drama of the world.... The peculiar thing about that is that if I can realize the world, if I can realize nature as an expression of the spiritual of God, if I can be in Spirit, then I am an expression of God.... I can have all of my conditioning, I can metaphorically let it all go and I know that I am one. I am who I am. It's not an inflamed ego, it's way beyond ego. That's the rejoining of the "I am" consciousness.... So we're in these boxes. What happens is that the spiritual unfolding exerts this magic within us and pushes us beyond limiting situation, limiting situation, limiting situation until we recognize that: "Hold on, Hold on, Hold on, Hold on," there is more to me than meets the eye. That's enlightenment. You just get it, and then when you kneel in this way, this is recognition of all that is. *And then you stand up and you're not the same.*

D: Were you raised with the sin and guilt of Catholicism?

J: Yeah, I was. I chose that, so I can wreak havoc with it. You know that was why I ended up studying psychology and philosophy. So I could have my own story, to not be vulnerable to preemptive impositions and so on.

D: There is a historical backdrop that makes this conversation possible. In fact, only at this time could we be having this kind of discussion. And there are lots of other people around having similar kinds of discussions.

J: There is a preliminary process of unraveling. Postmodernism is like an academic cover story for much bigger thought.

    This New Age, is one, Jon says, with not just the potential for renewal, for nature to come alive again, but for something more creative than renewal. As God made the possibility for free will for humans, and the duality of creation itself, something coming out of nothing, there is good and bad. Now the emerging consciousness has the possibility of creating a unity, one heart, that rises above that duality, rising above the original creative process. Fairies are not finished making the earth come into existence, not finished weaving material substance out of the etheric, not finished helping people come to recognize their connection to Nature.

Jon believes that more transformation comes about if one's mates or partners are also on the spiritual path of opening up to nature beings and mystical growth. The partner is a "mirroring companion of destiny," in which more parts of your self are being activated or encouraged by another person. Here he speaks more about spiritual growth.

J: The more of a sense of limitation you put down, the less expansive of a sense of reality can be brought to you. For many people it is like you enter what is the defining compromise of your life at age 20, 25, 30, whatever it is, and then you kind of sweat it out. It diminishes because you are going further and further away from your dream and you are dispensing with yesterday's framework.... So the more parts of yourself you have in order, then the more likely you connect. Almost invariably there is a part of one's self that has to be done mutually because it is not just a question of consolidating what is already there, but encouraging what is waiting to come out. It is a two way process. We are going through that in our separation. Before going into a new life, anything that might impede that should be addressed. So that is both an occasion and a necessity to bring all of these doubting parts, whatever their origin, into a new common order. It is good.

D: I guess I still have a personal problem, maybe an intellectual problem, about good and evil. I trust you as a good person, a loving person, but I think this kind of consciousness can be used in unloving and not good ways. I've seen it.

J: Okay, all right. The first thing is it has to be allowed, if the experiment and freedom are to mean anything. It has to be allowed. The second thing is an elaboration of that path. When people go to Auschwitz, even now, they know that something is wrong. How can you know that something is wrong without intuition? Something could be right. So automatically you know from the soul's exposure to the abyss. It's a wellspring of divine consciousness. You know you have this "God is dead" thing and it is permitted, this relativism.... But then you go into the glade and you have this mystical kind of experience, and you experience the temporary absence of Auschwitz. Something is wrong, something is wrong; I need to turn around so that I won't fear that something is wrong. I need to go home. This is the beginning of the journey.

D: I understand that intellectually. I know that intellectually... but it is as if the path is premised on the existence of that evil, on the absence of good.

J: Yes it is. On duality. Yes, that is the experience of duality. So as long as you have Arabs, Jews, Protestants, Catholics, and then you meet in the glade and a spark passes, then consciousness is not trapped on that level of self-identification. So it's actually the same process that breaks you out of the marriage which has tended towards stagnation or something. That's the frustration of life, being stuck in the self-identification as an x, y, or zed...

The impact of forgetting [past lives] comes in when you are born into the world. You just do whatever the local circumstances happen to be - the poverty, the sexism, the whatever it is. The inevitably self-driven unfolding of the spiritual essence begins, and with that the task of self-remembering, breaking beyond whatever boundaries, conditions, and limitations have been assigned. So then, insofar as I undertake this as a member of a particular culture, in terms of my conditioning and so forth, I am in the same place as everybody else. I have to go through the same kind of stages that other people have to go through. Insofar as I do that I'll find resources within myself, but I'm not stupid enough to think that the resources I have within myself are uniquely mine. *So when I talk to you about the truth of the heart and spiritual essence, you know what I mean. Not because I'm good at explaining it, because I'm not. Nobody is good at explaining it, but it resonates.*

Marita told me how she had been transformed and that her transformation enhanced her Christian self:

Marita: My sensitivity of the nature being has grown. My nature being essence has grown through being human and not hurting.

D: So your fairyness has contributed to your humanness?

M: Yes... I think that by feeling Christ and the sacred heart... and the suffering of man that our Lord went through for me, for us, that it has opened my heart to touch suffering, to not be afraid, to enter into it where I can..... There is a place inside myself that's so full, so full of love, so full of compassion, that there's so much that flows through me when I am connected.

Scholars (e.g., Shulman and Stroumsa 2002) differentiate transformation as arising from two different ideas about the self. In the one, say as in Zen Buddhism, the self is to be dismantled to its empty, or generative, core. Here practices like disciplined, regular meditation remove the surface layers or blockages, shrinking to get to an essential true self, to a no-mind or non-self. This is a centripetal process, spiraling downward, inward. In the more conventional Western process, on the other hand, transformation is more a centrifugal process of expansion.[6] Here linkages to the divine, or higher self, result from alignment or union with (initially) external divinity, God(s), or semi-divine beings to arrive at a true self. This latter expanding form of insight and transformation is the fairy way. It is a communion with and interaction with divinity, to intermittently connect with fairy energy. To eventually get to a state or quality of being which, regardless of specific event-connections with divine fairyness, becomes a more or less constant state of mind. Thus the Fairy Faith is in the Western tradition of transformation. It is similar to other Western mystical realizations, and lends itself to the Western mind and its own history of mystical practice and belief (knowledge). The very word "communion" in Christian contexts speaks to relationships merging the self with something outside the self, e.g., God.

Fairy consciousness with divinity utilizes, connects with, works with circumscribed, however fluid, intermediate fairy entities of God. God is ordinarily an unbounded or uncircumscribed force or energy. Thus in fairy work one can increasingly commune with representatives, messengers, of the divine. As mentioned early on, this system is an expansion of the hierarchy and organization of divine beings as monotheistic religions are ordinarily conceived today.

The dialogue of this chapter about transformation is relatively brief compared to other personal accounts of mystical or religious process. The anthropological literature, not usually about transformation, is scanty in this regard, although anthropologists' self-reflexive accounts in Blain, Ezzy, and Harvey (2004) and Young and Goulet (1994) portray some of the authors' own thinking and changes in their understandings of the universe – their being changed to incorporate native worldviews. But theologians, mystics, and transpersonal psychologists have written more in depth of their own process. Mystics such as Teresa of Avila (1972, 1991) and Meister Eckhart (in Blakney 1941) have written at length about their own realizations, experiences, changes and progress, and Kakar (1991) has written about the process of the famous 19th century Hindu mystic Ramakrishna.

Perhaps the fairypeople and fairyminded people here have just scratched the surface. There is no guidebook or extended discussion anywhere else on the seriously spiritual (but light-hearted!) use of fairy consciousness in personal transformation. Much more may able to be said. But, for now, we get a glimpse of how fairy consciousness is representative of some universal psycho-spiritual process open to people of all religious, mystical, or cultural walks of life.

The fairy experience, not necessarily grounded in daily ritual practice, spontaneously and briefly lived in visions of seeing or feeling fairy presence, sweeps up people – picks up people and their fairy "wings" – and transports them – runs with them – into a divine awareness. This provides a springboard for ongoing transformation. Some fairypeople and fairyminded folk "run" – realize and transform – faster than others. But all who truly have that "felt sense" and/or real eyeball vision of fairy allies are set on their path. It may start, as with Carol, as an accidental falling into the lake, or perhaps revealed in a book, a person, a conversation, an experience. But it sets people on a track, perhaps an additional track or coalescence with a previous track taken. Given some intent and ability to undergo psychic pain, fairy connection enables them to take part in a sacred process of psycho-spiritual change, using a language of transformation similar to other religious, spiritual or mystical seekers of the past or present.

As (transpersonal) psychology realizes, all people also have their own historical wounds and psychological disturbances which must be addressed and reconciled to one degree or another for individuation, maturation, and spiritual growth. As transpersonal psychologist Mack (1992) explains:

> A spiritual point of view stresses – paradoxically again – the transformative power of the affects associated with biographical wounds and other disturbing historical experiences. The spiritual element derives from the belief, which lies at the boundary between experience and faith, that each person possesses within him- or her-self a potential for wholeness. This does not mean, of course, that human beings do not have defects (especially biologically-based ones), limitations, and irreparable wounds. It is rather a point of view which gradually establishes its validity through enabling greater wholeness. (178)

With regard to the difficulties and psychic or emotional pain of the spiritual path, each of my informants have in part described or alluded to it. Kay, Marita, and Jon have particularly mentioned it. Such an experience of pain in the process of individuation and divine alignment is customary.

Episodes and crises of personal transformation have been described in the sacred literature of all times. Saints, mystics, theologians, psychotherapists, and scholars of mysticism have written about it, as well as anthropological scholars of, and firsthand accounts of, the psychological (and physical) travails of shamanic training in an indigenous society. (See, for example, Jakobsen 1999 or Prechtel 1998.)

Evelyn Underhill's classic 1911 treatise *Mysticism: A study in the nature and development of Man's spiritual consciousness* (published the same year as Evans-Wentz's *The Fairy-Faith in Celtic Countries*), like other works on the subject, speaks to the matter:

> Sometimes the emergence of mystical consciousness is gradual, unmarked by any definite crisis. The self slides gently, almost imperceptibly, from the old universe to the new. The records of mysticism, however, suggest that this is exceptional: that travail is the normal accompaniment of birth [of mystical awakening]. (177)

Continuing on in her chapter on "The Purification of the Self":

> The lives of the mystics abound in instances of… the deep-seated sense of necessity which urges the newly awakened self to a life of discomfort and conflict, often to intense poverty and pain, as the only way of replacing false experience by true. (200)

Underhill, giving an example of a mystic's own discussion, quotes the *Journal of George Fox*:

> One day I had been wrapped up in the love of God, so that I could not but admire the greatness of his love. While I was in that condition it was opened unto me by the eternal Light and Power, and I saw clearly therein… But O! then did I see my troubles, trials, and temptations more clearly than ever I had done. (Journal of George Fox, cap. I) (178)

This recognition that mystical religiosity entails working on the self, as in individuation, in a psycho-spiritual process of psychological and spiritual growth, has well been recognized in Western, Eastern, and indigenous mystical practice. The marginal or liminal period of many (indigenous) rituals is a period of often extreme discomfort. (Buddhism and Kabbalism, among other spiritual approaches, have specific terms for the not only for stages of spiritual development but also for the obstacles in the path.)

And relatively recently, in North America, with the rise of individualized spirituality, meditation, Jungian practice, and especially the adoption of

Yoga and Buddhism from the East, several authors have written about emotional and psychological problems encountered in Westerners seeking transformation.[7] The book *Spiritual Emergency: When Personal Transformation Becomes a Crisis* (Grof and Grof, eds. 1989) is perhaps the single best modern Western collection of work on this subject.[8] With regard to "spiritual emergencies" – crises of personal transformation, the authors say:

> When these states of mind are properly understood and treated supportively rather than suppressed by standard psychiatric routines, they can be healing and have very beneficial effects on people who experience them. This positive potential is expressed in the term *spiritual emergency*, which is a play on words, suggesting both a crisis and an opportunity of rising to a new level of awareness, or "spiritual emergence."(x)

Perhaps most specifically and directly describing the uncomfortable states that people on paths of spiritual transformation often experience are transpersonal psychologists. R. Assagioli (1989) in his "Self-Realization and Psychological Disturbances," describes a whole approach of psychosynthesis in which the subpersonalities of an individual need to be integrated into a whole. J. Kornfield (1989), with most attention to Buddhism for Westerners, emphasizes "Obstacles and Vicissitudes in Spiritual Practice." As the titles indicate, there are disturbances and obstacles in mystical/spiritual paths which need to be ongoingly addressed by the seeker, sometimes with the help of a guru or therapist.

A significant point that emerges here from the authentic mystic's admission of the necessity for personal psychological work in concerted attending to the Divine, "purification" in Underhill's terms, is that continued fairy alignment is not simply a process of believing in and talking to fairies, as some New Age books and self-help guides promote. Books on "working with fairies (or angels)" or "healing with fairies (or angels)" give the strong impression that belief is all that is necessary for enhancing one's life and becoming happy. Without ongoing individuation work in dissipation of the self with a small "s" to realize more a Self with a capital S, without watchful personal self-reflection and uncovering of the (Jungian) shadow into the light, without the exploration and integration of subpersonalities into a whole, there is a shallowness, perhaps even a danger, in pop alternative religion oversimplification of the spiritual process. Some call this "spiritual bypass." That happens when individuals avoid the self-reflection and self-work of an individuation or mystical process. Experienced, authentic practitioners observe that those in spiritual bypass are preoccupied with the external spirit, rather than with a balance between spirit and psyche. This can result in an inflated ego without much modesty in the face of working with Divinity, and/or in a presentation of self that may be bold, but hollow.

For me, my journal speaks loudly about transformation. My ruminations at the end of my summer stay 2004 still keep me aloft.

August 21, 2004

> It now seems to happen in my life, at a more conscious level, that most of what I do, experience, find myself in, is about the journey, about the pieces leading to one another, about wholeness, and seeing the parts fit together for myself. This experience is becoming holistic for myself, as the anthropologist comes to discover the holism in the culture and the mind. As my separation between observer and participant dwindles, I realize, personally interpret, my own fairyness.
> My quandary about being torn between two worlds, and separate selves, is just the issue of becoming whole in myself, whole in my person. About bringing my ego and unconscious closer together. About transcending myself of earlier days. About alchemically working on the parts of myself, the chemical constituents, to make a stable, aware, happy compound. The experiences that I have here in Ireland, and in North America, have interacted with my chemical constituents, have blessedly upset their semi-comfortable, but stagnating homeostasis. The chemical, emotional, intellectual bubblings, the impure gases produced in the mystical jarring of the liquid, create pain and movement towards a new compound, a purer, more contented form.

Chapter Fifteen

Fairyfolk Together

Most of the academic literature on the development of new religious groups discusses social and economic forces as the impetus for what are called "new religious movements" in sociology, or "revitalization movements" (Wallace 1956) in anthropology. Such collective (re) organizations or revampings of religious/spiritual pursuits are concerted group efforts to infuse or reawaken more meaning into people's lives. They originate from people feeling that their conventional religious beliefs and practices do not address their practical and/or spiritual challenges. They often come about as a consequence of charismatics, maverick thinkers, or of mystics' spiritual discoveries actively leading others to new perspectives. Organized to be more satisfying than previous beliefs and practices, all religions, and their various sects, were new at one point in their histories.

I was interested in the degree to which fairypeople and fairy conscious folks I met or heard about were indeed a group, and how much they communicated with one another. I wondered how dependent they are upon one another. I asked fairyfolk and others about the amount of social contact they had with like-minded others, on similar spiritual journeys through fairies or other elemental beings.

But among the fairypeople and the fairy conscious there is no organizational base, no place of gathering, no dogma, no doctrinal text. (You can go on the Internet and find fairy-related objects, happenings, and readings, but they are almost all commercial items, events, or disparate writings.) Although some fairy conscious and fairypeople had occasional contact with one another, it was often intermittent or happenstance, except for a visit in the past from an Irish person (Marita) to Questhaven in California. Whatever meetings there were in Ireland (or England), other than in the few "New Age" workshops or training programs which included fairy issues, gatherings were, except in a few rare instances, not much more than a handful of persons. Although there had long been a folk belief in the existence of fairies in Celtic lands it soon became apparent that the contemporary Fairy Faith was much more a personal spiritual or religious orientation, with an informal network of people, not even really approximating an individualist religious movement (Townsend 2004). It depended little on interaction with others. This corroborated my own notions that, despite there being a few books explicating the divinity of fairies, such as those of Kirk (1893, originally 1691), Russell (1918), Evans-Wentz (1911), Conan Doyle (1922), Newhouse (1955), Pogacnik (1996), and "pop" self-help New Age books, there was no ongoing structured social dimension to the belief in and knowledge of fairies as part of a psycho-spiritual path to transformation. As Kay has said more than once above, there was little to no precedent for her realization of fairyness as a mystical or psychological forum.

One, two, or rarely three fairypeople or fairy conscious persons visited Kay from time to time, sometimes in part because I was there collecting information for this book, and/or because, through word of mouth or newspaper articles, someone heard about Kay. Once in a while friends visited and stayed overnight for the company of friendship or like-mindedness, to share their perceptions, experiences, or just beingness, sometimes specifically with respect to fairy sensibilities, although it was me who directed much of the conversation for my study. Some of her friends had met each other through mutual friends, others came upon one another by chance. Kay and Carol originally met because Kay saw Carol displaying her art work at an arts and crafts show. Kay knew Carol was in touch with the Fairy Kingdom immediately by the style and content of her artwork.

(A hanging fairy sculpture made by Carol hangs above Kay's kitchen, and Kay had Carol paint two fairy murals along a wall surrounding Kay's spiral staircase to the second floor. Fairy conscious Kerstin, also an artist who senses nature beings, but who is not in direct contact with fairies, was also commissioned by Kay to paint murals in Kay's house. One is on a kitchen wall and another on a living room wall. There is a fairy figure or two lurking about in the mystique of wooded landscapes she painted. Kerstin clearly has an aptitude for fairy paintings, although she said she was jealous of the extent of Kay's connections.)

Jon met Kay through a mutual friend a year and a half before I met Kay. They share a lot. Jon said Kay was most articulate about the fairy world because Kay had worked through most of her sensitivity to being different, and had been working with her spiritual journey for some time. But Jon said that he hadn't consciously made contacts with fairypeople.

Here Jon describes his contacts with fairypeople:

Jon: I don't actively seek them out, but sometimes we find one another. I heard about Kay. Somehow there was something appropriate in me, in her, in you, to meet. It is equally likely that I will get an email from someone who got my address from somebody who met me at summer school last year. Sometimes there is a strong soul connection, sometimes not. It is not just a question of logistics, but it is part of a sense, a trans-rational sense, and therefore is not readily expectable. "The radar connection is over here, it is not over there, so get here." That tends to be the kind of contact with people I have. *It's like an expression of the truth of the heart to follow certain lines of exploration.* I stress the word *follow* because there is a sense of being carried by a wave. So there is no manipulation of the situation whatsoever. There isn't even any kind of active conspiracy. Increasingly, as these things happen, it becomes easier and easier to know that you're just going to meet the right people at the right time, and that will continue and continue and continue. So I have gone beyond the threshold where I doubt my connections. That's how the contacts are made. So it would be misleading to say that I seek these people out. I don't.

D: But sometimes you must choose to be, or not to be, with a person. You know when the potential is there to be with me or not to be with me. There is an element of choice involved in starting a conversation or continuing a conversation.

J: It flows more than that, and I will tell you why. These interactions in 3D, if they are to happen, are meant to be. If the potential of meeting is to be fulfilled it has to happen at the right time in the sense that both parties are prepared for the spark to leap across the gap and for communion to be established. So it wouldn't be the case that I would decide not to meet with you having assessed the information available, like "OK, is it right to meet now?" I don't even ask that question. I just know. It is something that I know intuitively. If I had been speaking these words to myself even two, certainly three years ago, the thought would be very strange. I would be questioning my own sanity. But this is part of the pattern of development.

Certainly as far as encounters with people in the network of spiritual contacts are concerned, this means that there is no kind of ego agenda or manipulation, or impression management. Meetings happen. It's time and they flow. I think that is really important, because as the fairyperson, the spiritual person, begins to come out of hiding, and begins to look around at a world that is remembered as being a little bit hostile, it is encouraging.

So the first range of compatible, sympathetic human contacts you make are very important in consolidating awareness, building confidence. It actually is efficient for these meetings to take place at the correct time under the right circumstances. *It seems that a higher intelligence or magic governs the timing of these events.* So you just kind of need to meet, talk to someone, so that it might accelerate development of the fairyperson by months. Because the spark leaps across the apparent gap between the hearts. Once the spark has leapt across the gap, there is no gap. So then confidence and awareness, imagination and daring, build with that and the ripples spread farther and farther and farther. Then you are in the discourse of the critical mass.

Here Minette describes the experience of meeting up with like-minded persons:

Minette: Once there is any connection with where they really come from, they feel the flow. It happens very quickly. It's very definite. Like this person I have in mind. When I met her she was into some real serious psychological stuff, but when I met her we just loved each other from the start. But I had nothing in common with what she was passionately chasing. But we just loved each other, and that was it. It was just obvious and absolutely she was just delightful. Then we would go our own ways. The minute we see each other again there is just this great delight, and everything lights up and the fairy kind of feeling comes out because it is just a natural flow. The inner joy is just really enchanting.

So while it is not necessary for fairy consciousness to come from contact with others, discussion or communion with others can corroborate one's beliefs and knowledge, accelerate and enhance awareness, and help in individuals' own ongoing spiritual ascent. As Rabbi Steinberg says in his *The Unlikely Nature of God:*

> As consciousness expands, the separation between mind, heart and soul diminishes until these become one. Once united, this unity more easily flows into and harmoniously connects with others who have also integrated their disparate elements of being. Yet, even if another remains separated in his inner self, the one who has united his elements of mind, soul and heart brings a concentration of being to bear that impacts this other more powerfully than if both persons try to relate while internally fragmented. The more one expands one's consciousness, the more one encompasses other realms of reality which then allows a better interface with a greater multitude of people, the principle being – the more one

experiences, the more likely one is to understand and relate to the experiences of others. (124)

Sometimes contact with another fairy sensitive person stimulates a dormant part of one's self.

One time Marita brought a non-fairyish friend to visit overnight at Kay's. Marita explained later that something happened to her friend in talking with all of us and later the three of us dancing together outside. The following morning Marita spoke of her friend:

Marita: It's magical. …. It was beautiful. She got so much out of the day, and the three of us being together. She really got a lot out of that, and gave a lot into it. It is very, very beautiful, the flow of that between us. She had a really lovely dream last night, and she might share with you her meeting of the wonderful child in her again. It was fantastic. So I held her today and we have deepened. We have a good relationship, but this side I never shared with her until now. It has done something to her.

As mentioned earlier, Jon and Kay sometimes go together to the glade, a special place in the forest a few miles from Kay's house where they experience Nature and Fairy energy as strong. One day I went with both of them to that special place. There was an opening in the forest canopy between where large trees stood and the luscious greenery seemed landscaped into the shape of an arena.

I asked Jon about his experience being with Kay.

D: This morning or yesterday in the glade did Kay see, feel, or experience similar things that you did?

Jon: I would say that Kay participated in the piece in her own way, because she told me that. The world is alive in different ways.

D: Did sharing that experience, or having another fairyperson there with you, help or change things? What's the effect of being with a similar person?

J: Moving out of the ordinary human world, into the glade, it makes it easier to enter into an altered state. It is tempting to speculate that another person intensifies the experience, but I don't think that that is actually the case. She comes with me for her own reasons, which overlap mine, and there is no strict distinction between them. It is part of the same unfolding.

So it's as if the energy potentials which I bring to that situation or the ones she brings to that situation possibly serve a great unfolding. Certainly a different unfolding than would have occurred if either of us would have been absent. As it happens, it is my understanding that Kay is the keeper of that place. She participates in the transformations which tend to happen when I come here.

Jon and Kay are friends, spiritual buddies. It is clear that their relationship is profound. They both said that they had/have a spontaneous affinity to one another. Jon said that there is "no need for history" in their relationship. It is similar in their other spiritual friendships.

Marita talks about Kay and their relationship:

Marita: Kay has been a great gift in my life because she hasn't disowned that part of herself. She came to Ireland to be her essence. And I left America, where I lived for a while, to come back to that part of myself, to find it again, to come home to it. Kay was the catalyst here that I would come to, to be humanly nurtured in myself, with the graciousness of simplicity. There is a bonding between us.

D: Is it automatic?

M: Yes. It's that way with Kay. There is just a sisterhood. It's built in me. I love to come up to Kay. I really, really just love to come up and just be. Even two days.

Marita, you may recall, became well formulated about her fairy connections as an adult after reading the work of the Christian mystic Flower Newhouse (1975). Marita had gone to the States to be with Newhouse and like-minded people in California.

Here Kay, who never met Flower Newhouse, describes how people were drawn to Newhouse and to one another:

Kay: Flower had a retreat center and she had all kinds of lessons and programs, and Christian mystical happenings. The fairy world is part of that – if you read any of her books, she did indeed see them, and certainly was in touch with beings of various Kingdoms. She told people that they were from those Kingdoms. People would gravitate towards her if they had an inkling of who they might be because they would find some correspondence there. So that happens. She is one of the few Christian writers that I know of who included the fairy realms in their writing. So then there were people connected to her who would form a bond, people like Marita, Anne and James Hubbell, and Peter. So they would become friends or have a common vision, which Flower would support.

Here Marita relates her own experience being with others from the Fairy or Nature Kingdoms.

Marita: You know there are some of them I know from other Kingdoms. With some you can sense it. You can sense the elemental realms that they come from, and you can feel the sound of the bigness of devas. There is one man that I have known in particular, a tree deva. And by God he is a big man, you know. And he knows it, and is very comfortable with it. He has a magic. It is very, very magic. He has a very free mind.

You know, I know people who are all kinds of beings, particularly those who are attached to Questhaven in southern California. Many of us know that side of ourselves and we are united from all over the world.

I think for yourself, for Dennis the nature being, that meeting others would open up doors, more doors, inside yourself, in your exploration and search for your own meaning, truth, and connectedness. The joy of knowing many others.

Marita, as discussed earlier, sometimes uses her fairyness, her nature beingness, and that of others, in her clinical practice. She explains:

M: I know one client in particular who is an out and out fairy[person]. How I recognize that is that we are very joyful in our pain together. We dance around, we really dance around. There is a lightness. We have moved along together into a lightness. We've lightened up. Literally we can jump up and down together. I took my client one day to one of the very infrequent workshops led by my teacher Flora Newhouse's daughter Athene, who is a clairvoyant and a nature being. Athene has been profound in my own journey of lightening up, before I met Kay. There were about sixty people at the workshop. Athene picked out this client of mine. She was lecturing and talking away about a lot of things, not necessarily fairies, and then, pointing to my client, she said "You in the first row, you were a little flower fairy."…. And there we had that connection in our therapy. Athene confirmed it in that way. And so that made our sessions together. We worked together for about four years and we have become very dear friends…. You would always know a fairy[person]- she is definitely one that I can know that with. An out and out fairy[person]. This client stands out as fairy and we did therapy in a different way. We connected so deeply in those ways, so we trusted each other.

I asked Marita if she was generally drawn to such fairy or fairy-concerned people and whether she makes an active attempt to be with them.

M: Since 1985, yes. Definitely since 1985. Since reading Flower Newhouse's books on the levels of beings in nature, the evolution of that, and the nature beings who evolve into the human line of evolution. I have remained friends with them to this day, and they are all over the world, but particularly in America. Because they open so many doors, and they visit me, or I occasionally visit them. We connect by phone, e-mail, whatever. So I do not frequently physically see them, but I have connections with a phone call. If I get too heavy, suddenly a phone call will come from somewhere "Marita, lighten up!" It is not part of my daily life to be around them, but it is necessary for me to come back to that in my life quite often. So I make it a point then of being with others who I need to replenish in myself. Then I go back and I feel renewed, by being sister/brother souls in that way.

I went regularly back to the States until about two or three years ago. Now I am going to India regularly. But people in America at Questhaven know me since 1985 and after, because then I went to live there and spent about six weeks there regularly for years. I went out there just to be in the lightness of what that is. And now I have met more people here at home in my country of birth, Ireland, who are connecting to those parts of themselves. I think fairies[persons] are everywhere, but particularly here and in the Scottish Isles.

D: How about in India?

M: I think that there is just a different name for them. In India it feels like I connect with Lord Krishna in that way, and I begin to dance in that magical, light, fairy aspect of me. It just makes you dance. The gopi [human follower of Krishna] in me, which is a nature being, comes out. It comes out very, very strongly, very freely there. Because everything is accepted in India.

D: So are you saying that, in addition to being a fairy, you are also other kinds of nature beings?

M: No. But I can resonate with the fairy aspect of myself in the countries where the essence of that playfulness, that joyfulness, is there.

And I always feel that when I go up into an airplane. I always, always feel that when I am up there, up above the clouds, in an airplane. Way up I touch another dimension in myself up in an airplane....

Occasionally there are workshops and retreats in Ireland and England led by fairyfolk, like R.J. Stewart, or, recently, by Jon. Such leaders help participants get in touch with themselves, their natural essences, and nature beings. Kay does not attend such events, preferring her own ways, although in years past she attended some spiritual retreats of other kinds.

Jon, as indicated earlier, recently quit his position as a college professor so he could devote himself fulltime to his own spiritual work and to help others with theirs. Kay says Jon's workshops are to awaken people to their own spiritual paths, not necessarily fairyness, although in one of Jon's workshop descriptions he talks about letting fairies into one's life. In this regard Kay describes Jon as a pioneer, as one of the first in Ireland. (R.J. Stewart's workshops on fairy contact and spirituality are usually in England.)

I do not want to give the impression that all of Kay's or other fairypeople's or fairy-minded people's friendships are mystical practitioners. Some friends are skeptics and some of their friendships contain no dialogue about fairies or even spirituality. I have been in the company of some of Kay's friends who are not aligned with fairy spirit. I do suspect, however, that fairypeople and the fairyminded think or know that some people they meet, or are friends with, are unconsciously connected to fairies or other elemental beings.

Most interactions among fairyfolk in the regions of and near Donegal are informal and impromptu. Like fairy-being and fairy energy alignment and experience, fairyfolk gatherings of at best a few people seem to erupt, like unannounced visits from friends, more than as a result of concerted planning. We could call the informal group of about twenty persons known to Kay and her cohorts a "cell," although a loose one. While I was Ireland in the summer of 2005, Denis, Lorraine, and Bob met Kay and me at Kay's house for the first time. They are part of what could be called a smaller cell of perhaps ten people in Northern Ireland, who also know about the divinity of fairies.

Even if spurred on by others in books, chance meetings, friendships, or even in reading New Age books, the fundamental and ongoing development is inner, in individualized mystical experience. Whether in time there will be more collective or structured contact, as in more traditional mystical or religious groups of established religions or sects, is yet to be seen.

The fact that fairy alignment (in Ireland), as part of a transformative path, is not wholly separate from Christianity (or other institutionalized religions) contributes to its free form nature, and makes it less likely to be institutionalized as separate. Its approach to reincarnation also likens it to Eastern religions or to the minority individuals or sects within Western religion that do believe in reincarnation. So the Fairy Faith cuts across Eastern, Western mystical, older Celtic folk religion, and even indigenous peoples' sensibilities to other-than-human persons.

It is difficult to sociologically locate the contemporary mystical Fairy Faith, difficult to quantify membership, or deem it a movement. Like fairies themselves, the Fairy Faith as an individualist quasi-movement or network is difficult to pin down and is effervescent, spontaneous, fluid, and sometimes capricious.

Chapter Sixteen

Ireland:
The Fairy Portal, Artistry

In the United States and Canada there are a number of people who identify with fairies, commercialize fairies, establish fairy websites, hold fairy festivals, etc. There is a magazine called "Faerie", which advertises products and events, and has short articles related to New Age thinking. There are several books in the New Age or Metaphysical sections of bookstores which purport to help people make contact with fairies. There is even now in bookstores an *Idiot's Guide* to *Elves and Fairies*, which joins the ranks in that large *Idiot's Guide* series to everything from computers to cooking to religion. It is as if fairies, and spirituality and religion in general, are part of a litany of vocational and recreational activities for the populace.

As mentioned above, Questhaven in California is one place in America that takes a mystical or religious approach to fairies and nature beings, although they are only a part of the Christian mystical approach there. My contact with three members of Questhaven who I met while they were visiting Kay demonstrated to me that they were uninterested in the popularity or commercialism of fairy things. Indeed the people that go there use the center as a spiritual gathering place, to expand upon Flower Newhouse's mystical experiences and writings. They are interested in communing with nature and in personal growth, connections with the Self, the Earth, Divinity. There is an authenticity about that place and those people which rises far above the pop interest in fairies.

And recently on the northwest coast of the US I met a couple who exude a bond with fairies, and the reality of fairies, and their benefit to the world. But they didn't appear to be interested in the transformational aspect of mystical discourse: they sell fairy objects over the Internet.

In Ireland, especially away from the big cities, Kay and several others from America that I have met in Ireland find that the Celtic people and consciousness seem more authentic. They found that the energy and environment in the States is, in general, too hard, too fast, too materialistic, too built-up, to allow or facilitate sensitivities to fairy things. Two women I met visiting Kay from the U.S. straightforwardly said that they can't invoke their fairymindedness in America. One said that that is part of the reason she comes back now and again to Ireland. Kay says it is "just so much more spiritually easier here [in Ireland] for me, which is why I am here."

D: Evans-Wentz said: "the natural aspects of Celtic countries impress man and awaken some unfamiliar part of himself that gives him unusual power to know and feel invisible or psychical influences." Kay, what you have said seems to agree with this statement from early in the twentieth century, that Ireland lends itself to the awareness of fairies.

Kay: One of the things that I have been able *to feel* is the energy. Here in Ireland is a softer, non-demanding energy that enables you to get to another dimension. You know anybody could feel that if they had some practice. It's not anything so mysterious. But most people wouldn't be interested in it.

Her sensitivities are overrun by just being in the States:

Going back to the States covers me up. I can operate my fairyness best here [in Ireland]. Anytime I get near a city or noise my psychic ability shuts down. It is like I am spending my energy building a wall. There is too much negative energy there [in the States] for me to be open and safe in. That is not necessarily a criticism. It is just an isness. Because most people have more protection against negative energies than I do.

This "lack of protection against negative energies" is especially so for the sylphs, the light, air fairies. But, even I, conceptualizing myself as more aligned with elves – earth fairies - still find it difficult to enter an alternate state and feel the energy or sense the presence of elemental beings in America. Only occasionally do I sense beings in the air here.

Some fairypeople and fairyminded people say that the belief itself in fairies affects the actual visible or invisible manifestation of fairies. That is, fairies are more likely to appear and be sensed in environments where there is support for them. It is not only that one has to have the perception of the possibility of real fairies existing for one to experience them, but they say that fairies also pick up on the consciousness of humans and will come to areas where they will be recognized.[1] In Ireland, believers and disbelievers told me about times when people who did not believe in fairies saw fairies, leprechauns, or other beings, despite the fact that they had been non-believers.

A friend of Kay's told me that a man I met, Paul, and his then girlfriend both saw a leprechaun, even though Paul was then the kind of person who would never believe in such things. She said they drove over a bridge and after passing looked at each other and said "Did you see I what I saw," both realizing that they each separately had seen a man with a hat and costume on, fishing or something by the river. But when they went back, nothing was there. (Their shared sighting is similar to the earlier discussion of Carol's and her friend Bernie's sighting of a green man mentioned in Chapter Three.)

Liz, (not a fairyperson), the friend of Marita who visited at Kay's one weekend, said that all Irish children grew up with fairies as a household term. Fairies is "not a foreign language," she iterated. She said fairies are part of the "saints and scholars" ethos of Ireland, even with the clergy. They know and have heard of people experiencing fairies, and thus it is part of the culture, particularly rural culture, even today. And even though there is often a jocularity and lightheartedness about fairies, about those who have seen fairies, and about people "running with the fairies," virtually all Irishmen and women have grown up in a culture that incorporates fairies, even if there are disagreements about their existence. People take it seriously. Even if an Irish person thinks fairies are the result of secular superstition, there is still a respect for the culture's and individual's history of being fairyminded. Belief in fairies is not a "weird" thing in Ireland. Liz said "Everyone knows people who have seen the fairies, or know people who know people who have seen the fairies. It's just common."

Carol said that all the west of Ireland is especially prone to fairies and imagination, and advised me that the longer I stay in Ireland the more I will see it. Val and Marc, both English and living mostly in England, say that they have met several people who came to Ireland for a social or tourist visit, people who had had no consciousness of the Fairy World, but who left Ireland with a "fairy connection". Val said "You can't connect unless it is already there, really within you. I think it is because the land is very alive, more so than a lot of other places in Europe."

Fairy spirit beings seen or sensed in particular places (re)locate Irish and Celtic people into familiar locales and also thereby act as counter-modern, counter-globalizing, counter-technological. At the same time there is connection with the universality of Spirit and mystical experience. There is spiritual immanence in the local appearance and association with fairies, and transcendence in their being representatives of a Divinity which transcends the local.

The magical nature of Ireland is evident in how people meet one another, and in the rapport easily gained between people of similar (fairyminded) ilks. Denis, the energy healer mentioned earlier, brought Robert and Lorraine with him that late summer 2005 day to talk with Kay and me. After they left I asked Kay why, as an energy healer, he was interested in fairies, and why he brought his fairyminded friends with him to talk with us. Kay said "energy work and healing go along with fairymindedness" ... "but that statement only makes sense in Ireland."

One night when I had dinner with Carol and Kay I found out that Carol had independently met Denis previously that summer. Carol and Kay had discussed how intriguing of a man Denis was. Carol said that she had detected a lot of energy when she first shook Denis' hand. I said that it was quite a coincidence that both of them had recently and independently met Denis, who lived in Northern Ireland. They both quickly turned to me and said "you should know better, after being in Ireland, that there is no such thing as coincidence."

Kay: Jeremiah said that there are parts of the world where they wouldn't place us [fairypeople]. It is obvious to me that *Ireland is the capital of the ingress. The cosmic spot for the Fairy Kingdom. The portal.*

But I think it is just so much in the Celtic soul to be in touch with the other worlds. And to be in touch with the other worlds in a light sense, in an impish sense, in a storytelling sense, in a mythic sense. Other cultures like some of the Oriental cultures, and to some extent the Indians and the Aborigines, have these qualities. But they have a different energy.

So Celtic people have that vibrational energy, and of course the land itself does. There is a geographical circle where most of the fairy paths, legends, come from. It encompasses Norway, Sweden, and Finland. Finland has a tremendous amount of fairy energy, and certainly so does Brittany.

Another time Kay was talking about her own work and path in Ireland:

K: Where else would we want to be when this is happening. So there is something here. It cannot happen so well other places. There is some kind of intensity here. Jeremiah said that Ireland is the primary vortex. He also emphasized that there are other vortexes, that this is not the only one. But it's the most available one. I think he said there is probably another one in Tibet, as I remember. He has also made special mention about South

America. But his emphasis was on Ireland being the primary location. *There are special energies all over the world.* But he did say some places can't harbor fairies because there is no love in the ground there. They can't survive there. It's not that they don't want to, they just can't. Just like some plants can't survive in some locations, fairies can't. And you take a look at some places and you wonder how even a spider could survive. But that's not where the fairies can be. Japan was another place that was awakening.

D: Japan?

K: Yes, Japanese people are awakening into consciousness about the fairies....And in the Appalachians. Well, because of the strong Irish and Scottish immigration to that part of the U.S. Because they believe. If somebody believes in the fairies, their belief system allows the fairies to manifest more than if they don't believe. (You can work that out scientifically if you want to). So the Appalachian people believe in the fairies. Appalachian architecture is fairy-like. You know I have never been there, but I imagine it is very fairy.

I asked Kay how her own harp music fits into all the fairy stuff: (The harp often is a symbol of Ireland):

K: You know the answer seems obvious. How could it not? Everything in harp music is everything in fairy, with its clear tones and its ability to crescendo. And its clear melody and the color of the strings. It's like a waterfall. It must be more than coincidence that the music I chose to play, even as a child, was connected to nature spirits.

[Kay's interest in harp playing long predated her own knowledge of the harp as a fairy, Celtic instrument and predated the general now-popular North American interest in Celtic subject matters.]

K: Many Irish musicians actually heard fairy music, especially the older people and the older generations. And in the folklore and in the archives you will find stories of people wandering in the woods or fields and they would hear the music.

Marc spoke of the same experience of Irish music and fairies:

Marc: Ireland is one of those places where if you could dance to fairy music, and if you could play fairy music, you were accepted by many. Not only that you were somebody, but you were living in the world where you could do that and people went out to get the experience. I mean you are going up to the fairy hill, lying on the fairy hill, and hearing the fairy music, and them coming down and writing it down. So some musicians in the olden days would seek out the fairy music and they would be quite proud of their fairy threads.²

D: Society was open to them.

M: Yes. The people, they were in-between. They were moving in between worlds, moving with the gentry and with the peasantry, writing music for both the peasantry and the gentry. It was quite a task. There was also a sense that you had to honor where it came from. ….

But I think what's going to happen, what I suspect, is that musicians inspired by Fairy are going to come back with that music, and elements of it. I think it's still coming, coming back…..You can hear the fairy music out there and you can hear it in rural Ireland and other parts of the world as well. *You can hear that music, and it might be in the forest or out in nature. I think we are still waiting for the return of it, and I think that that's part of what this process is all about.* Creating a space for them [the fairies] to return, and the meaning behind the music.

During the days I spent with Marc, Val, and Minette we had a long conversation about fairy inspiration, and the inspiration behind Minette's music and Val's artwork.

Marc: I think that the fairy language is still kind of an unspoken, or unheard, thing. I heard these two tunes that were so clear. I was singing and chanting them, and then the minute I walk off they're gone. They're still out there, if you walk around and reach behind a tree or something. You hear music and it's so intense. You hear the music, and hear the fairies, and then you walk away back on the country road and it's gone.

D: So when you hear the music is it in tonalities or notes of a kind that you recognize as from this realm also? How would you describe it?

M: It's different. You know it's strange. I've never used it or I've never played it. I could recognize some of it, and Jon said that he could recognize some of it. But they were tunes we both could recognize. It is kind of Japanese. It's almost kind of like a cross between a pentatonic scale and a chromatic scale.

But it's music that a lot of people won't like because they will wonder "what the hell is this, it sounds more like Indian music" or it will not sound like clinkity, clinkity, nice music. It's wild music, it's not music that is trying to be polite. It's quite wild music and when you hear it you know that this is music, not just dancing music, but it's actually music which has a very wild energy to it. So there isn't really that much fairy music out there in the courted arena of the world.

The fairies, it is like they are on drugs or something. Things played by a Japanese musician on a sitar. It's a very different kind of music. I think that it's in the language. Like when you're hearing the fairy singing. They're singing and speaking. It's kind of like listening to Chinese or Japanese people on the train, It sounds like music to us but we don't know what it means.[3]

D: But do you understand the communication in a way that is more than listening to music. Do you understand a phrase or a story or a communication other than in the musical tone?

Marc: You kind of translate. You're translating automatically into English. It's quite a leap from one thing to another, but you can do it. We have done it ourselves.

Minette: I'm just saying how they are tuned, you know the part that they are playing. If someone is a musician, they would be very sensitive to the energy and what's happening to the people around them when they are playing. It's just being in the flow of it. The very happy relationship that always makes them appear when I'm fluffing my hands. You know when some musicians get together, they recognize, they feel, this great flow of spontaneous friendship that just comes. It's very natural because you know the unity about it. There is always great unity about the whole experience. *It's a very different world from the standard Western or Eastern or whatever other kind of label we want to put on a human kind of view of life. The fairies and the fairy energy, and those people who pick up on it, just don't see things in the way of the conventional Western view.* It isn't how they operate at all. Absolutely not.

There is an invitation from them. With my poem, it was dreamy and everything, and the words just kept going on and on in my head. "Just come with me to the enchanted land, come with me to the enchanted land," and I said "I think I got it!" And it's just going around and around until actually I just took that away in my mind. And I went in and I got the computer and I just worked on it for about a day until I got it. *But it was like they wanted me to.* It's actually a lovely poem, isn't it. Full of life and the dance is in there. It's all in there. It's just an invitation, just come and Whooooo!!!!! *The feeling was just there, and the invitation, and away I go.*

In regard to Irish landscape and environment, Jon relates:

Jon: We have various areas in the country which are relatively unspoiled, so fairypeople are attracted to them, because there are features of the landscape which can evoke the souls' potential. *You won't jump into your awareness in the middle of New York or Dublin. So the landscape here can still be a mirror. So then the dialogue is reopened, and beyond that, to carry news of this unfolding dialogue out into the greater world. We are at a tender stage of this process.*

Kay had said that I was an unusual exception to the rule that Americans are unconnected to the Fairy Realm, as generally Americans are disdainful of the Fairy Realm or generally use fairies in a recreational, commercial way. As fairies feel most safe near their main portal in Ireland, it is easiest for humans to communicate with them there. Near the portal they are closest to their origins. Kay said fairies can get "locked" into human existences more easily if they are far from the portals. Too many people can prey upon the fairies and fairy-sensitive humans away from the portal. There are certain portals in the planet designed for different existences.

I felt supported and comforted when Kay said that the fairies will keep a connection with me, and would not abandon me, even when I was in the U.S. "They will risk it," she said, and they will not lose contact with me.

Ireland clearly made "it" possible for me, possible for me to experience that alternate consciousness of sensing Fairy things, however amorphous or uncrystallized. I know that because as I write this sentence here in the States, without having been back to Ireland for nine months, I have to rely on my previous journal and writings in Ireland to enable me to fully feel the feeling. Here and now, as I write, the energy fields surrounding Lorraine's fairy sculptures, Carol's fairy birdman painting of me, photographs of Ireland, etc., which punctuate my house, help me (re)invoke the Irish and fairy "space." The props around my house help keep fairymindedness available. Even silly things like "Fairy" brand hand soap (an Irish/English brand) and "Fairy" brand dishwashing liquid. They are icons, religious symbols with fairy *mana* in them. Yet even though I live much of the time in the rural countryside (in the US) amongst lots of nature, it is much harder for me to sense the Fairy or elemental realm here.

The degree of availability to spirit beings is both environmental and personal. Howard and Mageo (1996), in their review of Akin's article about the Kwaio of the Solomon Islands, state "....spirits personify a sense of place and associated virtues of stability, continuity, and permanence" (7).

Music, Art, Creativity

There is clearly a relationship between artistry, creativity, and fairyfolk. Many fairyfolk are painters, sculptors, musicians, intellectuals, and creative thinkers. Carl Jung, in his treatment of the transcendent function, discusses artists. He says that while artists may have some disadvantages in directed, rational thinking, they have advantages in their access to the unconscious and to the transcendent function which "arises from the union of the conscious and unconscious contents" (Jung 1971, originally 1957:273). They have more of "the permeability of the partition separating the conscious and the unconscious" (275).

Some (neuro)psychologists and scholars have written about right-brained people as naturally operationalizing their creative, holistic parts (Sperry 1966). Some transpersonal anthropologists are neuro-phenomenologists, and Winkelman (2004:59-60) argues that

> the reality of spirits should be understood in terms of fundamental aspects of the operation of the brain and mind. [The] underlying methodological and theoretical approach is one of neurophenomenology (Laughlin, McManus, and d'Aquili 1992; Winkelman 1997, 2000) that seeks linkages between the neurological functions of the brain and phenomenal experiences, particularly those manifested in universals and cross-cultural patterns....Spirits reflect necessary and fundamental principles of human consciousness and aspects of human nature referred to as innate processing modules and cognitive operators (e.g., d'Aquili and Newberg 1999).

While it may be so that spirit experiences are (neurologically) potentially universal in all human groups, specific cultural and environmental conditions prevail so as to lend (sub)culture members to specific interpretations of the nature of and characteristics of spirits and the spiritual world.

Fairyfolk and fairy conscious people, whether or not right-brained or particularly neurologically programmed for seeing or sensing spirit beings, embody the intuitive, holistic, flowing nature of the artistic temperament. (See also Chapter Eight above.) Their artful sensitivities and practices, initially unknown to me, are often avenues for their spirituality. It is not coincidental that Kay is a harpist, Carol a painter/sculptress, Jon a writer and philosopher, Minette a pianist and composer, Val a painter, Marita a poetess and writer, Debbie a sculptress, Kerstin a sculptress/painter, and so forth. They may not all earn their livings in these ways, as it is quite difficult to earn one's entire living as an artist or musician, although Kay and Marita earlier spoke about some famous musicians and artists they knew were fairy.

Kakar (1991:xi) links three interacting factors in the making of a mystic: "particular life historical experiences, the presence of a specific artistic or creative gift, and a facilitating cultural environment." His view is cross-cultural, historical, and perennial:

> Mystical experience, then, is one and – in some cultures and at certain historical periods – the preeminent way of uncovering the vein of creativity that runs deep in all of us. For some, it is the throes of romantic love that gives inklings of our original freshness of vision.
>
> Others may strive for creative experiencing in art or in natural science. In the West, the similarities between mystics and creative artists and scientists have been pointed out since the beginning of the century. Evelyn Hill in her path-breaking work on mysticism emphasized the resemblance between artistic geniuses and mystics – though one should hesitate to see the terms as interchangeable ... In China, we know that it was the mystical Taoists stressing spontaneity, "inaction," "emptying the mind," rather than the rational Confucians, who stimulated Chinese scientific discovery. In India, too, in different epochs, the striving for mystical experience through art, especially music, has been a commonly accepted and time-honored practice. And Albert Einstein writes of his own motivations for the scientific enterprise, "The most beautiful, the most profound emotion we can experience is the sensation of the mystical. It is the fundamental emotion that stands at the cradle of true art and science."

Fairyfolk seem to epitomize Kakar's understanding. Creative people with particular life experiences, in the spiritually supportive context of Celtic Christianity and Irish natural landscape, mystically engage with Fairy.

Here Kay muses:

Kay: Marita says James Galway is also from the Fairy Kingdom. You'll have to talk to her about that. He certainly looks like he might be. The way he's bringing forth his music, the way he's used the flute in the symphony, for instance, is completely organic, and completely bringing that instrument in. That's a gift from the Fairy Kingdom.

D: And she suggests that he knows that.

K: She was so correct about James and Anne Hubbell. It doesn't mean that everybody who is creative is from the Fairy Kingdom, or anything like that. But there is a sense of continuity to it all.

Kay says everything the architect James Hubbell does "comes from the Fairy Kingdom." She talks of his work:

K: James Hubbell speaks it so clearly as to what the earth fairies are trying to do. I haven't met him, but to have seen what he did with architecture is enough. When I saw that chapel in California, bumping into such a perfect sculpture, *I just wept. I knew it*. It was so perfect that you know that that kind of beauty, brought into the manifestation of architecture, would change the whole world. I mean it would take a long time for that to happen, but it is a perfect representation of what architecture is supposed to be. The magnificence of it has to be instantly familiar and illuminated for everybody, not just me.....Why was I in my so-called innocence so unbelievably moved by that place? Why could I not do anything but weep? Why would that be an appropriate reaction for me if I didn't know better about something?

Later I was always tracing him via the Internet, finding out where he was. He has volumes of books, and people have written about him. You meet someone like James Hubbell and you know. Just even looking at his website you know what he's bringing forth from the Fairy Kingdom, a whole organic sense of building. It's just so unbelievably rich that it's mind-boggling.

Here Marita talks about her own writing of poetry, prose, and her own journals:

Marita: In the last few years I started writing some poetry in these deep moments, sacred moments inside myself that come through.

D: Are you interested in sharing that?

M: Not now. It's for the universe, and it's of the universe... but I don't feel the time is right yet to put it out there. When I go out to nature, particularly to the places that I visit and revisit, the fairy aspect of myself brings me there and I write.... I think this writing is a bit more prose. It's opening, it's very fresh in me, it's so very new. I don't know that I would put this in a book, but if I do I will dedicate all of it to a particular orphanage in India that I am involved with. That's my purpose. If that comes, if I do, it will be for the children, I think, because it is my old heart child, and the tragedy that I experienced at the overcoming of that, and coming back to myself. This writing at some stage can be for children who are orphans somewhere in the world, so they can have the opportunity to know that there is another space that will bring them truth.

Kay said that when Carol does her art work: "It is constantly fairy and it comes out in a physical form that you can see." Carol herself said that every piece of her art work incorporates forms of spiritual beings, fairies or elemental beings. She said "It's not that I set out to do that." I asked Carol if she had been chosen by the Fairy Kingdom to communicate with them. She said "Yes!"

As Kakar suggested earlier, individual life experiences, an artistic bent and spiritually supportive environs set the scene for mystics. Perhaps we need to extend his notion of spiritually supportive environs to include not only the human social and cultural environments of mystics, but also to include the kinds of spirits and gods which people interpret as existing on other planes of reality. In the often unconscious taking on of local or even idiosyncratic ideas, interpretations, and worldviews, believers and mystics consider specific beings as existing independently of humans, beings indigenous to other planes of existence. Ireland (and Celtic lands) are a location on the planet where it is thought that fairies most easily access the human plane, where the portal for fairies is most open, where the veil between fairy and human is thinnest. Thus a perennial or transpersonal anthropology of religion might recognize that particular kinds of spirits and gods, and mystical experiences thereof, are accessible in different geographic contexts. The variability of human spiritual experience is also a function of the varying cosmogeographic entry points of spirits and gods.

In this light, the varying content and sacrednesses of different religious/spiritual understandings are in great part a function of the multiplicities of planes or realms of the ethereal. Thus "mazeway" configurations and reconfigurations (Wallace 1966), through particular human experiences in particular geographic locations, as also for me in

Ireland, arise not just through exposure to humans with different perspectives than one's own, but also through exposure to the ideas of differing spiritual planes with particular occupants who inhabit near or in particular landscapes of the earth.

Chapter Seventeen

Consciousness, Evolution, Planet

Anthropologists' interests in consciousness studies manifested in the development and continuation of the peer-reviewed journal "The Anthropology of Consciousness." M. Winkelman (e.g., 2004, 2002, 1994), interested in the evolution of consciousness, suggests, as mentioned in the last chapter, that there is a human neurophenomenology that accounts for the apprehension of spirits. Accordingly, he is critical of transpersonal psychologist's Ken Wilber's (1981) work on the evolution of consciousness, *Up From Eden,* in its avoidance of studies in paleontology, archaeology, and anthropology, and for its general model of the development of consciousness over the millennia from lower-to-higher stages of consciousness, even though some individuals exceed the norm. Yet, as we have seen, Wilber's contributions to a perennial cross-cultural psychology, religion, and mysticism can be helpful. My interest here is not to locate the Fairy Faith in the context of a debatable evolutionary model of stages (or not) over time or space.

I present the ideas of fairyfolk in their understanding of the modern need for more spiritual consciousness, which would incorporate more respect for and communing with the sanctity of Nature and the closeness of God. There does seem to be agreement among fairyfolk, theologians, mystics, many scholars, and of spiritually-minded people in general that there is, or can be, a progression towards higher states of spiritual awareness, for both the individual and the collective.[1]

With respect to the evolution of consciousness at the collective level, Western writers like Bucke (1901) in his *Cosmic Consciousness* (acclaimed by William James); Teilhard de Chardin (1959) in his promulgation of evolution of a 'noosphere'; Redfield (1993, 1997) in his best-selling *Celestine Prophecy* and *Celestine Vision*; and Wilber (e.g., 2005) discuss how individuals participate in the creation of a supra-individual spiritual atmosphere and/or how collective consciousness evolves.[2] Indigenous traditions of Native Americans and Mayans; Jewish, Christian, and Islamic sects; and Eastern traditions such as Hinduism, Buddhism, and Yoga speak of the presence or absence of collective spiritual realization, readiness for states of spiritual awakening and practice, and human relationships to the earth and Nature. Native peoples especially consider human-to-nature relations and the human treatment of the earth as key to spiritual balance and the state of humankind.

Many agree with professor of psychiatry Mack (1992):

> The threats on a global scale confronting us and much of the earth's life can be thought of as a spiritual crisis, for at its core it represents the separation of human beings from one another and of humankind from nature (181)....What is called for then is a means of discovering a wider human identity, not one that denies the polarity of nature and human feeling, but one that integrates them in a larger sense of purpose and connection. (182)

Understanding the immanence of God, in nature beings like fairies, has consequences for human treatment of the earth:

> The traditional creation-providence story in Christian history has underscored God's power more than divine love, God's transcendence more than divine immanence, and God's distance from the world rather than involvement in it. This need not, should not, be the case: an interpretation of the God-world relationship based on the belief that *God is incarnate in the world* implies re-thinking the issues of creation and providence in light of the world as internally related to God – The world as within God or the world as God's "body" – rather than externally related as an artist is to his or her production. Our doctrines of creation and providence do not stand alone: they are offshoots of our deepest beliefs about the nature of God's relation to the world. If this belief is that God and the world are wholly other, creation and providence will be seen in that light; if this belief is that God and the world are intrinsically intimate, creation and providence will be understood from within that perspective. An incarnational context for understanding the God-world relationship has implication for our response to climate change. It means that *God and we are in the same place* and *we share responsibility for the world.* (McFague 2010:53)

As mentioned in Chapter Eight, fairy connection with the timeless divine, a realm of reality which can be responsive to human reaching, can not only affect the mortal on earth, but the divine in another realm(s). It is part of a process in which humans can affect divinity. Thus the fairy experience, like Jews repairing the world in doing good deeds (*tikkun*), or Kabbalists in interacting with old souls, improves both earthly and divine realms. The interaction heals not only humans but can heal God. Touched together, humans and humans' spiritual entities - fairies and God - participate in cosmic evolution.

***

D: I feel sadness when ugly buildings are built in the middle of a hilltop or when natural places are destroyed. It is actually saddening. It raises emotions. You can actually cry over it. Is that what you feel?

Kay: Well, it's not just nature. Many things happen in the world that are cruel. You know, human beings being cruel to one another.

D: It seems there is an increase in people talking about fairies or people engaged with fairies, although it is a small minority of people. I wonder if the world is getting worse or more cruel. I guess it is just at this point in history, when things seem so complicated and cruel, that there is a need for people to realize their fairyness.

K: I think that fairypeople coming into their awareness of who they are has more to do with the so-called "New Age." As the New Age continues, of course there will be more and more fairy awareness. Even eventually to the point where there is actually interaction. But right now what is sad to the fairypeople and sad to me is that: Are we going to make it before we blow ourselves up? You know there are some intelligent reasons to believe that we are not going to make it. So as far as we are sure that we can make it through, and really go into the golden age that has been prophesized, that would be wonderful.

D: From a left-brained perspective, I try to legitimize this. .... This book that we are now working on is part of that process. And I have a sense that that is part of our relationship, that we are collectively carrying out part of the mission, however grandiose it sounds.

K: Yes, absolutely. It doesn't sound grandiose..... This is a whole new idea. Somebody actually talking about the fairypeople. Or even to identify somebody as a fairyperson. Who has the balls to say that they used to be a fairy. It is a completely different concept, even though they may have thought so themselves or known people who they thought were fairy... I don't believe it is in the Protestant or Catholic religious doctrines to give an idea about reincarnation, or about changing stream. You have to get deeply into metaphysical material, like Flower Newhouse. The Protestants are much more strict than the Catholics regarding the possibility of fairies.

Ana asked about the evolution of an individual's fairy consciousness:

Ana: And what you are saying is that the fairyness continues to evolve as very positive, even with unknowns. That it is very positive, and yet there is no blueprint. So sometimes you are making the road as you go.

Kay: Yes, that is what we are supposed to do. The forerunners, the pioneers. This is the beginning. Nobody else in the world has ever done this so there are no books. There is no data. Nothing. I like that job. Yes…. It is a great job. [Laughter] Nobody can tell me what to do. [Laughter] … I wouldn't want any other job than the job I've got now. No way. If I were not aware of what I'm doing, and I were me thirty, forty years ago, and I was reading about me, I'd say, that's what I would want to do.

A: That's wonderful .

K: That's not arrogance, that's just true….This is a great job.

D: That is fantastic to hear.

K: I mean it is a weird job. But it's great.

***

D: Some of the books and people that you are steering me towards are what I will call "New Age" healers. I don't mean to make that hokey or trivial, but I will call them that, whether or not they are fairypeople or fairyminded, because we are living in the so-called New Age. Why do you encourage me to look into that or talk to those people? What are the connections for you between the Fairy Kingdom or being a fairyperson and these people or practices of healing that seem to be independent of the fairy world or being a fairyperson?

K: They all have to do with the energy and the comprehension of energy as a divine force. And that is very much connected to the fairy world, because of our energy or divine force. So the more they know about it, and I get knowledge from them, the more I understand it, and the more they want to know about the Fairy World. The more knowledge they have of the Fairy World, the more we will all see ourselves as being quite connected.

Kay says that when there is a fairy contact there is a quality of awe, andwith the fairypeople a quality of enchantment, which is what the fairies want to bring across. Fairies want to "bring through to mankind, a joy, a beauty, and mystery, and a lack of deadness". Communing with Nature and places within nature facilitates the enchantment.

Jon says "when that fairy consciousness comes into human form it becomes a source we can draw upon, to rise above the problems our humankind creates."

He continues, in discussion with Kay:

Jon: We come in with this innocence, this openness, and it is harshly assaulted by the world. We experience this sense of betrayal. But we also have this resource deep within ourselves which tells us that there is more, we are more, and that we can create more. So we continue to do so. In other words, we don't despair.

Kay: We get out of despair.

J: Yes, like the phoenix. Like James Hubbell rebuilding after the fire last year. That is a chemical process of transmutation. Once a number of human beings have done that, it becomes easier for others, because it is no longer just a metaphysical possibility. It is actually being charted and explored. It's been realized. So the horizon of aspiration shifts, more and more models become available, and we become more visible to ourselves, to each other, and to the world at large.

K: Why we as fairypeople are here now is to be bridges. Like Jon said, we're living bridges. We bridge between the Fairy Kingdom and mankind. We act as a conduit and our job is to make whoever will listen to it aware of the reality of the Fairy Kingdom.

D: For the purpose of?

K: If we were working actively with the Fairy Kingdom, the Fairy Kingdom would help us make the planet into a green paradise. And that would inspire us with color and music and dance, gifts that the fairies can bring. They have an ability to neutralize anger and therefore eliminate war.

Spirit talks a lot about what the fairies can do when they're allowed to do it as our assistants. It all has to do with the greening of planet. That's the job of the fairies.

D: Environmentalists.

K: Yes. Somebody said that the fairies have definitely inspired the green movement. The inspiration for that whole movement comes from the Fairy Kingdom. ... And a task of the Fairy World is to help overcome the pain of dissociation from Nature and the Divine.
Yes... We will make it, but it will take so much longer without their help. *As I understand it we* [fairypeople] *came over to help with the transition. They hope that the transition will take place. The transition for people to wake up to their spiritual reality. So that they will take responsibility for the planet. Or for each other. Or for the cosmos. The transition to become awake.* Now Raj says it is going to happen, that it is already happening. That there are enough people now awake. Even though there will be turmoil and climate changes and eruptions, it is going to happen.

Thus individual evolution of consciousness is related to collective evolution of consciousness, as suggested earlier. Even this book could only have been written in a certain moment in history and in the history of the potential acceptability of what it shares. And, as fairypeople's and others' words above have indicated, the level and activity of Spirit depends in part on the human connection to it. Fairies are "living in their connection to you." Such connections and actions repair the world, and enable it to continue. Thus general or collective evolution of consciousness can affect the appearance and volume of Divinity in its various forms. Jon spoke of his practice of "bringing frequencies together for harmony."

Yet the force of growing collective consciousness of Fairy is not (yet) strong enough to overcome other forces. At this time, according to Kay's channel, there are not many fairies who are being reincarnated as human beings. There are especially a limited number of air fairies, sylphs. That makes Kay and others particularly important and cognizant of the Fairy World, and may make her mission all that more crucial.

It is at this time in human history that fairy consciousness as a divine pathway has come to be most fully realized. Consciousness has evolved. As Kay, Jon, and many others have stated, "the membranes are thinning." I asked Kay whether the thinning of the membranes was a result of humans being open to the other side of the membrane, or whether the membrane works on its own. She said it was a function of human consciousness. "The other side is always there, it's just that we're not there. It is because of the evolutionary capacity, evolutionary growth."

Kay's channel recently told her about the current difficulty for fairies because of the growing crisis in non-fairy and non-spiritual human consciousness. The human climate, in local and global senses, in the twentieth and early twenty-first centuries continues to be full of the destruction of people and environment. Thus the environment, literally and spiritually, is not very receptive to perceptions and interpretations which highlight added (or even previous) spiritual perspectives which include nature beings such as fairies or other elemental beings in human life ways.

The crisis contains a paradox. On the one hand there is the growing ability of some people to connect with the Fairy World, and, on the other, an increasingly materialistic and violent world in many places. Kay is not sure that her channel is correct about this halt in air fairies reincarnating as humans. Her own uncertainty itself indicates that ambiguity abounds, that much is unclear about the dawning or not of a real New Age.[3] The Fairy Faith can be considered a response to transpersonal social scientist Duane Elgin's (1980) call for "restoring the balance" of the "ecological flow of the universe" through the "Tao" of social transformation and personal transformation.[4]

Kay: The fairies are not coming in so much as people, now. Not at this time in physical form. At least temporarily, the sylphs have stopped reincarnating into human form. They are coming in a different form, as ambassadors. They are here not in a form that can currently be seen. It is just too hard to be in physical form. They are not seen, but they are still present. We [fairypeople] are often too tender and trusting to make it here. There are other ways of getting through. But that may change again as we become more effective or the plan works out.

There are some twenty kingdoms all together on the elemental levels. That includes the fairies. Worldwide there are less than 1,100 fairypeople. Given the current status of mankind, other elemental fields feel such efforts are not appropriate. *But the fairies are the only ones who did not give up.*

I asked Billie if I will stay here as a human being when I die. Will I be reincarnated? She said *They* won't leave me behind. A choice will be given me. There is a timeframe to accomplish human awakening. In other words, there are no more of the unknowns coming in until it is decided what is going to happen with the earth changes, as to whether we will be waking up or not, or whether the earth will be taking another direction. Until that time fairies will not be coming in, until it is decided....

We continue to discuss the progress of our times:

D: It seems like the crisis is heightening with respect to the earth's ecology.

Kay: Jon alludes to the culminating crisis in the aspect of time. There is a time when the decision will be made to go ahead or not. OK. That is in most of the prophecies, too. For Mayans it is 2012.

D: Many Native Americans believe the same thing.

K: That is what Billie is saying here, and that is why there are no new fairies being born at this time.

D: If it is true that fairies on the other side do not work according to a human timeframe, then maybe it is not necessarily bad news about the crises that might be impending. It is only from a human perspective of time that if bad things happen to the earth now it might take 3000 years, or whatever amount, for the earth to get better again. Maybe from a spiritual world's perspective, from the fairies' perspective, that doesn't matter.[5]

K: Yes, it doesn't. And with the fairies' perspective, eventually everything will happen correctly in time. It just may take longer. For the fairies time is almost meaningless. But I can see now that, if in fact there is a crisis coming, why there wouldn't be any more fairies coming in. But the forerunners have done their job.

D: It doesn't make sense for them to work on a long term project, if the project is not going to be around.

K: I just thought that out recently, and even going over it with you, it makes sense. The fairies can't do anything, the gnomes can't do anything, until the decision has been made.

D: It also implies that the fairies are not decision-makers, do not have access to the decision, however it is made. So they are like humans in that respect, in that they are workers, like bees. They might not have access to the Queen's agenda.

K: And some of them may not even know that there is a project. They are just called on, or not called on.

D: You are not sure about what Billie says is the temporary halt of fairies coming into human form?

K: No. I think she may have just thought that, for the same reason that I tried to explain that there wouldn't be any more fairies coming in. She may have just unconsciously thought that. There is possibly no catastrophe coming up, but she definitely thinks there is. Jon, and Marc and Val are sure that there are going to be massive changes very soon. It is in all their literature, and in their channeled literature coming through. And maybe that is the case. But you read other channels that say there is not going to be any catastrophe. So I don't know which channel has got the correct information. Or maybe it is all going to happen.

Raj never said there was a cut off period, if we didn't get through. I think what Billie says is incorrect. She is prey to misconception, she is not misleading me intentionally. But big in Billie's theory is the deadline date. Raj maintains that there are not going to be any massive earth changes. No disaster day in 2012.

But Kay, like Jon, sees fairy consciousness coming into human form as a source for human beings to draw upon, to permeate human consciousness with hope and joy:

K: Fairypeople are taking on a secondary consciousness. There is still hope. The hope is eternally there. It has to be. It can't be erased, because God can't be erased. Ultimately we are going to make it back home. We divorced God, God didn't divorce us. Fairypeople have been coming in to rescue in the way of divine awareness, of beauty.

I don't know what's going to happen in the future. It depends on humans' free will, how many of us are actually going to be part of the changeover.

D: According to Jeremiah, your mission or one of your jobs is to find as many fairypeople as you can, and eventually get together. And then at that point things will happen?

K: Jeremiah said that there were originally 5000 sylphs[people] who "volunteered", and that there are only about 2000 of them left. But not all

2000 of them know that they are sylph[persons]. What did he say, one hundred and fifty-seven know their origins?

D: He said that two thousand have evolved [been reincarnated], and 157 of them know who they are.

K: I certainly don't know 157 at this point.

D: He said that every year you will get to know one or two more. Has that happened?

K: Yes, kind of. It's growing. It's not growing fast, but more is going to be happening.

D: More is going to be happening?

K: Yes, I mean I have seen the connections happening over the years. So it is getting bigger and quicker. When it reaches a certain mass it is going to have some substance. It can't be erased. It could never be erased, the nowness that we think we live in. So it's fun to be here now.

Near the end of my last stay in Ireland, driving home in my rented car, after having taken Kay out to dinner, Kay summarized things and advised me. My journal the following morning reads:

> On the drive home Kay started talking about how this fairy "trip" she is on is exponential. Once you let go into the mystery of things, it just keeps growing by leaps and bounds. Kay was again thankful out loud about how she made the correct decisions on how to lead her life on the fairy path in Ireland. She also lamented the lack of progress she, and the earth and the fairies have made. She is glad for her mission, the importance of her work, and would not have it otherwise. And she is wonderfully thankful that at 75 she has, and has had, such a wonderful fairyperson existence of late. ..."Once you let go into the unknowing, life is far from ordinary."

***

Fairy faith and fairy knowledge - fairy consciousness - is a continuous process, not a static mental or spiritual state. To fairyfolk, fairies are enablers, whether of a fairyminded fairyperson or of fairy conscious folk. Fairies in general enable an ongoing spiritual and psychological dialogue between the human and the spirit world. They are lighteners. For fairyfolk

Fairies are part of a path of increasing awareness and connection, often enhanced by, but not dependent upon, dialogue with humans. Continued fairy consciousness is an inner transformative process. It is akin to individuation in Jungian terms, the realization of the higher self in Pathwork, turning lead into gold in the symbolism of alchemy, liberating the "sparks" of God in Kabbalistic terms, undoing the ego in Buddhist terminology, communing directly with God in Christian terms - all mystical, ego-dissolving traditions. Fairy knowledge is one form, one language, of the search and realization of the divine.

Kay and Marita epitomize the constancy as well as the evolution of a fairy consciousness. Kay said that she grew happier over time. When I said goodbye to Marita on the telephone, when I again asked her about her fairyness, she responded: "It is always in my soul," "I go to the woods whenever I can," and "My fairy nature is most essential to me – life is empty without it."

Kay's, Marita's, and others', like Jon's, Lorraine's, Carol's, awakenings are representative of the transition, the necessary transition of our time, to return to a spiritual worldview, to fairy consciousness. To go beyond the old paradigm in which fairies were generally considered bad and not understood as divine agents or celestial beings helpful for personal and societal transformation and evolution. They are now especially helpful in going beyond the materialistic, scientistic paradigm, in connecting us to our spiritual and innate capacity to dialogue with Nature and the Divine. The world of verifiable, empirical science must allow the unverifiable spiritual and mystical worlds to coexist alongside.

Earlier Jon spoke of how the primary role of the fairy dimension is to participate in the process of evolution. Here he describes his own experience and process, and its relation to the wider context and progression of our time:

Jon: When a fairyperson comes into the human world there is a difficult situation to be overcome. So each of us is apparently to undergo our own version of the strand of loss and redemption..... And that feeds into the potential of the culture, particularly as it is used in creative potential, for transformation......

So yesterday was a very strong coming together of the worlds, the various dimensions, looking at it from just my own point of view, which I wasn't doing when I was there in the glen. I, as Jon the speaker now, was scarcely present, but I am now reconstructing from the point of view of Jon the speaker. Now I would say that elements of my own self history were coming together and being woven into a more coherent whole. But at the same time, that was happening in the context of the transpersonal encounter of coming together.

The way I understand that is that all of these beings which exist in different frequencies are coming together. This morning, it was very peaceful, very harmonious, and my heart was the center of creation. It was clear. So all these frequencies are coming in and being clarified there. They were going out again and they were coming in. They were being sent out, they were coming in again, but each time they came in they were more and more in accord. And I think that is as close as we can come to putting it into human language. The experience was a wonderful harmony, a belonging. In that reconciliation I ceased to be a doer or observer.

D: Earlier you mentioned that devas and fairies, and such, are beings that spin or manifest reality.

J: That is a matter of descriptive sociology, or something like that. Beyond that if you are asking me what is the final answer, I don't know. Because it is subject to all of the relativities of perception and conceptualization. One thing that I have noticed a lot in spiritual circles of my persuasion is that people tend to think differently when you are talking about the other world, or a higher reality. That it really is real, and that *there is something, a truth there, that isn't available here.* And all the human relativities are suddenly set aside when you are talking about something that you can't see. That proves to be the case.

The real thing that happens is that there are people who are capable of having direct experience in one way or another, and then there are many more people who aren't. Human cultures are religiously ordered and it is necessary to devise conceptions of existence which would render some impression of the quality of this invisible reality to use it to pattern the experience..... So you need to be really clear and pure. *The history of humanity can be seen as a history of repeated failures in our trying to institutionalize heaven on earth.*

So talking about this, or writing about this, is certainly very difficult, as you try to connect with something that allows you to represent it in a positive light. But it might be misrepresenting it in the process, or it may be a provisional framework for attempting to communicate something.

There aren't many people who are coming through the confusion that tends to go along with this refined sensitivity. There is a lot of confusion. You won't get many clear informants because people are still in the middle of it. The revolution is incomplete.

The evolution of one's own consciousness can be painful. It is like the hero's journey when you finally meet the dragon. Actually the dragon has been on your side all along, because it's only when you find the strength within yourself to slay the dragon that she is available to you, that you are able to hack it out there. So you need to be a little bit careful about this. In the end we are all on the same side, and this feeds back into what you were saying about duality. Take this back to individual experience and you know that the quality of your inner experience achieves reflection in the kind of experiences the outside world presents you with.... Every step you take is stepping beyond whatever is the fear or the limitation of the moment in your consciousness, and *every step is for human consciousness as a whole.*

Jon said that his and others' "alignment" with divinity has to be activated by one's own will. He said it can't be one hundred percent God's gift. There is an element of personal responsibility for the alignment:

Jon: There is a great responsibility. It would seem to me that going through this process of pitfalls that we've been talking about is going through it from the perspective of human consciousness. It's creating a blueprint that will allow other people to follow. To redefine the horizons of possibility and to chart the way by means of which this possibility can be realized…..

I guess what happens is that the knowledge of good and evil comes in so we take our cue in relation to social codes, rather than the unconstrained prompt of the truth of the heart. So as that happens we begin to fall out of the state of grace, because the state of grace is to be in the truth of the heart. So then you get the history of civilization, warfare, technology….. And then you come back into the truth of the heart. We have that opportunity that is present now, and that's why we're going through difficult times. … *These hybrids [fairypeople] are appearing now in order to rescue human consciousness from the abyss.*

This is a definition of, and call for, personal mystical experience and development, beyond social conventions, towards a purposeful evolution of consciousness and action. Steinberg, in *The Unlikely Nature of God* suggests that expanded states of consciousness stimulate a social consciousness, a feeling of unity with all creation:

> Whoever reaches into other realms of consciousness has the potential of moving mankind a step further in our evolution as may be evidenced from individuals such as Newton and Einstein.

Kay and Jon speak further:

D: Without that other un-free willed consciousness of the Fairy, elemental Realm, free willed humans would make the human condition fall on its face?

Kay: The destiny of human beings is to return to grace, and the Fairy Realm helps to accomplish this, as do other realms coming in from other dimensions. With Fairy, a sense of joy and grace, it's faster. To say that fairies are only responsible for mankind to return to grace, that's not correct. *They're responsible for bringing man quicker to grace*, and to bringing humankind an awareness of joy and creativity in humankind's return which, according to many traditions, would take a million years. But fairies are quickening agents. … Do you agree with that, Jon?

Jon: Yes I do, and I think that there is a specific context in which this is happening now. Humanity has begun to shrug off the limiting effects of three centuries of materialistic perspectives and activity. So we're on the threshold of recognizing that. *There is a place opening up in human consciousness which can relate to fairy-human partnership. So in order to facilitate that coming together again you have this generation of hybrids who can look in both directions, and bring those communities together.* And by writing anthropology books and stuff, and saying 'hey guys look there is something over here to pay attention to.' So it's a coming together.

D: Was there a period of time when human beings lived in a state of grace? When fairies occupied the earth in a more active fashion, centuries ago, and had to retreat?

K: It would have to be answered yes. Because why did, and do they, exist. There are immense histories about them being seen and the things that they did. So yes, it had to exist in time. There was a time when we were more aligned. But there is also going to be a time in the future when we are going to be more aligned, realigned.

Val also thinks that there is a re-evolution of beings on the planet:

Val: As humans originally, we were very light, extremely light. But certain things happened. That's why we are turning full circle and becoming lighter and lighter. I really do suspect that with these new kids coming in there is actually a big change. I suspect that physically they are changing more rapidly than before. So I think that it takes time. It takes generations, I think. But I think they got lighter, these new kids. I suspect that their genes, the ones that are coming through now, are going to be structurally different. I mean it is already beginning. They don't know why it is happening. I think that it is going to be more and more apparent.

Jon sent me some writing about experiences that he had regarding having contact with fairies. I quote at length from his "The Return of Fairy":

> Early in February 2006 I had a strong intuition that the stone beings of Connemara would soon be relaying important information to me. On the day I felt this was to happen, I went walking in the mountains, tuning in to stones as I walked. My feeling was that I might meditate on a mountaintop and perhaps receive illumination in this way. It didn't happen. On the way down I was feeling quite disappointed when suddenly I noticed a little valley that had never come to my attention before. Something about it seemed to be calling strongly to me. I left the beaten track and went closer.
>
> The valley was shaped like a horseshoe with layers of stone raised as if in tiers at its closed end. Facing these to one side was an imposing mound of rock and clay, grassy on one flank, poised like a dragon waiting to take off. Both the mound and the tiers of stone were calling to me, saying that fairies from all over the world would be coming there to confer and receive instruction from an exalted being whom I found myself intuitively referring to as ' the Over-lighting Deva of the universe'. I had and have no idea what this means but it is the expression which occurred to me. It resonated because it suggested that the intended gathering was somehow to have Cosmic as well as Earthly impact.
>
> Suddenly then, I 'saw' the close end of the valley reconfigured as a parliament of stone, brimful with fairy delegates. I knew that the Overlighting Being would descend into the mound and communicate with fairies on the valley floor and raised rock formations from this vantage point. At first I was dubious. I had not been anticipating anything on this scale, and especially not the sense I now had that this was to be an important event aimed – my intuition told me – at bring about a new beginning for Earth and a renewed opportunity for human beings and Fairy to come back into a creative, mutually beneficial relationship. My job was to prepare the venue to receive these beings. I shared these impressions with Tim, who is very attuned to the fairy realm, and asked him to see what he could find. His guidance coincided with my intuition and also confirmed my sense that the event was due to happen soon, beginning at the next New Moon and lasting until the Full Moon, February 28th to

March 15th 2006. Since this was only a matter of weeks away, I began visiting the site regularly......

This process was repeated several times over the next weeks. Increasingly, I had the impression that my participation was required to exemplify the role of stewardship that humanity can serve in renewing links between Heaven, Earth and the Fairy world. I also had a sense that my frequent meditations at the Ocean were somehow feeding into this process, although it was not at first clear to me how......

Eventually, it was time for the conference to begin. On the evening of the New Moon, the stones were singing, calling delegates in. I had a sense that many beings had gathered from many dimensional levels to witness this event. At one point I felt myself attuned to the energies of a pre-Celtic priest who had stood in this place long ago, calling on beings from all levels and dimensions to come and participate in a Great Dance to celebrate the inter-connectedness of All That Is. On this occasion, my intention was directed primarily towards calling the fairy beings in and extending a welcome to them from the depths of my own human longing to participate once more in a fully integrated Earth community.

Tim came next day and I brought him to the valley as we both sensed that he had a part to play in opening the proceedings. A light snow began to fall as we drew near. The fairies had already arrived but the Over-lighting Being had not yet entered the mound. We were drawn down to the valley floor. Many of the fairies were in bad shape and needed healing themselves. They waited in trust as we approached. (It is relevant to note that we had presented a course together the previous week which involved calling fairies into our human cycle to receive gratitude, recognition and healing for all they had done to assist our world. The grace of that occasion evidently helped us gain acceptance on this one.) I was directed to a rock in the centre of the valley. I knelt there and sang a healing song that seemed to affect all members of the assembled community. Tim was directing light to heal particularly wounded fairies. It seemed clear that a secondary purpose was to introduce us as trustworthy and beneficent human beings. Snowflakes continued falling as we worked. The fairies nibbled on them and were tangibly rejuvenated as a result. We left before dark with the intention of returning early the next morning.

.... Then Tim began singing the first waves of an oration, welcoming the fairies and assuring them that their assembly did indeed mark a new beginning for Earth. The Over-lighting Being was here to transmit information required to set Earth's unfolding back on course. Tim fell silent. The transmission continued energetically. Snow fell gently like manna. I watched all from above, a human witness wedded to the consciousness of Earth....

I dream then of visiting 'the other side' and befriending a fairy child who asks to stay with me as the veil between dimensions falls again. S/he agrees to live in my heart. On my next visit, several days after, I am moved to participate as a Child. My inner "fairy child' comes to the fore. Sensing this, the fairies want to dance and play. I oblige them on the soft, boggy ground for a long time....

By the time of my next visit, proceedings have begun to wind down. The fairies are preparing to leave on the following night of the full moon. They have been directed to inform their home communities that the possibility will soon exist of coming once again into right relationship with human beings and to pass on all instruction received from the Over-lighting Being. As yet, I have no sense of what these entail. I am directed to attend for a closing ceremony under the Full Moon....

I can't remember exactly what happened when I reached the end of the walk, such was my altered sate. I have a memory of singing and executing quite precise geometric dance steps, I think to honour and unite dimensions in the awareness of that moment. I turned back to face the mound then and sang my gratitude, very conscious of my position as a human being standing (figuratively) at the head of a legion of fairies drawn from all over the world. When I finished, I was directed to retrace my steps back to the mound. There I sang again of my gratitude and joy at having been allowed to participate in such an event....

There is no conclusion to my tale except to say that the fairy realm is preparing once again to play its intended role in fulfilling a renewed covenant between humanity and Mother Earth. Inspiration towards this end is currently being shared by fairy delegates with the home communities all over the world. Concerned humans are requested to do likewise at this time.

Thus we see that Jon and his friend are sometimes consciously seeking contact and work with fairies in behalf of the evolution of consciousness and the benefit of the planet.

We can talk about the development or evolution of consciousness at both the level of the individual and the level of the group. Both levels of consciousness interact in that the possibilities for individual awareness and evolution are at least in part connected to, and affect, the cultural milieu. It is like Jung's collective unconscious evolving into a collective consciousness.

As I mentioned in Chapter One, without my knowledge, there was a more or less parallel development of participatory and transpersonal anthropology during the end of the 20th and beginning of the 21st centuries with my own experiences and fieldwork in Ireland after 2000. Perhaps that was for the best because at the time I was not trying to fit my work and personal development into others' writings, experiences or models. The fact that there was some parallel evolution in these regards may in itself be indicative of a supra-individual evolution of consciousness within anthropology and in general. This is not unlike the unfolding of which fairyfolk have discussed.

Theorists of pure consciousness, perennial psychologists, like Forman (1998), say that all humans have an innate capacity for the mystical. And that beyond a particular culture's or religion's terminologies and practices for attaining enlightenment, there is a universal, pure consciousness recognizable by all human beings. In this way all mystics – perhaps all people – are striving for the same goal and experience. From the perspective of a perennial philosophy or transpersonal anthropology, in which all religions share some basic concerns and goals, fairymindedness is but one particular form not substantially different from whatever religious, mystical, or spiritual orientation one might have.

Jon affirms:

> In so far as fairypeople can discover the gift of transformation within themselves, they can chart the course. In particular they can participate in the urgent task at the present time of transforming our view of nature, our relationship with nature, and realizing and bringing forth various expressions of the magic that is inherent in life.

***

The day before I left Ireland I found a large straight scratch on my right cheek, all the way back to my hairline. I vaguely remember being scratched, perhaps by a bramble along the footpath. The scratch and irritation remind me of the nettles sting I got upon entering the footpath to the cottage at the beginning of the summer. Nature's – the fairies' – way of marking my passage into, and now with the scratch, out of, the life at the cottage. Also, last evening I saw for the first time seeing it well, the rabbit that lives at the corner of the road to Derryhassen. As I drove up the way, as it stopped and sat in the heather, I clearly saw into the rabbit's eye.
– The rabbit hole is real.

I stopped again, peering out over the wild coast on the road out of Baile an tSleibhe, to raise my hands to the sky in view of Hornhead and the Atlantic. Dancing Mind. Divinity.

On the plane

I just slipped out of my journey on this big island in the North Atlantic. As I was climbing up the airplane steps, I looked around to the landscape of Ireland around the airport. I got a sense of being a special being, smiling inside my head at the amusing knowledge. It borders slightly on mania. And I am smiling and laughing to myself right now, as if I am an emissary. Wait till they find out I am a hybrid. I laugh again.

NOTES

Chapter One - Introduction

1. The only recent scholarly book on fairies is *The Good People: New Fairylore Essays* (Narvaez, ed. 1991) which is a collection of articles on the folklore of fairies. Only one of the articles (Rojcewicz 1991) treats fairies as possibly something other than stories.

2. See Laughlin (1994c) for a review of anthropological studies in which researchers experienced altered (alternate) states of consciousness.

3. The book's dedication reads:

> I dedicate it to two ... brethren in Ireland: **A.E.**, whose unwavering loyalty to the Fairy Faith has inspired much that I have herein written, whose friendly guidance in my study of Irish mysticism I most gratefully acknowledge; and **William Butler Yeats**, who brought to me at my own alma mater in California the first message from Fairyland, and who afterwards in his own country led me through the haunts of Fairy Kings and Queens.

See A.E's *The Candle of Vision* (1965) and Yeats' *The Celtic Twilight* (1962).

4. Madame Blavatsky's Theosophy, among many other things, speaks of the existence of a variety of elemental, normally invisible beings – nature spirits, etc. – who populate the cosmos. See, for example, *The Secret Doctrine* (1888).

5. Transpersonal anthropologist Laughlin (1994a:3) describes James' radical empiricism:

> To be radical, an empiricism must neither admit into its constructions any element that is not directly experienced, nor exclude from them any element that is directly experienced. For such a philosophy, the relations that connect experiences must themselves be experienced relations, and any kind of relation experienced must be accounted as "real" as anything else in the system.

6. As anthropologist D. Young (1994:169-70) points out, Carl Jung (1960 [1920]:303) has commented on the universality of the appearance of spirits:

> It is generally assumed that the seeing of apparitions is far commoner among primitives than among civilized people, the inference being that this is nothing but superstition, because civilized people do not have such visions unless they are ill. It is quite certain that civilized man makes much less use of the hypothesis of spirits than the primitive, but in my view it is equally certain that psychic phenomena occur no less frequently with civilized people than they do with primitives. The only difference is that where the primitive speaks of ghosts, the European speaks of dreams and fantasies and neurotic symptoms, and attributes less importance to them than the primitive does. I am convinced that if a European had to go through the same exercises and ceremonies which the medicine-man performs in order to make the spirits visible, he would have the same experiences. He would interpret them differently, of course, and devalue them but this would not alter the facts as such. It is well known that Europeans have very curious psychic experiences if they have to live under primitive conditions for a long time, or if they find themselves in some other unusual psychological situation.

7. Beebe (2003) lauds Evans-Wentz, as opposed to Carl Jung, in Evans-Wentz's treatments of Eastern concepts on their own terms.

8. For a survey discussion of the "biology of religion" see Stevens, Jr. 2011, pp 38-41.

9. Here Ingold (2000:166) describes new perceptions of the physical environment:

> Throughout life one can keep on seeing new things in an otherwise permanent world, not by constructing the same sense data according to novel conceptual schemata, but by as sensitization or 'fine-tuning' of the perceptual systems to new kinds of information. Novel perceptions arise from creative acts of discovery rather than imagining, and the information on which they are based is available to anyone attuned to pick it up.

10. In older, common usage in Ireland, the English word "fairyfolk" referred not to humans, but to the usually not visible fairies themselves, as did words and phrases such as "the little people," "hill folk," "the wee ones," and "the good people." Here I have changed its meaning for a shorthand method of referring to humans who have sensibilities to fairies.

11. Cosgrove, et. al., eds. (2011) do discuss new religious movements in Ireland but there is virtually no mention of fairies, and no mention of the Fairy Faith. Therein Butler (2011) briefly discusses fairies for some Neo-Pagans, but, as I

demonstrate below, the new Fairy Faith cannot be classified as a (neo-)Pagan religion.

12. Taylor (2010:10) distinguishes between "green religion" (which posits that environmentally friendly behavior is a religious obligation) and "dark green" religion (in which nature is sacred, has intrinsic value, and is therefore due reverent care).

13. Vincett and Woodhead (2001:329) explain:

> Although spirituality often retains its historic opposition to 'religion', there are increasing signs of a crossing of the boundaries between new forms of spirituality, and aspects of traditional theistic religious practice.
>
> Theologically, one of the points of incompatibility has been that theistic religions conceived God as a personal, often male, being with authority over the individual. Another has been an exaltation of the 'Creator' over the creation as a whole, which may imply a hierarchy of value in which the natural world comes at the very bottom. How then can the two come into closer contact and rapprochement with one another?
>
> One way is by highlighting the mystical tradition within theistic religions. Christianity, Judaism, and Islam all have mystical strands, often with distinctive teachings, traditions, and rituals. In some cases these downplay the 'hierarchy' of God, and emphasize the unity between God and the believer. They may also present God as ineffable (beyond name), and unknowable. Another way is by emphasizing the extent to which theistic religions venerate the whole creation, which is understood as brought into being and upheld by God. For example, the sacramental emphasis of Roman Catholicism views the natural world as a sign and gateway to the divine, and 'Celtic' Christianity (the Christianity of parts of the early British Isles before it was Romanized) has some features which resemble a nature-mysticism.

14. Christian Jr. (1981:8) describes apparitions:

> Apparitions documented for Spain fall into two categories. The first is the kind common in the twentieth century – one or more divine figures who appear to one or more seers "in the flesh," as it were. [The second category is "signs" which can be independently verified by the senses of other people]. They usually speak, sometimes touch the seers: often they walk with them and show them things; and sometimes they leave sacred objects for the seers. These are apparitions proper. Those I know about in Spain occurred mainly in two periods; from around 1400 to about 1525 (the subject of this book): and from 1900 to the present.

Fairy "apparitions" are not quite like these in which divine figures "speak" or sometimes "walk" with them. Fairy appearances in general seem to be less interactive.

15. As Stevens, Jr. (2011, personal communication) writes:

> When we are confronted with an extraordinary claim, we have three ways to respond to it: 1) it is a lie, a fabrication. The only fruitful pursuits of this option would be to examine the claimant's motives for lying, and/or people's reasons for believing it. 2) It has no basis in science, it cannot be measured, therefore we cannot verify or falsify it, and we must acknowledge that it may be true, it may have happened just as reported. This is the option we must accept in dealing with people's claims to the existence of supernatural beings and forces, and the intervention of such in people's lives. These are matters of faith; we accept that and move on. 3) It has no basis in science, it cannot be measured, *but it was perceived by the claimant*, recorded in his/her brain/mind, and therefore *it is real for him/her* – the claimant really did have this experience, he/she is not lying. This latter option we can deal with through the principles of science, we know how the biological process of perception works and how it can be distorted by various psychological, physiological, and chemical means and how it is modified by cultural expectations, and this whole process of investigation is fully scientific.

16. Knecht and Feuchter (2008), one an ethnologist, the other a historian, respectively, in *Religion and Its Other*, look at the interplay, rather than separation, between the secular and the religious.

17. One might be tempted to call the Fairy Faith a modern esoteric spirituality (to use Western terms), but, using Faivre's (1992) criteria of esoteric spirituality to include the four "intrinsic" characteristics of 1) correspondences, 2) living nature 3) imagination and mediation, and 4) the experience of transmutation and the "nonintrinsic" characteristics of the 5) practice of concordance and 6) transmission (by master to disciple) (xix), fairyfolk cannot be said to practice esoteric (Christian) spirituality.

Fairyfolk do share with some esotericists the certainty of intermediary spirits, such as angels or fairies, but a difference between esotericism and mysticism is not definitive:

> Perhaps it is this notion of mediation, above all, which makes the difference between that which is mystical and that which is esoteric. A little simplistically, we might consider that mystics – in the most classic sense – aspire to a more or less complete suppression of images and intermediaries because such things soon become hindrances to the experience of union with God. In contrast, esotericists seem more interested in intermediaries revealed to their interior gaze, by virtue of their

creative imagination, which is essentially directed toward union with the divine; esotericists prefer to stay on Jacob's ladder, upon which angels (and doubtless other entities as well) climb and descend, rather than to go beyond. The distinction has only practical value; there is sometimes a great deal of esotericism in the mystics (e.g., Saint Hildegard of Bingen), and a mystical tendency can be seen in many esotericists (e.g., Louis de Saint-Martin). (Faivre 1992: xvii)

Fairyfolk experience fairies and fairy energy as intermediary beings, and thus could be considered esoteric in this regard, but also know the intermediaries as part of the earthly dimension of God and are thus, indirectly or directly, experiencing union with God, and therefore could be considered mystic. Since esoteric spirituality is very much a group phenomenon and has other characteristics which do not fit well, it is better to consider the Fairy Faith as mysticism and animism, more than esotericism, also because both mysticism and animism incorporate less Western bias and permit a more cross-culturally relativist perspective.

As Needleman (1992) emphasizes, the esoteric is usually considered as "existing outside or independent of the known religious traditions" (xxvii), and, in this regard, perhaps it is also best to refrain from using esoteric to describe the Fairy Faith. I also wish to get beyond categorization as much as possible.

18. Although the word "vision" is occasionally mentioned in the (transpersonal) anthropology of religion, as in Laughlin, McManus and Shearer's (1983) "Dreams, Trance and Visions: What a Transpersonal Anthropology Might Look Like" there is little to no discussion of visionary experience.

19. Laughlin (1994a:117) describes eidetic intuition:

> .... It is the absolute certainty of this kind that allows the contemplative to transcend the "natural attitude" (i.e., the cultural and personal historical loading) of the everyday lifeworld (Husserl 1977:152-153).

20. For examples, recently Garrett (2008) traces the history of changing Christian conceptualizations and functions of angels, historian Isaiasz (2008) recounts the official Lutheran church's ambivalent reaction to lay experiences of angel appearances, and Huss (2008) discusses trends in the content, acceptance and popularity of Kabbalism.

21. For a review and discussion of religious *belief* and anthropology see Glazier (2011) 32-37.

22. See, e.g., Nelstrop's (2009) recent book *Christian Mysticism: An Introduction to Contemporary Theoretical Approaches* which posits four main theories.

23. During my fieldwork in the early 80's on the Faeroe Islands locals told me that the advent of electricity drove away most of the elves (*huldufolk*). Likewise, twenty years later, locals in Ireland told me that electricity drove away many of the fairies (*sidhe*). Anthropologists in other contexts, e.g., in Mageo and Howard (1996), reported similar situations with respect to the diminishing appearance and sightings of spirits in the context of social and technological change.

24. Indeed, not wishing to erode my participatory approach and fairy sensibility, my first draft of this ethnography was written as a non-academic work. Only after reading and digesting numerous works, familiarizing myself with the literature did I come to locate this ethnography into the wider academic anthropology of religion discussed in this introduction and elsewhere in the book.

25. Laitman (2008:305) discusses the transmission of religious views:

> ....when a person is among religious people, and begins to converse and argue with him, he immediately mingles with their views. Their views penetrate his mind below the threshold of consciousness to such an extent that he will not be able to discern that these are not his own views, but what he received from the people he connected with.

26. Anthropologist Needham, after reviewing major philosophers' discussions of the idea of belief, concludes that 1) belief is a state of mind, 2) belief entails the *feeling* that is appropriate to some belief, 3) belief is in part an emotional commitment 4) we do not decide to believe, and 5) we do not actively change our minds. "We say transitively that *we* change our minds, as though it were in our power to foresee a new idea. Yet all we know, and necessarily only in retrospect, is that we now entertain or express thoughts which are different from those that we were conscious of before." (241)

> When a man utters a belief-statement he is not reporting an inner experience of a discriminable kind, and he cannot intend (mean) to impart to his hearer any distinctive property of such an experience. He is using a word by which he can convey a judgment, supposition, expectation, commitment, doubt, or many another statement about a position that he holds; and in using the word 'believe', in a certain grammatical form and in a particular social situation, he assumes a recognizable part in the play of communication. The meaning that he expresses in a belief-statement is the effect that he intends to procure, and this is an expectation that he has learned by his familiarity with the linguistic and other conventions of the culture. Conversely, the meaning that he is taken to express by that belief-statement is the effect actually produced in a hearer who similarly interprets the situation in the light of his knowledge of the cultural conventions. *This act of social intercourse does not depend on the existence of belief as a distinct mode of experience that is reported by the*

speaker, nor does it require that the hearer shall himself be familiar with such an experience. (242, my emphasis)

Thus we need to remember that there are social and emotional dimensions to our acceptance or rejection of other's beliefs – and our own. If we come to recognize this more thoroughly, then authenticity becomes even more so a matter of inner voice. It is assessed by the person him/herself and picked up on, or not, by someone else with a similar sensibility or opening to that sensibility, rather than through dogma. Thus when religious leaders or mystics, or people below like Jon and Kay, say that they cannot really convey their experience or talk fully about their experience, they use verbs such as "open up (one's heart)," "experience," "connect." It is the only way to understand in the widest sense of the word "understand," rather than through thinking and "believing."

27. Campbell (1976) appears to be the originator of the term "transpersonal anthropology." For reviews of transpersonal anthropology see Laughlin (1994c) and Sheppard (2007).

28. Bernstein (2005) explains:

> By transrational reality I mean objective, nonpersonal, nonrational phenomena occurring in the natural universe, information and experience that does not readily fit into standard cause and effect logical structure. These are the kinds of experience that typically are labeled and dismissed as superstition, irrational, and, in the extreme, abnormal or crazy.(xv-xvi)

He says that transrational experience is "nothing short of sacred" (xvi).

I suggest that fairyfolk are "borderland personalities" having transrational experiences.

Chapter Two - Overview

1. Fairies exist, and are agencies, on what Stevens, Jr. (2011:41) calls a "horizontal dimension" in relation to humans, which contrasts with the vertical dimension along which gods and elevated divinities reside:

> It is useful to consider religion ethnologically as including simultaneously a vertical relationship between people and elevated divinities, its popular meaning in the West, and a horizontal dimension, the active recognition of supernatural agencies on the level of human society…
> …'Other spirits' are spiritual beings of non-human origin, including nature spirits and cultural variants like pixies and fairies, some 'trickster' figures and demons, all of which are conceptualized as sharing the same level of existence as human society.

2. Regarding anthropomorphism and the attribution of agency to supernatural entities Boyer and Bergstrom (2008:119) summarize:

> The human imagination tends to project human-like and person-like features onto nonhuman or nonperson-like aspects of the environment; such representations are attention-grabbing or enjoyable; they are found in all religious traditions (Guthrie 1993). But anthropomorphism in religious concepts is also rather selective. That is, the domain of intuitions and inferences that is projected is intentional agency, more frequently and consistently projected than any other domain of human characteristics (Barrett & Keil 1996).
>
> In this sense, concepts of religious agency can be described as derived from (and a possible by-product of) evolved dispositions to represent physical objects and intentional agents. But what is remarkable in religion is not just the production of supernatural concepts but also their social and emotional importance, which in a cognitive account also derives from evolved dispositions to morality and social interaction (Boyer 2000).

3. N. Williams (1991:462-3), in his article "The Semantics of the Word *Fairy*: Making Meaning Out of Thin Air," gives a detailed etymology of the word "fairy":

> In the first place its etymology is by no means clear, although one etymology now seems to be generally accepted. Etymologies for *fairy* have generally been derived from words denoting female supernatural creatures in other languages. Thus it has been derived from the last syllable of Latin *nympha*, and from Arabic *peri*. Alternatively it has been derived from words with supernatural associations, or words connoting properties regarded as attributes of fairies. Amongst these are derivations from *fair*, Old English *fagan* and Latin *fatua*.
>
> The accepted etymology also follows the pattern of derivation from a word taken to mean female supernatural creatures. Ultimately it would seem to be derived from Latin *fatum* ="thing said." This gave *fata* = "fate," a neuter plural which, it is supposed, was misinterpreted in the Dark Ages as feminine singular, *fata* = 'female fate, goddess," and.........
>
> This identification [with Celtic goddesses] firstly gives a noun *fai, fae, fay* referring to an individual female with supernatural powers, probably best translated as "enchantress," so that we must suppose that the substantive *faerie* is derived from this, meaning "enchantment." Later, this was again misunderstood or perhaps extended to signify "fairyland," and as a plural "enchantresses," whose singular was then mistakenly taken to be not *fay* but *faerie*.

Williams summarizes:

> .... I want to argue that *fairy* in particular, but more generally *any* supernatural name, is necessarily amorphous, and to show that from its

earliest use in English, from the earliest occurrences of fairies in England, no single meaning has ever been paramount. At the same time, I will also argue that there is a central concept, that of "fatedness" which antedates the earliest occurrences of *fairy* and is captured by both the earliest and much later use of the word, and that this central concept perhaps best characterizes the *fairy* concept from its first use. (457) (author's italics)

4. Here E. Turner (2009, originally 1993) describes the terms "spirit manifestation" and "energy" from her own experiences:

> Moreover, there is disagreement about terms. "Spirits" are referred to in most cultures. Some Native Americans refer to 'power." "Energy," *ki* or *chi*, is known in Japan and China, and has caught on among Western healers. "Energy" was not the right word for the blob that came out of the back of the Ndembu woman; it was a miserable object, purely bad, without any energy at all, and much more akin to the miserable ghost of suicides. One thinks of energy as formless, but when I *see* internal organs, the organs aren't "energy"; they had form and definition. Or, when I saw the face of my Eskimo friend Tigluk on a mask, as I saw it in a waking dream, and then saw Tigluk himself by luck a few minutes afterwards, the mask face wasn't "energy," laughing there --- it was not in the least abstract. The old-fashioned term, *spirit manifestation*, is much closer. These are deliberate comings of discernable forms with a conscious intent to communicate, to claim importance in our lives. On the other hand I have indeed sensed energy, very like electrical energy, when submitting to the healing passes of Spiritist women adepts in a mass meeting in Brazil. (313) (author's emphasis)

5. I decided to concentrate my first-hand experiences with about a dozen people, rather than search out and less intensively briefly interact with many more. It is my interpersonal style and my scientific understanding, as an anthropologist and as a social actor, that the best information and best experience is attained by immersing oneself intensively in a small group, by talking with and living by a small number of people to get to know them well.

6. On life forces see Harvey (2006:129ff). In discussing life forces in the anthropological literature he writes:

> ... Nurit Bird-David argues that [south Indian Nayaka] *n/um* is a 'kind of potency' that is not best understood using 'Western material imagery' (i.e. electrical forces), but is better thought of, using local imagery, 'in immaterial terms of sociality and personal relatedness.... [*n/um* is] invisible, strong, usually beneficial, has to be "awakened", whereupon "it awakens the heart" etc.' Given the disagreement between these expert interpreters, any other putative 'power' must be considered with care.

> Perhaps the problem here is that Western interpreters attempt to systematize fluid and resistant metaphors. When the Lakota define something or someone as *wakan* they may indicate a degree of mystery about it. Similarly when John Matthews writes of how the older men among the Osage 'added new thoughts to the fumblings toward an understanding of *Wah'Kon*, the Mystery Force', he is attempting to speak of one who is personal and relational but ultimately different and approached through intermediaries if at all. Another example is the reification of breath as a 'life-force'. While breathing is a common sign of life, it can also be foundational to the understanding of 'soul' or 'spirit'. Whether the Hawaiian word *ea* means anything different to breath is debatable – but this does not diminish the power of breath as a metonym of *everything* else that is significant about the breathing person. In Maori and Hopi contexts (which may of course be nothing like the Hawaiian one) sharing breath is vitally important and socially empowering, but does not require notions of the transmission of mystic powers.
>
> Discussions of West African (or West African diaspora) religious traditions commonly refer to a power variously translated as *ashe, ache, ase* and so on. While this is often said to be something that can be stimulated and utilized as if it were a vitalising force, it is equally often discussed as the power to act, the power manifest in relationships, and creativity. (131)

7. Winkelman (2004:87):

> The consistency of religious experience across time and place illustrates their naturalness and innate source. The naturalness of spirit experiences is illustrated in studies of spontaneous religious experiences among contemporary people (Stark 1997). Contemporary religious experiences primarily involve perceptions of contact with a spirit that has a relationship with the individual. This experience of the divine other involves perceptions of a presence with volitional characteristics like one's self. The experiences vary in terms of the degrees of interaction with the spirit entity experienced. These range in terms of the intensity of interaction, beginning with a confirming experience, the self's awareness of the divine other. The experience may also be responsive, a sense of the divine other's awareness of self. More intensive experiences are an ecstatic union of self with the divine other, a revelatory message from the divine other, and the experience of the control of the self by the divine other, exemplified in possession. The ubiquity and primordial nature of these spirit experiences are illustrated by their universal presence in shamanism.

8. Rojcewicz (1991:496) continues:

> Human witnesses may actually play an unwitting role in how, or even if, they see fairies. Tradition suggests a symbiotic or participatory relationship

between the human perceiver and the entity perceived. From this perspective a fairy encounter is a mutually constructed reality. Poet and mystic W.B. Yeats once commented on this interdependent function: "Many poets and all mystics and occult writers, in all ages and countries, have declared that behind the visible are chains and chains of conscious beings, who are not of heaven but are of earth, who have no inherent form, but change according to their whim, or *the mind that sees them*. (author's emphasis)

9. Laughlin (1994a:117) continues in this regard with an important methodological point:

Methodologically speaking, the ethnographer cannot infer uncertainty or incompleteness of knowledge from the apparent fuzziness or lack of crispness of native categories, or the inarticulateness of reports of experience. This is an important point, not only in conceptually bridging from fuzziness to apodicticity of knowledge, but also in understanding the structure of ethnological material cross-culturally.

10. Although channeling is a New Age term for receiving words and wisdom from invisible sources, historically all religious traditions, mainstream and esoteric, recognize specially endowed or experienced individuals, leaders, and "translators" of divine messages. They have transmitted divine will and communication. Moses, other prophets, and saints received revelations from "on high" and communicated them to other humans. In some traditions, entire religious texts have been revealed or "channeled."

11. One or two twentieth century writers on metaphysical phenomena, such as Jacques Vallee (1969), have suggested that human experiences with fairies and with UFOs have so many resemblances that fairies and UFOs are different manifestations of attunement to the same energy. This, Vallee says, is a result of the same synchronicity with a spiritual force of the invisible world. In *Passport to Magonia* he states "the mechanism of the apparitions [of fairies and UFOs] in legendary, historical, and modern times is standard and follows the model of religious miracles."

Similarly, P. Rojcewicz (1991), more conventionally scientific, is interested in the epistemology and nature of mind as revealed in stories of fairies and UFOs:

the archetypal patterns in [fairy and UFO] folklore are instinctively related to the structures inherent in nature itself. ... The psychophysical nature of the archetype [behind fairies and UFOs] is closely related to Jung's concept of 'synchronicity', an unexpected meeting of one or more psychic states with a physical event....From this peculiar fusion of time and space and inner and outer-worlds, something of the original unity of life becomes visible and can be experienced. Synchronistic phenomena, like fairy and UFO encounters, with their parallel mental and material aspects, must be regarded as the 'coming to consciousness' of an archetype....strange encounters with fairies and UFOs are 'signals from the unitary reality... (501)

However, *Running with the Fairies* here does not deal with folklore, nor tries to explain the appearance of UFOs. And it is especially clear to me that, as ethereal nature beings of the divine, fairies are quite unlike UFOs, big mechanical or technologically advanced devices. None of the knowledgeable, knowing people discussed and quoted below ever mentioned UFOs.

Chapter Three – Opening Up

1. Carol's experience aligns with what Underhill (1910) describes in her classic work *Mysticism*:

> Commonly, however, if we may judge from those first-hand accounts which we possess, mystic conversion is a single and abrupt experience, sharply marked off from the long, dim struggles which precede and succeed it. It usually involves a sudden and acute realization of a splendor and adorable reality in the world – or sometimes of its obverse, the divine sorrow at the heart of things – never before perceived. In so far as I am acquainted with the resources of the language, there are no words in which this realization can be described. (178)

2. Henceforth, all italics and underlinings within quotes are my emphases.

3. In psychology this half-awake state is termed hypnagogic, when falling asleep, hypnopompic, when awakening.

4. James Redfield (1997), in *The Celestine Vision,* discusses "luminosity," and the luminosity of an object, in which there is an out-of-the-ordinary special light or attraction about an object that draws a person to it, even in the midst of other objects in the visual field. Something jumps out at you.

Chapter Four - Lightness, Drama, and the Natural World

1. In the Introduction to their edited volume on ritual levity and humor in South Asian religions, editors Raj and Dempsey (2010:3) mention how, despite the general notion that levity denotes "lacking appropriate seriousness," that "ritual levity - as we understand it - denotes ritual actions that are at once lighthearted and serious."

2. Fairyfolk are, of course, familiar with non-fairyfolk's not uncommon notion that fairy belief is silly, frivolous and not really serious. Fairyfolk, though, in their own lightness, sometimes play with that notion, making fun of themselves, knowing

that the lightness of fairyness can recognize and incorporate or co-optate that outsider's perspective that fairy belief is not serious at all. Thus, at times, to be amused or laugh at one's self as a fairyperson reinforces the lightness of being of fairies, fairyfolk, and fairypeople, maintaining its lightheartedness in part by not getting angry or overly earnest about not being recognized or accepted as also serious in their fairyness.

Raj and Dempsey (2010:9) propose six basic types of ritual levity: " (1) *vertical levity*, which bridges the gulf between human and divine realms and establishes intimacy between the two, (2) *horizontal levity*, which softens social divides among humans and enhances human relationships and intimacy, (3) *transgressive levity*, which challenges established conventions, hierarchies, and institutions, often through role reversals, (4) *restorative levity*, which restores order hierarchy, and conventional distinctions, (5) *redemptive levity*, which provides a glimpse into the meta or transcendent dimension of existence and bridges both vertical and horizontal distinctions and hierarchies, and (6) *competitive levity*, which is designed to edge out competition and display contests (religious, professional, and ritual) between rival participants within a religious group or between competing, if not conflicting, traditions. This type of levity also helps mark and reinforce boundaries."

I suggest that fairyfolk may engage in all these types of levity - perhaps primarily vertical levity, transgressive levity, and redemptive levity - but their humor is usually spontaneous and less formal and ritualized than much of the South Asian religions' "sacred play" and "ritual levity" as portrayed by the authors in Raj and Dempsey, eds. (2010), who, in their academic analyses take levity quite seriously. This "serious," analytical approach to levity runs a bit counter to the "fairy way."

3. Ken Wilber (2000:179) describes the Witnessing (or Observing) Self:

> This observing Self is usually called the Self with a capital S, or the Witness, or pure Presence, or pure awareness, or consciousness as such, and this Self as transparent Witness is a direct ray of the living Divine. The ultimate "I AM" is Christ, is Buddha, is Emptiness itself: such is the startling testimony of the worlds' great mystics and sages.

4. As mentioned earlier, the advent of electricity was also the reason many Faeroe Islanders gave me for the disappearance of *huldufolk* ("elves").

Chapter Five - Fieldwork and Personalwork

1. I put the word "believe" in quotation marks to indicate that, as Ruell (2011:278-9) suggests, that belief is 1) not "central to all religions in the same way as it is to Christianity", that 2) the belief of a person or people does not "form the ground of his or their behavior", that 3) belief is not "fundamentally an interior state, psychological condition" and that 4) the determination of belief is not "more

important than the determination of the status of what it is that is the object of the belief.

2. With respect to rapport and subjectivity in fieldwork in the anthropology of religion Hume (2007:16) writes:

> ....Fieldwork and emotional intersubjectivity, in fact, are probably essential to good ethnography. Wikan (1992:471) insists that the importance of 'resonance' cannot be underestimated, and one should willingly 'engage with another world, life or idea', and use one's experience to try to grasp the meanings and values of members of other cultures. This deep engagement with alternative religious groups has produced some very exciting work in the field of the anthropology of religion (see for example, Rountree (2004); Blain (2002); Greenwood (2000); and the classic, Young and Goulet (1994), *Being Changed by Cross-cultural Encounters*), where fieldworkers have plunged into the beliefs and ritual practices and experienced at first hand the events described by informants.

3. See footnote 3 to Chapter Two above for a fuller discussion.

4. Psychologist P. Nelson (2000:55) describes "knowing" and ontic shifts in *Transpersonal Knowing: Exploring the Horizon of Consciousness:*

> Knowing is that moment to moment reflexive, retrospective activity of awareness that we engage as we navigate the waters of consciousness. It is both the act of immediate experiencing as well as the experience of that experiencing. In its immediacy it appears to be our way of "touching" reality – of directly accessing the who, what, where, and when of our existential worlds. For most of us, most of the time, knowing has a consistency and constancy that allows us to feel and believe that there is an ontologically solid and unchanging world "out there" that we access through our senses. However, on some occasions the regularity and certainty of this daily style of knowing undergoes a radical transformation – such as when one has a mystical experience. To those of us who have had such encounters, mystical experiences appear to be a radically altered way of knowing where reality is experienced afresh, illusions are penetrated, and self and other seem to lose their rigid boundedness. The world appears to become both imminent and transparent. Thus, mystical knowing appears to be both broader and deeper – encompassing a more complete contact with reality.

Chapter Six – Perspectives and Writings on Fairies

1. In a long footnote in his *Tibetan Yoga & Secret Doctrines* Evans-Wentz (1935:219-220) describes Tibetan propitiation of elementals, and then compares it to Celtic offerings for fairies:

> It is held by learned *gurus* that at this stage [of practice on the "path of knowledge"], or under this circumstance, elementals, comparable to the elementals of medieval mystics, and similar non-human entities, try to prevent the *yogin* from acquiring *siddhic*, or supernormal, powers, which are essential in this *yoga*. Consequently, before the *yogin* can establish himself securely on the 'astral' plane and be quite free of all such interference, he must make friends with its inhabitants, the elementals, called in Sanskrit *Viras* ('Heroes') and *Dakinis* ('Fairies'). When a traveler from a far country enters into a new and unexplored country peopled by uncouth savages, he first appeases them by simple gifts. Similarly, in the view of the *guru*, the inhabitants of the strange realm into which the *yogin* hopes to enter and make exploration must first be propitiated. The ritual offerings are of food, whence the 'Heroes' and 'Fairies' extract the invisible spiritual essences, upon which they feed. The modern Tibetan, and also Hindu, practice parallels that of the ancient and highly cultured Greeks of sacrificing to the daemons, believing that daemons enjoy the odour of burnt offerings. …. And the Gaelic peasant, on November Night, still makes food-offerings to the 'good people', 'pucks', 'leprechauns', and other fairy folk, as the Breton peasant does to the spirits of the dead, that these dwellers in the Celtic Otherworld may be friendly rather than inimical, and so bless the hearth and family and cause increase of the flocks and bountiful harvest during the year to come.

2. Words all in capital letters refer to other entries in her dictionary. For example, elsewhere in the dictionary, GLAMOUR refers to

> a mesmerism or enchantment cast over the senses, so that things were perceived or not perceived as the enchanter wished. Gipsies, witches, and above all, the FAIRIES had this power…   (Briggs 1976:191)

3. Ken Wilber (2005) suggests that the less than spiritualized rationality of recent times is a necessary part of the evolution of consciousness toward a "transrational" understanding of the true spiritual nature of the universe.

4. Stewart prefers the f-a-e-r-y spelling of fairy, to differentiate the recreational, entertainment kind of fairy in people's minds, from the true, more mystical consciousness and experience.

Chapter Eight – The Unconceptual

1. As indicated above, scholar-believer Evans-Wentz, who worked intensively with both the Celtic Fairy Faith and Tibetan Buddhism, wrote in the early twentieth century that Tibetan dakinis <u>are</u> fairies.

2. The heart often has been conceptualized in diverse cultures as the spiritual center or source of unity. See, for example, the Mahayana Buddhist "Heart Sutra," which from the Sanskrit directly translates to "Heart of the Perfection of Transcendent Wisdom."

3. For longer discussions of the nature of mystical experience, there are numerous books and articles, some by mystics themselves, e.g., Teresa of Avila (1963-72), and others by scholars. See, e.g., Underhill (1974 (1910)) and Bishop (1995).

Chapter Nine - Realization

1. Individuation is a term commonly used by Carl Jung and others since which refers to the process of becoming aware of one's self, one's own psychological make-up, to reach one's true inner self, an integrated personality in which a person becomes conscious of his/her personal and collective unconscious.

2. See Chapter Twelve for a discussion of physical traits of fairypeople.

Chapter Ten – Incarnation and Reincarnation

1. In reincarnation in Tibetan Buddhism actually any person or being may take on buddha qualities, or even be a Buddha, even if they are not Buddhist:

> The availability of the tulkus of the buddhas and adepts is not limited to so-called Buddhists. For example, Buddha and Buddha-qualities have arisen from the ultimate and universal nature and they can appear in any form, at any place, and for any being who is ready to receive them. (Thondup 2011:11)

2. Opal Whiteley, a nature writer, who some considered a fairyperson, had a very popular childhood diary which was published in the US in 1920. She also wrote an unpublished manuscript entitled *The Fairyland Around Us*. Similar to Kay, Whiteley claimed that her parents were not her real parents. In her environmentally conscious works Opal wrote about her interaction with fairies in the woods of Oregon. See Benjamin Hoff's (1986) *The Singing Creek Where the Willows Grow: The Mystical Nature Diary of Opal Whiteley*.

3. In Buddhism, a bodhisattva is an enlightened human being who chooses to reincarnate again as a human being to help other humans, although he/she has the

option to end the cycle of reincarnation because he/she is now fully enlightened and able to become one with the divine.

Chapter Eleven – Mission, Purpose, Responsibility

1. Even though this perspective is embedded in the monotheistic West, it is often neglected. As Stendhal (1992:143) points out:

> To be created in the image of God is a definition of the self. In Greek this *imago*, this *ikon*, came to be referred to as the *doxa*, the "glory."…. the inviolable and sacred nature of humanity in the West is rooted in this idea of *imago dei*, the image of God. (my underlining)

Chapter Twelve – Fairypeople Traits

1. Somewhat akin to astrological birth signs, in that individual personalities have in part been destined by birth, the Enneagram is a psychological and spiritual system of understanding in which individuals fall into different personality types, different constitutional types, which explain personal traits. The information also leads the way for understanding one's self and working on personal transformation.

The Enneagram system was first published by P.D. Ouspensky (1947), a student of Gurdijeff, in *In Search of the Miraculous: Fragments of an unknown teaching.*

Chapter Thirteen – Healing and Well-being

1. Laughlin, McManus and Shearer (1983) discuss "cross-phasing" in consciousness and nervous system functions, and, in this regard, the differences between our own and traditional societies.

> The manner in which phenomenological phases will be cognized by a person will largely be determined by his or her socialization. Society molds the experiences of its members (1) by providing conditions, often ritually controlled, under which experience arises, and (2) by providing a hermeneutic system (usually cosmological) through the organization of which elements of experience may be recognized and integrated into the Ec [cognized environment].

> Put in negative terms, a society may inhibit access to and integration of experience by systematically ignoring or negatively sanctioning the phase of consciousness under which the experience is derived….. Experiences derived in alternate phases are given negative valence by being labeled "dream", "crazy", or "mad", "illegal", "bestial", "out of his mind", "wrecked", "on a trip", etc., thus inhibiting the integration of experiences

> confronted in trance, dream or what-have-you into a totally integrated Ec. At worst, rampant monophasia may provide the sufficient conditions for a disintegrated personality – one mediated by fragmented, disentrained structures storing information differentially and contradictorally at different loci in the nervous system (see Grinder and Bandler 1976 , Jung 1966, Maslow 1968, McManus 1975).
>
> Of immense anthropological significance is the fact that most human societies operate upon multiple realities (Schutz 1945), experienced directly by some or all group members through *polyphasic consciousness* …….. That is, the formation of Ec's in most societies requires integration of experiences (Maslow's "unitive consciousness"; see Krippner 1972) derived from two or more alternative phases (e.g., integration of waking and meditative consciousness among North American Indian cultures, see Underhill 1946, Eggan 1966; and waking, meditative and dream consciousness in Tibetan tantrism, see Evans-Wentz 1958). As we have said, it is quite possible to argue that failure to integrate polyphasic experience may result in psychopathology. In fact, many traditional (as well as modern) therapies would seem to exist to alleviate such problems (Stewart 1951, Roszak 1975). (author's italics)

2. The guardian angel, in earlier Christian and some New Age Christianity, is personal. But Raff and Vocatura differentiate further between inner images or figures that are simply of the unconscious and those in the imagination that come from outside the person:

> Hundreds of years before Jung, a Sufi Islamic mystic explored the nature of the imaginal world and the figures that inhabit it. This master, Ibn 'Arabi, wrote that the imagination was intermediary between the world of human life and the Divine Reality. Events from the ordinary human world could appear as images in the imaginal realm. This certainly occurs in dream life, where our daily experiences are represented in symbolic terms. However, the beings from the higher Divine world may also present themselves in the imagination. The Divinity manifests, along with spirits, in the intermediate world. *When a messenger or a being from the higher world wishes to communicate with a human being, it does so through the imagination.* Ibn 'Arabi wrote that one way the spirits communicate is to take on form and become inner figures. Moreover, he assures us that the inner figure is identical with the spiritual being who appears in that form. …The spiritual beings of the psychoid realm take on form within the imagination, and though the form is an inner experience, it is identical with the psychoidal being who adopts it. (117) (my emphasis)

In a description which fits well the variety of fairy experience as related by the people in this book, Raff and Vocatura further explain:

Inner figures may in fact embody the psychoid as well as contents of the unconscious. Such inner figures may express themselves in a visual image, or speak, or create feeling states….. The visual images they create are often more intense and sometimes are perceptible even when one has one's eyes open. Sometimes they are accompanied with intense colors and bright lights, and they seem more autonomous than inner figures…. Our language is not well suited for explaining such different feeling states, but as a rough approximation, I might state that psychoidal figures generate more profound feelings than other figures. The feelings are often ecstatic, and the entity creating them feels alien to the ego. It is therefore possible to discriminate between psychic and psychoidal inner figures by the nature of the experiences they create. (116-117)

3. See Fine's (2003) book, *Physician of the Soul, Healer of the Cosmos: Isaac Luria and His Kabbalistic Fellowship*, especially the two chapters on "Healing the Cosmos."

Chapter Fourteen – Individual Transformation

1. Raff and Vocatura (2002) discuss trust, and trusting the process of working with an ally. See especially pages 203-6.

2. See Grof and Grof's (1989) *Spiritual Emergency: When Personal Transformation Becomes a Crisis.*

3. Indian spiritual psychoanalyst Kakar (1991) states that mysticism is the mainstream of Hindu religiosity.

4. Wilber is perhaps the foremost systematist of spiritual development and of a perennial philosophy, a transpersonal developmental psychology, in which all religious/mystical pursuits and worldviews can be conceptualized as particular courses of a universal process of seeking spiritual transformation. See Wilber (2005), especially pages 69-81.

5. A similar heart-oriented, emotional basis for forward personal, mindful movement is discussed by best-selling spiritual teacher Eckhart Tolle (2005) in *The New Earth: Awakening to Your Life's Purpose.* He says that spiritually-aligned attitudes for action - "the three modalities of awakened doing" - include acceptance, enjoyment, and *enthusiasm.*" (295) Enthusiasm is "deep enjoyment in what you do plus the added element of a goal or vision that you work toward." (301).

6. In a similar manner Shulman and Stroumsa (2002) use the terms centripetal and centrifugal (13) to describe personalities (and religious cultures), differentiating

between a religious self that expands and those that ultimately shrink out of existence.

7. And Jungian analyst Bernstein discusses the difficulties sensitive, aligned-with-nature persons with "borderland consciousness," who are sometimes labeled "pathological," can have in adapting to modern urban life.

8. See also *Meeting the Shadow: The Hidden Power of the Dark Side of Human Nature* (Zweig and Abrams, eds. 1991).

Chapter Sixteen – Ireland: The Fairy Portal, Artistry

1. On the interdependence of belief in fairies and the perception of fairies see Rojcewicz (1991), as in footnote 8 of Chapter Two.

2. Westwood (2009), a folklorist, has collected tales of the phenomenon of "fairy tunes" being received from the "Good People," being composed and/or learned by musicians, often in altered states of consciousness. Known fairy sites, usually mounds and earthworks, or near the sounds of water, are the places where musicians and singers have heard and learned fairy music. "The tune may be secretly learned and stolen from the fairies, or the musician may be wanted by the fairies to play at one of their festivities and the tune is gifted to him." (138)

3. Flower (1944) distinguishes between fairies' own music and music which they shared with people. Westwood (2009:140) discusses two kinds of fairy music, traditional jigs and reels, and fairy music with an "ethereal, otherworld" nature. This latter music may be the kind of "strange" music Marc is discussing here.

Chapter Seventeen – Consciousness, Evolution, Planet

1. At a less metaphysical level, Taylor (2010) traces the development of "green religions" in North America and their replacement for many of traditional religious views. Fairy Faith adherents have not replaced traditional religious worldviews, only modified or added to them.

Taylor also considers the (planetary) future, hypothesizing about the "winner" of the conflict between radical environmentalist green religion(s) and continuing environmental decline. As understandable, he reaches no definitive conclusions.

2. Wilber (1983), who has systematized in detail "structural" realms of consciousness and the potentially progressive evolution of spiritual consciousness writes:

> ….Ontogenetically…an individual today can develop beyond exclusively rational forms of mentation to some sort of higher stage or stages of consciousness as yet unspecified. Phylogenetically, it means that evolution

is still continuing and that human culture at large faces further and higher levels of (r)evolutionary structuralization.

But that idea reminds us immediately of Hegel, who saw history as eventually transcending mental self-consciousness in the absolute knowledge of spirit as spirit. There are Aurobindo, who maintained that evolution is driving toward supermind realization; Teilhard de Chardin, who saw it culminating in omega point, or Christ consciousness at large; and the great Russian philosopher Berdyaev, who concluded that evolution moves from subconsciousness to self-consciousness to superconsciousness (his words). Despite the excesses of some of these presentations, the point is that the general concept of evolution continuing beyond its present stage into some legitimately transrational structures is not a totally outrageous notion.

Based upon his studies of the psychology of Buddhism, Hinduism, Sufism, Kabbalah, neo-Confucianism, mystical Christianity, and other esoteric traditions he concludes:

> ... they were perfectly aware of the general features of the level-structures so intensively investigated in the West (i.e., physical, sensorimotor, emotional-sexual, lower mental, and logic-rational). Nonetheless, they universally claimed that these levels by no means exhausted the spectrum of consciousness – there were, beyond the physical, emotional, and mental levels, higher levels of structural organization and integration.
>
> For instance, Vedanta Hinduism claims there are six major structure-levels of consciousness. The first and lowest is called annamayakosha, literally the level made of physical food, or the physical body. The second is pranamayakosha, the level of emotional-sexuality (prana is an almost exact equivalent of libido). The third is manomayakosha, the level of mind. This level also includes, besides rationality, the "dream aspects" of mentation; dreams, says Shankara, are basically wish-fulfillments, composed of the person's "fantasy and desires." The fourth is vijnanamayakosha, higher mental or transrational or intuitive cognition, the beginning of actual spiritual insight. The fifth is anandamayakosha, the level of ecstatic illumination-insight. The highest state is turiya, or Brahman-Atman itself, although it is not so much one level among other levels but the ground, reality, or suchness of all levels (tathata, the Buddhists call it.)...
>
> The conclusion was that it is indeed plausible that there are higher stages of structural organization and integration, and that these higher stages increasingly display what can only be called a spiritual or transcendental tone. (74-5)

3. The phrase "New Age" itself speaks to collective changes in consciousness as a result of changes in positions of the sun and stars during the precession of the spring equinox bringing on the Age of Aquarius. The precession of the spring equinox is:

> a slow westward motion of the point of the spring equinox along the apparent path of the sun's annual motion among the fixed stars, caused by the conical motion of the earth's axis. A complete revolution takes about 25,800 years, called the 'Platonic Year'. Consequently, the spring equinox moves clockwise through the twelve zodiacal signs, the precession through each taking an average of about 2,150 years, a 'Platonic Month'."(Main 2002: 220)

Even Carl Jung expected changes in the collective psyche as a consequence of astronomical changes.

4. Elgin (1980) points to how the industrial period, in its environmental degradation, creates a "disruptive flow" in nature. He calls for a "voluntary simplicity":

> Economic necessity (which dictates either enforced or voluntarily assumed simplicity), Taoistic 'necessity' (which impels us to evolve our awareness to assume evolutionary trusteeship), and human possibility (to evolve to higher levels of awareness/consciousness) all combine to create what seems to be a gentle but increasingly insistent evolutionary imperative toward individual and societal transcendence. (254-5)

He suggests that during this 'new frontier' of social and human possibility that we must develop two major ethics:

> First is Self-Realization Ethic, which asserts that each person's proper goal is the evolutionary development of his fullest human potential. Accordingly, this ethic insists that social institutions provide an environment supportive of self-realization. Second, we must develop an Ecological Ethic, which accepts our earth as limited, recognizes the underlying unity of the human race, and perceives man as an integral part of the natural environment. (255)

5. The Hindu Vedas speak of different *yuga*s, eons of time during which there are long periods of human spiritual ascent, and of descent. The yuga cycle, like the Platonic Month and Platonic year mentioned in footnote 3 above, is seen as the precession of the equinox, caused by celestial motion.

According to a newer version of the yuga cycle by yogi Swami Sri Yukteswar Giri (1949) in *The Holy Science*, the sun takes about 24,000 years to revolve in its orbit around a star. Depending upon where the sun is in its orbit, there are periods in which man can comprehend the "mysteries of Spirit" or not.

BIBLIOGRAPHY

Abram, David. 1996 *The Spell of the Sensuous: Perception and Language in a More-Than-Human World.* New York: Random House.

—. 2010 *Becoming Animal: An Earthly Cosmology.* New York: Pantheon Books.

AE 1965 *The Candle of Vision.* New Hyde Park, NY: University Books.

Anderson, Rosemarie. 1998 *Celtic Oracles: A New System for Spiritual Growth and Divination.* New York: Harmony Books.

Ashlag, Baruch Rav. 2008 'Concerning the Importance of Society.' In Michael Laitman, ed. *Kabbalah for the Student.* Toronto: Laitman Kabbalah Publishers. 305-7.

Assagioli, Roberto. 1989 'Self-Realization And Psychological Disturbances.' In Stanislav Grof and Christina Grof, eds. *Spiritual Emergency: When Personal Transformation Becomes a Crisis.* Los Angeles, CA: Jeremy P. Tarcher, Inc. 27-48.

Basso, Keith. 1996 *Wisdom Sits In Places: Landscape and Language Among the Western Apache.* Albuquerque, NM: University of New Mexico Press.

Barrett, J.L. and F.C. Keil. 1996 'Conceptualizing a nonnatural entity: anthropomorphism in God concepts.' *Cognitive Psychology* 31:219-47

Bastine, Michael and Mason Winfield. 2011 *Iroquois Supernatural: Talking Animals and Medicine People.* Rochester, Vermont: Bear & Company.

Bauman, Z. 1992 *Intimations of Postmodernity.* London: Routledge.

Beddoe, Stella. 1998 'Fairy Writing and Writers.' In Jeremy Maas et. al, eds.*Victorian Fairy Painting.* London: Royal Academy of Arts. 23-31.

Beebe, John. 2003 'Response to William McGuire.' *Journal of Analytical Psychology* 48:447- 452 (following McGuire 2003).

Benedict, Ruth. 1922 'The Concept of the Guardian Spirit in North America.' *Memoirs of the American Anthropological Association* 29, 1-7.

Bernstein, Jerome. 2005 *Living in the Borderland: The Evolution of Consciousness and the Challenge of Healing Trauma.* London: Routledge.

Bird-David, Nurit. 2002 "'Animism' revisited: Personhood, environment, and relational Epistemology.' In Graham Harvey, ed. *Readings in Indigenous Religions*. London: Continuum Press. 72-105.

Bishop, Donald H., ed. 1995 *Mysticism and the Mystical Experience: East and West.* Cranbury, NJ: Associated University Presses, Inc.

Blain, Jeremy. 2002 *Nine Worlds of Seid-Magic: Ecstasy and Neo-shamanism in North European Paganism.* London: Routledge.

Blain, Jeremy, Douglas Ezzy and Graham Harvey. 2004 'Introduction.' In Jeremy Blain, Douglas Ezzy and Graham Harvey, eds. R*esearching Paganisms.* Walnut Creek, CA: Altamira Press. 1-12.

Blain, Jeremy, Douglas Ezzy and Graham Harvey, eds. 2004 *Researching Paganisms*. Walnut Creek, CA: Altamira Press.

Blakney, Raymond Bernard. 1941 *Meister Eckhart: A Modern Translation.* New York: Harper & Row.

Blavatsky, Madame. 1988 *The Secret Doctrine: The Synthesis of Science, Religion and Philosophy.* London: Theosophical Publishing Co.

Bock, Heike, Jorg Feuchter, Michi Knecht, eds. 2008 *Religion and Its Other: Secular and Sacral Concepts and Practices in Interaction.* Frankfurt/New York: Campus Verlag.

Bourke, Angela. 1999 *The Burning of Bridget Cleary: A True Story*. New York: Penguin Books.

Bown, Nicola. 2001 *Fairies in Nineteenth-Century Art and Literature.* Cambridge: Cambridge University Press.

Boyer, Pascal. 2000 'Functional origins of religious concepts: conceptual and strategic selection in evolved minds.' (Malinowski Lecture 1999) Journal of the Royal Anthropological Institute 6:195-214.

Boyer, Pascal and Brian Bergstrom. 2008 'Evolutionary Perspectives on Religion.' In William Durham, Donald Brenneis, and Peter Ellison, eds. *Annual Review of Anthropology.* Palo Alto, CA : Annual Reviews.

Boyer, Pascal and Sheila Walker. 2000 'Intuitive Ontology and Cultural Input in the Acquisition of Religious Concepts.' In Karl Rosengren, Carl Johnson, and Paul Harris eds. *Imagining the Impossible: Magical, Scientific, and Religious Thinking in Children*. Cambridge: Cambridge University Press. 130-156.

Briggs, Katharine. 1976 *A Dictionary of Fairies*. London: Allen Lane, Penguin Books Ltd.

Bronson, Matthew and Fields, Tina, eds. 2009 *So What? Now What? The Anthropology Of Consciousness Responds To A World In Crisis*. Newcastle upon Tyne, UK: Cambridge Scholars Publishing.

Brown, Thomas Kingsley. 2003 'Mystical Experiences, American Culture, and Conversion to Christian Spiritualism.' In Andrew Buckser and

Stephen Glazier, eds. *The Anthropology of Religious Conversion.* Lanham, MD: Rowman and Littlefield. 133-145.

Bucke, Richard Maurice. 1991(1901) *Cosmic Consciousness: A Study in the Evolution of the Human Mind.* New York: Penguin.

Buckser, Andrew and Glazier, Stephen, eds. 2003 *The Anthropology of Religious Conversion.* Lanham, MD: Rowman and Littlefield.

Butler, Jenny. 2011 'Irish Neo-Paganism: World-View and Identity.' In Olivia Cosgrove, Laurence Cos, Carmen Kuhling and Peter Mulholland, eds. *Ireland's New Religious Movements.* Newcastle upon Tyne, UK: Cambridge Scholars Publishing. 111- 130.

Campbell, Alan T. 2003 'Submitting.' In Graham Harvey, ed. *Shamanism: A Reader.* New York: Routledge. 123-43.

Campbell, Joseph. 1971 *The Portable Jung.* New York: Viking Press.

Campbell, Ronald. 1976 *The Concept of Man in Integral Psychology.* University Microfilms: Ann Arbor.

Campbell, Ronald and Philip Staniford. 1978 'Transpersonal Anthropology.' *Phoenix: The Journal of Transpersonal Anthropology* 2(1):28-40.

Christian Jr., William A. 1981 *Apparitions in Late Medieval and Renaissance Spain.* Princeton, NJ: Princeton University Press.

Conan Doyle, Arthur. 1921 *The Coming of the Fairies.* New York: Samuel Weiser, Inc.

Corbin, Henry. 1994 *The Man of Light in the Renaissance.* New Lebanon, NY: Omega Publications.

—. 2000 *Avicenna and the Visionary Recital.* Ann Arbor: UMI Books on Demand.

Cosgrove, Olivia, Laurence Cos, Carmen Kuhling and Peter Mulholland, eds. 2011 *Ireland's New Religious Movements.* Newcastle upon Tyne, UK: Cambridge Scholars Publishing.

Cosgrove, Olivia, Laurence Cos, Carmen Kuhling and Peter Mulholland . 2011 'Editors' Introduction: Understanding Ireland's New Religious Movements.' In Olivia Cosgrove, Laurence Cos, Carmen Kuhling and Peter Mulholland, eds. *Ireland's New Religious Movements.* Newcastle upon Tyne, UK: Cambridge Scholars Publishing. 1-27.

Crapanzano, Vincent. 1980 *Tuhami: Portrait of a Moroccan.* Chicago: University of Chicago Press.

D'Andrade, R.G. 1992 'Schemes and motivation.' In R.G. D'Andrade and C. Strauss, eds. *Human motives and cultural models.* Cambridge: Cambridge University Press. 23-44

d'Aquili, E. and A. Newberg. 1999 *The Mystical Mind.* Minneapolis: Fortress Press.

de Chardin, Pierre Teilhard. 1959 *The Phenomenon of Man.* New York: Harper & Row.

Deikman, Arthur. 1966 'Deautomatization and the mystic experience.' *Psychiatry* 29, 324-338.

Eggan, D. 1966 'Hopi Dreams in Cultural Perspective.' In G.E .von Grunebaum and R. Caillois, eds. *The Dream and Human Societies.* Berkeley, CA: University of California Press.

Elgin, Duane. 1980 'The Tao of Personal and Social Transformation.' In Roger Walsh and Frances Vaughn, eds. *Beyond Ego: Transpersonal Dimensions in Psychology.* Los Angeles: J.P. Tarcher, Inc. 248-256.

Ezzy, Douglas. 2004 'Religious Ethnography: Practicing the Witch's Craft.' In Jeremy Blain, Douglas Ezzy and Graham Harvey, eds. *Researching Paganisms.* Walnut Creek, CA: Altamira Press. 113-128.

Evans-Wentz, W.Y. 1911 *The Fairy-Faith in Celtic Countries.* London: Oxford University Press.

—. 1927 (ed.) *The Tibetan Book of the Dead.* London: Oxford University Press.

—. 1935 (1958) *Tibetan yoga and secret doctrines or, Seven books of wisdom of the great path, according to the late Lāma Kazi Dawa-Samdup's English rendering.* London, Oxford University Press.

—. 1951 *Tibet's great yogi, Milarepa: a biography from the Tibetan.* English rendering (2d ed.), edited with introd. and annotations by W. Y. Evans-Wentz, London, New York : Oxford University Press, 1951.

—. 1954 *The Tibetan book of the great liberation.* According to English renderings by Sardar Bahādur S. W. Laden La and by the Lāmas Karma Sumdhon Paul, Lobzang Mingyur Dorje, and Kazi Dawa-Samdup. Introductions, annotations, and editing by W. Y. Evans-Wentz. With psychological commentary by C. Jung. London, New York: Oxford University Press.

Faivre, Antoine. 1992 'Introduction I.' In *Modern Esoteric Spirituality.* Eds. Antoine Faivre and Jacob Needleman. New York: Crossroad Publishing Company. xi-xxii.

Feinberg, Richard. 1996 'Spirit Encounters on a Polynesian Outlier: Anuta, Solomon Islands.' In Jeannette Marie Mageo and Alan Howard, eds. *Spirits in Culture, History, and Mind.* London: Routledge. 99-120.

Fine, Lawrence. 2003 *Physician of the Soul, Healer of the Cosmos: Isaac Luria and His Kabbalistic Fellowship.* Stanford, CA: Stanford University Press.

Flower, Robin. 1944 *The Western Island or The Great Blasket.* Oxford: Clarendon.

Forman, Robert K. 1990 *The Problem of Pure Consciousness*. New York: Oxford University Press.
—. 1998 'Introduction: Mystical Consciousness, the Innate Capacity, and the Perennial Philosophy.' In Robert Forman, ed. *The Innate Capacity: Mysticism, Psychology, and Philosophy*.45-81.
Forman, Robert K., ed. 1998 *The Innate Capacity: Mysticism, Psychology, and Philosophy*. New York: Oxford University Press.
Froud, Brian and Alan Lee. 1979 *Fairies*. New York: Harry N. Abrams, Inc.
—. 1998 *Good Fairies, Bad Fairies*. New York: Simon & Schuster.
Gaffin, Dennis. 1996 *In Place: Spatial and Social Order in a Faeroe Islands Community*. Prospect Heights, IL: Waveland Press.
Garrett, Susan R. 2008 *No Ordinary Angel: Celestial Spirits and Christian Claims about Jesus.* New Haven, CT: Yale University Press.
Glazier, Stephen D. 2003 'Limin' wid Jah': Spiritual Baptists Who Became Rastafarians and Then Became Spiritual Baptists Again.' In Andrew Buckser and Stephen Glazier, eds. *The Anthropology of Religious Conversion*. Lanham, MD: Rowman and Littlefield. 149-170.
—. 2011 'Anthropology and Religious Belief." In Phillips Stevens, Jr., ed. *Anthropology of Religion: Critical Concepts in Religious Studies*. 4 vols. London: Routledge. 32-37.
Goody, Jack. 1996 *The East in the West*. Cambridge: Cambridge University Press.
Goulet, Jean-Guy. 1994 'Dreams and Visions in Other Lifeworlds.' In David Young and Jean-Guy Goulet, eds. *Being Changed: The Anthropology of Extraordinary Experience*. Peterborough, Ontario: Broadview Press.16-38.
Goulet, Jean-Guy and David Young. 1994 'Theoretical and Methodological Issues.' In David Young and Jean-Guy Goulet, eds. *Being Changed: The Anthropology of Extraordinary Experience*. Peterborough, Ontario: Broadview Press. 298-235.
Greenwood, Susan. 2000 *Magic, Witchcraft and the Otherworld.* Oxford: Berg.
—. 2009 *The Anthropology of Magic*. Oxford: Berg.
Grindal, Bruce T. 1983 'Into the heart of sisala experience: witnessing death divination.' *Journal of Anthropological Research* 39(1):60-80.
Grinder, J. and R. Bandler. 1976 *The Structure of Magic II: A Book about Communication and Change*. Palo Alto, CA: Science and Behavior Books.

Grof, M.D., Stanislav and Christina Grof, eds. 1989 *Spiritual Emergency: When Personal Transformation Becomes a Crisis.* Los Angeles, CA: Jeremy P. Tarcher, Inc. Grossinger, Richard

—. 1980 *Planet Medicine: From Stone Age Shamanism to Post-Industrial Healing.* Berkeley, CA: North Atlantic Books.

Guthrie, S.E. 1993 *Faces in the Clouds: A New Theory in Religion.* New York: Oxford University Press.

Hallowell, A. Irving. 1960 'Ojibwa Ontology, Behavior, and World View.' in Stanley Diamond, ed. *Culture in History: Essays in Honor of Paul Radin.* Columbia University Press: 19-52. (Reprinted in Graham Harvey, ed. 2002:18-49).

Harner, Michael. 1980 *The Way of the Shaman: A Guide to Power and Healing.* New York: Bantam Books.

Hart, Tobin, Peter L. Nelson, and Kaissa Puhakka. 2000 'Introduction.' In Tobin Hart, Peter L. Nelson, and Kaissa Puhakka, eds. *Transpersonal Knowing: Exploring the Horizon of Consciousness.* Albany, NY: State University of New York Press. 1-9.

Tobin Hart, Peter L. Nelson, and Kaissa Puhakka, eds. 2000 *Transpersonal Knowing: Exploring the Horizon of Consciousness.* Albany, NY: State University of New York Press.

Harvey, Graham. 1997 *Contemporary Paganism: Listening People, Speaking Earth.* New York: New York University Press.

—. 2003 'General Introduction.' In Graham Harvey, ed. *Shamanism: a reader.* London: Routledge. 1-23.

—. 2006 *Animism: Respecting the Living World.* New York: Columbia University Press.

Harvey, Graham, ed. 2002 *Readings in Indigenous Religion.* London: Continuum.

Heschel, Abraham J. 1951 *Man is Not Alone: A Philosophy of Religion.* New York: Farrar, Straus, and Young.

—. 1955 *God in Search of Man: A Philosophy of Judaism.* New York: Farrar, Straus, and Cudahy.

—. 1959 *Between God And Man: An Interpretation of Judaism.* New York: Free Press.

—. 1962 *The Prophets.* New York: Harper & Row.

—. 1965 *Who is Man?* Stanford, CA: Stanford University Press.

Hillman, James. 1971 'Psychology: Monotheistic or Polytheistic?' *Spring* 193-208, 230-232 (Expanded in appendix to *The New Polytheism*, by David Miller, 109-142. Dallas: Spring Publications, 1981)

—. 1975 *Re-Visioning Psychology.* New York: Harper & Row.

—. 1985 *Anima: An Anatomy of a Personified Notion.* Dallas: Spring Publications.

—. 1996 *The Soul's Code: In Search of Character and Calling.* New York: Random House.

Hoff, Benjamin. 1995 *The Singing Creek Where the Willows Grow: The Mystical Nature Diary of Opal Whiteley.* With a biography and an afterword. New York: Penguin.

Howard, Alan and Jeannette Marie Mageo. 1996 'Introduction.' In Jeannette Marie Mageo and Alan Howard, eds. *Spirits in Culture, History, and Mind.* London: Routledge. 1-10.

Hume, Lynne. 2007 *Opening Doorways to other realities through the senses.* Oxford: Berg.

Huss, Boaz. 2008 'The Formation of Jewish Mysticism and Its Impact on the Reception of Rabbi Abraham Abulafia in Contemporary Kabbalah.' In Heike Bock, Jorg Feuchter, and Michi Knecht, eds. *Religion and Its Other: Secular and Sacral Concepts and Practices in Interaction.* Frankfurt/New York: Campus Verlag. 142-162.

Husserl, Edmund. 1931 *Ideas: General Introduction to Pure Phenomenology.* New York: McMillan

—. 1977 *Phenomenological Psychology.* The Hague: Marinus Nijhoff.

Idowu, E.B. 1973 *African Traditional Religion.* Mary Knoll, NY: Orbis Books.

Ingold, Tim. 2000 *The Perception of the Environment: Essays in livelihood, dwelling, and skill.* London: Routledge.

Isaac, Stephen, ed. 1995 *Flower A. Newhouse's Angels of Nature.* Wheaton, IL: Quest Books.

Isaiasz, Vera. 2008 'The Devil in Spandau: Demonology between Religion and Magic at the End of the Sixteenth Century.' In Heike Bock, Jorg Feuchter, and Michi Knecht, eds. *Religion and Its Other: Secular and Sacral Concepts and Practices in Interaction.* Frankfurt/New York: Campus Verlag. 165-184.

Jakobsen, Merete Demant. 1999 *Shamanism: Traditional and Contemporary Approaches to the Mastery of Spirits and Healing.* Oxford; Berghahn Books.

James, William. 1985 (1902) *The Varieties of Religious Experience.* Cambridge, MA: Harvard University Press.

Jung, Carl. 1966 *Two Essays on Analytical Psychology* (2nd edition). Princeton, NJ: Princeton University Press.

Kakar, Sudhir. 1991 *The Analyst and the Mystic: Psychoanalytic Reflections on Religion and Mysticism.* Chicago: University of Chicago Press.

Kalff, Martin M. 1978 'Dakinis in the Cakrasamvara Tradition.' In Martin Brauen and Per Kvaerne, eds. *Tibetan Studies Presented at the Seminar of Young Tibetologists, Zurich, June 26-July1, 1977.* Zurich: Volkerkundemuseum der Universitat Zurich. 149-62.

Katz, Nathan. 1992 'Dakini and Anima: On Tantric Deities and Jungian Archetypes.' In Daniel J. Meckel and Robert L. Moore., eds. *Self and Liberation: The Jung-Buddhist Dialogue*. Chicago: Paulist Press. 302-29.

Katz, Steven T., ed. 1983 *Mysticism and Religious Traditions*. New York: Oxford University Press.

—. 1992 *Mysticism and Language*. New York: Oxford University Press.

Keightley, Thomas. 1978 (orig 1880) *The World Guide to Gnomes, Fairies, Elves, and Other Little People*. New York: Crown Publishers.

Kinney, Jay, ed. 2004 *The Inner West: An Introduction to the Hidden Wisdom of the West*. New York: Penguin Group.

Kirk, Robert. 1893 (1815, originally 1691) *The Secret Commonwealth of Elves, Fauns and Fairies.*

Knecht, Michi and Jorg Feuchter. 2008 'Introduction: Reconfiguring Religion and Its Other.' In Heike Bock, Jorg Feuchter, and Michi Knecht, eds. *Religion and Its Other: Secular and Sacral Concepts and Practices in Interaction*. Frankfurt/New York: Campus Verlag. 9-20.

Kohut, Heinz. 1985 *Self Psychology and the Humanities: Reflections on a New Psychoanalytic Approach*. New York: W.W. Norton & Company.

Kornfield, Jack. 1989 'Obstacles and Vicissitudes In Spiritual Practice.' In Stanislav Grof and Christina Grof, eds. *Spiritual Emergency: When Personal Transformation Becomes a Crisis*. Los Angeles, CA: Jeremy P. Tarcher, Inc. 137-169.

Krippner, S. 1972 'The Plateau Experience: A. H. Maslow and Others.' *Journal of Transpersonal Psychology* 4(2):107-120.

Lambek, Michael. 1996 'Afterword: Spirits and Their Histories.' In Jeannette Marie Mageo and Alan Howard, eds. *Spirits in Culture, History, and Mind*. London: Routledge. 237-249.

Larkin, David, ed. 1978 *Faeries*: Described and Illustrated by Brian Froud and Alan Lee. New York: Harry N. Abrams, Inc.

Laughlin Jr., Charles D. 1994a 'Apodicticity: The Problem of Absolute Certainty in Transpersonal Ethnology.' *Anthropology and Humanism* 19(2): 115-129.

—. 1994b 'Psychic Energy & Transpersonal Experience: A biogenetic structural account of Tibetan Dumo Yoga Practice.' In David Young and Jean-Guy Goulet, eds. *Being Changed: The Anthropology of*

Extraordinary Experience. Peterborough, Ontario: Broadview Press. 99-134.

—. 1994c 'Transpersonal Anthropology, Then and Now.' *Transpersonal Review*(1):7-10

Laughlin, C.D and E.G. d'Aquili. 1974 *Biogenetic Structuralism*. New York: Columbia University Press.

Laughlin, C.D., J. McManus, J., and d'Aquili, E. 1992 *Brain, Symbol, and Experience: Toward a Neurophenomenology of Consciousness*. Boston: Shambhala.

Laughlin, Charles D., John McManus, and Jon Shearer. 1983 'Dreams, Trance and Visions: What a Transpersonal Anthropology Might Look Like.' *Phoenix: Journal of Transpersonal Anthropology*. VII (1 & 2):141-159.

Lee, Raymond L. M. 1987 'Amulets and Anthropology: A Paranormal Encounter with Malay Magic.' *Anthropology and Humanism Quarterly* 12 (3&4). 69-74.

Leenhardt, Maurice. 1979 [1947] *Do Kamo: Person and Myth in the Melanesian World*. Translated by Basia Miller Gulati. Chicago: University of Chicago Press.

Letcher, Andy. 2001 'The Scouring of the Shire: Fairies, Trolls and Pixies in Eco-Protest Culture.' *Folklore,* vol. 112, 147161.

—. 2004 'Bardism and the Performance of Paganism: Implications for the Performance of Research.' In Jeremy Blain, Douglas Ezzy and Graham Harvey, eds. *Researching Paganisms*. Walnut Creek, CA: Altamira Press.15-41

—. 2006 'There's Bulldozers in the Fairy Garden': Re-enchantment Narratives within British Eco-Paganism.' In Lynne Hume and Kathleen McPhillips, eds. *Popular Spiritualities: The Politics of Contemporary Enchantment*. Surrey, UK: Ashgate. 175-186.

Levy, Robert I, Jeannette Marie Mageo, and Alan Howard. 1996 'Gods, Spirits, and History: A Theoretical Perspective.' In *Spirits in Culture, History, and Mind*. Ed. Jeannette Marie Mageo and Alan Howard. London: Routledge. 11-27.

Levy-Bruhl, Lucien. 1926 *How Natives Think*. Translated by Lilian A. Clare. London: Allen & Unwin.

—. 1938 *L'Experience mystique et les symbols chez les primitives*. Paris: Alcan.

Lossiah, Lynn King. 1998 *The secrets and mysteries of the Cherokee Little People: Yunwi Tsunsdi*. Cherokee, NC: Cherokee Publications.

Lowie, Robert H. 1954 'The Vision Quest Among the North American Indians.' Reprinted in William Lessa and Evon Vogt, eds. *Reader in*

Comparative Religion: An Anthropological Approach (1965). New York: Harper and Row.194-197.

Luhrmann, Tanya. 1989 *Persuasion of the Witch's Craft: Ritual Magic in Contemporary England.* Cambridge, MA: Harvard University Press.

Maas, Jeremy, Pamela White Trimpe, Charlotte Gere, and others, eds. 1997 *Victorian Fairy Painting.* London: Royal Academy of Arts.

Macdonald, J.L. 1981 'Theoretical Contributions in Transpersonal Anthropology.' *Phoenix: The Journal of Transpersonal Anthropology* 5(1):31-47.

Mack, John E. 1992 'Psychoanalysis and the Self: Toward a Spiritual Point of View.' In Leroy S. Rouner, ed. *Selves, People, and Persons: What Does It Mean to Be a Self?* Notre Dame, IN: University of Notre Dame Press. 169-186.

Maffesoli, Michel. 1991 'The Ethic of Aesthetics.' *Theory, Culture and Society* 8:7-20.

Mageo, Jeannette and Alan Howard, eds. 1996 *Spirits in Culture, History, and Mind.* London: Routledge.

Main, Roderick. 2002 'Religion, science and the New Age.' In Joanne Pearson, ed. *Belief Beyond Boundaries: Wicca, Celtic Spirituality and The New Age.* Burlington, VT: The Open University and Ashgate Publishing. 173-222.

Maramay, Marc and Young, Val. 2007 *Earth Will Be Reborn.* Winchester, UK: O Books.

Marcus, George. 1999 *Critical Anthropology Now: Unexpected Contexts, Shifting Constituencies, Changing Agendas.* Santa Fe: SAR Press.

Martineau, Jane, ed. 1997 *Victorian Fairy Painting.* London: Royal Academy of Arts and Merrill Holberton Publishers.

Maslow, A. H. 1968 *Toward a Psychology of Being* (2nd edition). Princeton, NY: Van Nostrand.

McCoy, Edain. 2000 *A Witch's Guide to Faery Folk: Reclaiming our Working Relationship with Invisible Helpers.* St.Paul, MN: Llewellyn Publications.

McFague, Sallie. 2010 'A New Climate for Theology: God, the World, and Global Warming.,' *Tikkun* March/April. 53 (adapted from chapter 4 of same title 2008 Fortress Press.)

McGuire, William. 2003 'Jung, Evans-Wentz and various other gurus.' *Journal of Analytical Psychology* 48:433-445.

McManus, J. 1975 'Psychopathology as Errors in Cognitive Adaptation.' Presented at Annual Meeting of American Anthropological Association, San Francisco.

Mills, A. 1992 'Are children with imaginary playmates and children said to remember previous lives cross-culturally comparable categories?' Paper presented at the American Anthropological Association, San Francisco.

Milton, Kay. 2002 *Loving Nature: Towards An Ecology of Emotion.* London: Routledge.

Moore, Thomas. 1989 *A Blue Fire: Selected Writings by James Hillman.* New York; Harper & Row Publishers.

Morris, Brian. 2006 *Religion and Anthropology: A Critical Introduction.* Cambridge: Cambridge University Press.

Mullin, Kay. 1997 *Wondrous Land: The Faery Faith in Ireland.* Berks, England: Capall Bann Publishing.

Myers, Fred. 1986 *Pintupi Country, Pintupi Self: Sentiment, Place and Politics among Western Desert Aborigines.* Washington, D.C.: Smithsonian Institution Press.

Naess, Arne. 1973 'The shallow and the deep, long-range ecology movement: a Summary.' *Inquiry* 16:95-100.

—. 1989 *Ecology, Community and Lifestyle: Outline of an Ecosophy.* Cambridge, England: Cambridge University Press.

Narvaez, Peter, ed. 1991 *The Good People: New Fairylore Essays.* Lexington, KY: University of Kentucky Press..

Needham, Rodney. 1972 *Belief, Language, and Experience.* Chicago: University of Chicago Press.

Needleman, Jacob. 1992 'Introduction II.' In eds. Antoine Faivre and Jacob Needleman, eds. *Modern Esoteric Spirituality.* New York: Crossroad Publishing Company. xxiii-xxx.

Neitz, Mary Jo. 2002 'Walking between the Worlds: Permeable Boundaries, Ambiguous Identities.' In James Spickard, James, J. Shawn Landres, and Meredith McGuire, eds. *Personal Knowledge and Beyond: Reshaping the Ethnography of Religion.* New York: New York University Press. 33-46.

Nelson, Peter L. 2000 'Mystical Experience and Radical Deconstruction: Through the Ontological Looking Glass.' In Tobin Hart, Peter Nelson and Kaisa Puhakka, eds. *Transpersonal Knowing: Exploring the Horizon of Consciousness.* Albany, NY: State University of New York Press. 55-84.

Nelson, Richard K. 1983 *Make Prayers to the Raven.* Chicago: University of Chicago Press.

Nelstrop, Louise. 2009 *Christian Mysticism: An Introduction to Contemporary Theoretical Approaches.* Burlington, VT: Ashgate Publishing.

Newhouse, Flower A. 1955 *The Kingdom Of The Shining Ones*. Escondido, CA: The Christward Ministry.
—. 1975 *Insights into Reality*. (ed. by Stephen and Phyllis Isaac) Escondido, CA: The Christward Ministry.
O'Donohue, John. 1997 *Anam Cara: Spiritual Wisdom from the Celtic World*. London: Bantam Press.
O'Driscoll, Robert, ed. 1982 *The Celtic Consciousness*. New York: George Braziller, Inc.
O Giollain, Diarmuid. 1991 'The Fairy Belief and Official Religion in Ireland.' In Peter Narvaez, ed. *The Good People: New Fairylore Essays*. Lexington, KY: University Press of Kentucky.199-214.
Orion, Loretta. 1995 *Never Again the Burning Times – Paganism Revisited*. Prospect Heights, IL: Waveland Press.
Ornstein, Paul H. 1978 *The Search For The Self: Selected Writings of Heinz Kohut:1950-1978*. New York: International Universities Press.
Otto, Rudolph. 1923 *The Idea of the Holy: An Inquiry into the non-rational factor in the idea of the Divine and its relation to the rational*. London: Oxford University Press.
Ouspensky, P.D. 1947 *In Search of the Miraculous: Fragments of an Unknown Teaching*. New York: Harcourt Brace.
Pearson, Joanne, ed. 2002 *Belief Beyond Boundaries: Wicca, Celtic Spirituality and The New Age*. Burlington, VT: The Open University and Ashgate Publishing.
Pelletier, Kenneth . 1978 *Toward a Science of Consciousness*. New York: Delacorte Press.
Petroff, Elizabeth Alvilda, ed. 1981 *Medieval Women's Visionary Literature*. Oxford: Oxford University Press.
Piaget, Jean. 1932 *The Moral Development of the Child*. London: Routledge and Kegan Paul.
Pogacnik, Marko. 1996 *Nature Spirits and Elemental Beings: Working with the Intelligence in Nature*. Findhorn, Scotland: Findhorn Press.
Prechtel, Martin. 1998 *Secrets of the Talking Jaguar: A Mayan Shaman's Journey to the Heart of the Indigenous Soul*. New York: Tarcher/Putnam.
Prince, Ruth and Riches, David. 2000 *The New Age in Glastonbury: The Construction of Religious Movements*. Oxford: Berghahn Books.
Puhakka, Kaisa. 2000 'An Invitation to Authentic Knowing.' In Tobin Hart, Peter Nelson and Kaisa Puhakka, eds. *Transpersonal Knowing: Exploring the Horizon of Consciousness*. Albany,NY: State University of New York Press. 11-30.

Raff, Jeffrey. 2000 *Jung and the Alchemical Imagination*. Berwick, Maine: Nicolas-Hays, Inc.

Raff, Jeffrey and Vocatura, Linda Bonnington. 2002 *Healing the Wounded God: finding your personal guide on your way to individuation and beyond*. York Beach, Maine: Nicolas-Hays, Inc.

Raj, Selva T. and Dempsey, Corinne G. 2010 'Introduction: Ritual Levity in South Asian Traditions.' In Selva T. Raj and Corinne G. Dempsey, eds. *Sacred Play: Ritual Levity and Humor in South Asian Religions*. Albany, NY: State University of New York. 1-18.

Raj, Selva T. and Dempsey, Corinne G., eds. 2010 *Sacred Play: Ritual Levity and Humor in South Asian Religions*. Albany, NY: State University of New York Press.

Rambo, Lewis R. 1993 *Understanding Religious Conversion*. New Haven, CN: Yale University Press.

Redfield, James. 1993 *The Celestine Prophecy: An Adventure*. New York: Warner Books.

—. 1997 *The Celestine Vision: Living the New Spiritual Awareness*. New York: Warner Books.

Robbins, Richard H. 2009 *Cultural Anthropology: A Problem-Based Approach*. Fifth Edition. Belmont, CA: Wadsworth Publishing.

Rojcewicz, Peter M. 1991 'Between One Eye Blink and the Next: Fairies, UFOs, and Problems of Knowledge.' In Peter Narvaez, ed.. *The Good People: New Fairylore Essays*. University Press of Kentucky. 479-514.

Roney-Dougal, Serena. 2003 *The Faery Faith: An Integration of Science with Spirit*. London: Green Magic.

Rorty, R. 1980 *Philosophy and the Mirror of Nature*. Princeton: Princeton University Press.

Roszak, T. 1975 *Unfinished Animal*. New York: Harper and Row.

Rose, Deborah Bird. 2000 *Dingo Makes Us Human: Life and Land in an Australian Aboriginal Culture*. Cambridge: Cambridge University Press.

Rosengren, Karl S., Johnson, Carl N., and Harris, Paul L., eds. 2000 *Imagining the Impossible: Magical, Scientific, and Religious Thinking In Children*. Cambridge, UK: Cambridge University Press.

Rothschild, Fritz A. 1959 *Between God and Man: From the Writings of Abraham Joshua Heschel*. New York: Harper & Row.

Rouner, Leroy S., ed. 1992 *Selves, People, and Persons: What Does It Mean to Be a Self?* Notre Dame, IN: University of Notre Dame Press.

Rountree, K. 2004 *Embracing the Witch and the Goddess*. London: Routledge.

Ruel, Malcolm. 1982 'Christians as Believers.' In John Davis, ed. *Religious Organization and Religious Experience*. London: Academic Press. 9-31.
Salomonsen, Jone. 2004 'Methods of Compassion or Pretension?' The Challenges of Conducting Fieldwork in Modern Magical Communities.' In Jeremy Blain, Douglas Ezzy, and Graham Harvey, eds. *Researching Paganisms*. Walnut Creek, CA: AltaMira Press. 43-58.
Schultz, A. 1945 'On Multiple Realities.' *Philosophical and Phenomenological Research* 5:533-576.
Schuon, Frithjof. 1975 *The Transcendent Unity of Religion*. New York: Harper Torchbooks.
Shaked, Shaul. 2002 'Healing as an Act of Transformation.' In David Shulman and Guy Stroumsa, eds. *Self and Self-Transformation in the History of Religion*. New York: Oxford University Press. 12-130.
Sheppard, E. 2007 'Anthropology and the development of the transpersonal movement: Finding the transpersonal in transpersonal anthropology.' *Transpersonal Psychology Review* 11(1) 59-69.
Shulman, David and Guy Stroumsa, eds. 2002 *Self and Self-Transformation in the History of Religions*. New York: Oxford University Press.
Shulman, David and Stroumsa, Guy. 2002 'Introduction: Persons, Passages, and Shifting Cultural Space.' In David Shulman and Guy Stroumsa, eds. *Self and Self-Transformation in the History of Religion*. New York: Oxford University Press. 3-18.
Simmer-Brown, Judith. 2002 *Dakini's Warm Breath: The Feminine Principle in Tibetan Buddhism*. Boston, MA: Shambhala Publications.
Smith, Wilfred Cantwell. 1998 *Believing: An Historical Perspective*. Oxford: Oneworld Publications.
Sperry, R. W. 1966 'Brain bisection and mechanisms of consciousness.' In J.C. Eccles, ed. *Brain and consciousness experience*. Heidelberg: Springer-Verlag. 298-313.
Spickard, James, J. Shawn Landres, and Meredith McGuire. 2002 *Personal Knowledge and Beyond: Reshaping the Ethnography of Religion*. New York: New York University Press.
Sri Yukteswar, Swami. 1949 *The Holy Science*. Yogoda Satsanga Society of India.
Stark, R. 1997 'A Taxonomy of Religious Experience.' In B. Spilika and D. N. McIntosh, eds. *The Psychology of Religion:Theoretical Approaches*. Boulder,CO: Westview. 209-21.
Steinberg, Rabbi Jerry. n.d. The Unlikely Nature of God. Unpublished manuscript.

Steiner, Rudolph. 1996 *Angels*. London: Rudolph Steiner Press.
Steinsaltz, Adin. 1992 *The Thirteen Petalled Rose*. Northvale, NJ: Jason Aronson Inc.
Stendahl, Krister. 1992 'Selfhood in the Image of God.' In Leroy S. Rouner, ed. *Selves, People, and Persons: What Does It Mean to Be a Self?* Notre Dame, IN: University of Notre Dame Press. 141-49.
Stephen, M. 1989 'Self, the Sacred Other and Autonomous Imagination.' In G. Herdt and M. Stephen, eds. *The Religious Imagination in New Guinea,* New Brunswick: Rutgers University Press. 41-64.
Stevens, Jr., Phillips, ed. 2011 *Anthropology of Religion: Critical Concepts in Religious Studies*. 4 volumes. London and New York: Routledge.
Stewart, K. 1951 'Dream Theory in Malaya.' *Complex* 6:21-34.
Stewart, RJ. 1990 *Robert Kirk: Walker Between Worlds*: A New Edition of *The Secret Commonwealth of Elves, Fauns, & Fairie*. Longmead, Dorset, England: Element Books.
—. 1995 *The Living World of Faery*. Glastonbury, England: Gothic Image Publications.
Soderblom, Nathan. 1975 *Till mystikens belysning*. Lund. C. Strauss.
—. 1992 'Models and motives.' In R.G. D'Andrade and C. Strauss, eds. *Human Motives and Cultural Models*. Cambridge: Cambridge University Press. 1-20.
Taylor, Bron. 2010 *Dark Green Religion: Nature Spirituality and the Planetary Future*. Berkeley, CA: University of California.
Teresa of Avila (1515-1582). 1963-72 *Complete works of St. Teresa 1-3*. ed. by E. A. Peers. London.
Thondup, Tulku. 2011 *Incarnation: The History and Mysticism of the Tulku Tradition of Tibet*. Boston: Shambhala Publications.
Tolle, Eckhart. 1999 *The Power of Now: A Guide to Spiritual Enlightenment*. Novato, CA: Namaste Publishing and New World Library.
—. 2005 *A New Earth: Awakening to Your Life's Purpose*. New York: Penguin Group.
Townsend, Joan B. 2004 'Individualist Religious Movements: Core and Neo-Shamanism.' *Anthropology of Consciousness* 15 (1):1-9
Turner, Edith L. B. 1994 'A Visible Spirit Form in Zambia.' In David Young and Jean-Guy Goulet, eds. *Being Changed: The Anthropology of Extraordinary Experience*. Peterborough, Ontario: Broadview Press. 71-97.
—. 2003 'The Reality of Spirits' In Graham Harvey, ed. *Shamanism: A Reader*. London: Routledge. 145-152.

—. 2009 'The Reality of Spirits: A Tabooed or Permitted Field of Study?' In Matthew Bronson and Tina Fields, eds. *So What? Now What? The Anthropology Of Consciousness Responds To A World In Crisis.* Newcastle upon Tyne: Cambridge Scholars Publishing. 308-316.

—. 2012 *Communitas: The Anthropology of Collective Joy.* New York: Palgrave Macmillan.

Tylor, E.B. 1871 *Primitive culture: researches into the development of mythology, philosophy, religion, art, and custom* (2 vols). London: John Murray.

Underhill, Evelyn. 1974 (1910) *Mysticism; A study in the nature and development of Man's spiritual consciousness.* New York: New American Library.

Underhill, R.M. 1946 *Papago Indian Religion.* Columbia University Contributions to Anthropology, No. 33. New York: Columbia University Press.

Vallee, Jacques. 1969 *Passport to Magonia: From Folklore to Flying Saucers.* Chicago: Henry Regnery Company.

Vincent, Giselle and Linda Woodhead. 2001 'Spirituality.' In Linda Woodhead, Hiroko Kawanami, and Christopher Partridge, eds. *Religions In The Modern World: Traditions and Transformations.* London: Routledge. 319-337.

von Franz, Marie-Louise. 1996 *The Interpretation of Fairy Tales*: Revised Edition. Boston: Shambhala.

Wallace, Anthony. 1956 'Revitalization Movements: Some Theoretical Considerations for their Comparative Study.' *American Anthropologist*, LVII: 264-81

—. 1966 *Religion: An Anthropological View.* New York: Random House.

Walsh, Roger and Frances Vaughn, eds. 1980 *Beyond Ego: Transpersonal Dimensions in Psychology.* Los Angeles: J.P. Tarcher, Inc.

Washburn, M. 1995 *The ego and the dynamic ground.* Albany: State University of New York Press.

Weil, Andrew. 1972 *The Natural Mind.* New York: Houghton Mifflin Co.

Wellman, H.M. 1990 *The Child's Theory of Mind.* Cambridge, MA: MIT Press.

Weltecke, Dorothea. 2008 'Beyond Religion: On the Lack of Belief During the Central and Late Middle Ages.' In Heike Bock, Jorg Feuchter, and Michi Knecht, eds. *Religion and Its Other: Secular and Sacral Concepts and Practices in Interaction.* Frankfurt/New York: Campus Verlag. 101-114.

Westwood, Jennifer. 2009 'Music from the Mound.' *Time and Mind: The Journal of Archaeology, Consciousness and Culture* 2(2): 135-152.

Wilber, Ken. 1977 *The Spectrum of Consciousness*. Wheaton, IL: Quest.
—. 1983 *A Sociable God: Toward a New Understanding of Religion*. Boston: Shambhala Publications.
—. 1985 (1979) *No Boundary: Eastern and Western Approaches to Personal Growth.* Boston: Shambhala Publications.
—. 1998 *The Essential Ken Wilber: An Introductory Reader*. Boston, MA: Shambhala Publications.
—. 1998 *The Eye of Spirit: An Integral Vision for a World Gone Slightly Mad.* Boston: Shambhala Publications.
—. 2000 *A Brief History of Everything*. Boston, MA: Shambhala Publications.
Wikan, U. 1992 'Beyond the Word: The Power of Resonance.' *American Ethnologist* 3: 460-82.
Wilkie, Rab. 1994 'Spirited Imagination: Ways of approaching the shaman's world.' In David Young and Jean-Guy Goulet, eds. *Being Changed: The Anthropology of Extraordinary Experience.* Peterborough, Ontario: Broadview Press. 135-165.
Williams, Noel. 1991 'The Semantics of the Word *Fairy*: Making Meaning Out of Thin Air.' In Peter Narvaez, ed. *The Good People: New Fairylore Essays.* Lexington, Kentucky: University of Kentucky Press. 457-478.
Willis, Janice Dean. 1987 'Dakini: Some Comments on Its Nature and Meaning.' In Janice Willis, ed. *Feminine Ground: Essays on Women and Tibet.* Ithaca: Snow Lion Publications. 96-117.
Willis, Roy, with K.B.S. Chisanga, H.M.K. Sikazwe, K.B. Sikazwe, and S. Nanyangwe 1999 *Some Spirits Heal, Others Only Dance: A Journey into Human Selfhood in an African Village.* Oxford: Berg.
Winkelman, Michael. 1982 'Magic: A Theoretical Reassessment.' *Current Anthropology* 23. 37-44,59-66.
—. 1990 'The Evolution of Consciousness: An Essay Review of Up From Eden (Wilber 1981).' *Anthropology of Consciousness* 1(3-4): 24-31.
—. 1993 'The Evolution of Consciousness: Transpersonal Theories in Light of Cultural Relativism.' *Anthropology of Consciousness* 4(3):3-9.
—. 1994 'Multidisciplinary Perspectives on Consciousness.' *Anthropology of Consciousness* 5(2):16-25.
—. 1997 'Altered States of Consciousness and Religious Behavior.' In. S. Glazier, ed. *Anthropology of Religion: A Handbook of Method and Theory.* Westport, CT: Greenwood Press. 393-428.
—. 2000 *Shamanism: The Neural Ecology of Consciousness and Healing.* Westport, CT: Bergin & Garvey.

—. 2002 'Shamanism and Cognitive Evolution.' *Cambridge Archaeological Record.* 12: 71-101.

—. 2004 'Spirits as Human Nature and the Fundamental Structures of Consciousness.' In J. Houran, ed. *From Shaman to Scientist: Essays on Humanity's Search for Spirits.* Lanham, MD: Scarecrow Press. 59-96.

Wood, Christopher. 2000 *Fairies in Victorian Art.* Woodbridge: Antique Collectors Club Limited.

Yeats, Willam Butler. 1962 *The Celtic Twilight and a Selection of Early Poems.* New York: Signet.

—. 1990 *Fairy Tales of Ireland.* London: HarperCollins Ltd.

Young, David E. 1994 'Visitors in the Night: a creative energy model of spontaneous Visions.' In David Young and Jean-Guy Goulet, eds. *Being Changed: The Anthropology of Extraordinary Experience.* Peterborough, Ontario: Broadview Press. 166-194.

Young, David E. and Jean-Guy Goulet, eds. 1994 *Being Changed: The Anthropology of Extraordinary Experience.* Peterborough, Ontario: Broadview Press.

Young, David E. and Jean-Guy Goulet. 1994 'Introduction.' In David Young and Jean-Guy Goulet, eds. *Being Changed: The Anthropology of Extraordinary Experience.* Peterborough, Ontario: Broadview Press. 7-13.

Zaczek, Iain. 2005 *Angels & Fairies: The World's Greatest Art.* London: Flame Tree Publishing.

Zweig, Connie and Abrams, Jeremiah, eds. 1991 *Meeting the Shadow: The Hidden Power of the Dark Side of Human Nature.* Los Angeles: Jeremy P. Tarcher, Inc.

INDEX

ally, 182, 184, 185, 186
angel, 1, 4, 7, 9, 13, 18, 25, 26, 34, 40, 56, 95, 98, 100, 101, 105, 106, 109, 119, 130, 142, 170, 182, 183, 184, 185, 186, 190, 204, 254, 255, 268
Angel, 186
animism, 3, 7, 8, 9, 164, 187, 255
apodicticity, 12, 35, 121, 261
authenticity, 13, 16, 17, 18, 31, 39, 41, 68, 79, 84, 91, 104, 187, 204, 217, 257
Buddhism, 3, 4, 18, 25, 28, 64, 66, 68, 96, 122, 133, 142, 150, 172, 178, 189, 193, 201, 203, 204, 231, 241, 266, 271
Celtic, 2, 3, 10, 11, 13, 16, 18, 26, 33, 35, 36, 44, 50, 71, 73, 74, 78, 80, 92, 94, 99, 104, 113, 123, 125, 137, 207, 216, 217, 218, 219, 220, 221, 226, 228, 246, 253, 258, 265, 266
changeling, 94, 99, 106, 107, 110
channel, 28, 29, 35, 43, 50, 53, 73, 87, 236, 237, 239, 261
children, 3, 13, 26, 30, 37, 38, 39, 40, 42, 43, 44, 45, 46, 47, 49, 57, 69, 70, 88, 94, 96, 101, 105, 107, 108, 139, 158, 160, 169, 170, 171, 172, 190, 211, 219, 228, 247, 266
Christianity, 1, 2, 9, 11, 14, 15, 18, 22, 25, 26, 28, 33, 39, 64, 92, 97, 98, 100, 101, 102, 105, 122, 124, 133, 134, 135, 165, 182, 183, 200, 201, 212, 213, 216, 217, 226, 231, 232, 241, 253, 254, 255, 263, 268, 271
communitas, 20

Conan Doyle, A., 91, 96, 97, 104, 149, 208
consciousness, 7, 10, 12, 17, 18, 19, 21, 22, 24, 27, 28, 30, 31, 40, 46, 51, 57, 66, 67, 69, 79, 84, 91, 92, 100, 101, 102, 116, 120, 121, 131, 140, 148, 149, 150, 156, 163, 168, 170, 172, 175, 178, 179, 180, 181, 183, 186, 187, 189, 191, 192, 193, 194, 195, 197, 198, 199, 200, 203, 210, 217, 218, 219, 221, 225, 231, 236, 237, 239, 243, 244, 246, 247, 248, 256, 262, 263, 264, 265, 268, 270, 271, 272
  altered, (alternate), 2, 5, 6, 9, 16, 17, 20, 21, 22, 33, 79, 122, 168, 224, 251, 270
  anthropology of, 231
  borderland, 182, 270
  fairy, 6, 14, 22, 30, 33, 41, 46, 48, 53, 66, 70, 72, 101, 102, 110, 113, 121, 122, 127, 143, 147, 148, 170, 175, 182, 187, 191, 193, 195, 196, 197, 201, 202, 210, 234, 235, 236, 239, 240, 241
  phases of, 10, 168, 267
  polyphasic, 10, 268
  spectrum of, 18, 31, 193, 271
  stream of, 3, 18
  transrational, 121, 265
daemon, 1, 34, 98, 187, 265
dakini, 3, 4, 25, 27, 94, 96, 133, 134, 265, 266
eidetic, 12, 50, 51, 255
elemental being, 2, 3, 9, 25, 48, 99, 101, 128, 134, 170, 189, 207, 215, 218, 228, 237

elf, 33, 35, 44, 78, 92, 94, 95, 96, 97, 98, 99, 101, 105, 153, 155, 156, 217, 218, 256
enchantment, 8, 32, 36, 39, 66, 78, 153, 210, 223, 235, 265
Enneagram, 153, 267
epoche, 77
Evans-Wentz, W.Y., 2, 3, 4, 11, 15, 36, 91, 94, 97, 99, 104, 203, 208, 218, 252, 265, 266, 268
Faeroe Islands, 72, 78, 79, 92, 256, 263
fairy doctor, 45, 100, 116
fairy garden, 130
fairy music, 43, 61, 70, 95, 117, 153, 191, 221, 222, 223, 270
fairy painting, 95, 103, 104, 208
fairy path, 71, 77, 93, 131, 174, 182, 195, 220, 240
fairy portal, 217, 220, 224, 228
fairy portrait, 114
fairy tree, 47, 55, 71, 74, 75, 93, 105, 116
fairy vortex, 220
FairyLands, 29, 30, 74, 75, 93, 105, 130
fairyology, 13, 22
fieldwork, 2, 21, 22, 29, 30, 72, 77, 79, 81, 248, 256, 264
frequency, 31, 57, 119, 128, 148, 179, 193, 197, 236, 242
glamour, 32, 35, 39, 94, 265
gnosis, 121, 189
harp, 27, 29, 30, 42, 43, 44, 177, 221, 226
Harvey, G., 1, 6, 7, 8, 9, 11, 89, 187, 201, 259
Heschel, A., 15, 64, 68, 77
Hinduism, 10, 25, 28, 64, 133, 134, 142, 193, 201, 231, 265, 269, 271, 272
huldufolk, 72, 78, 92, 256
imagination, 4, 19, 20, 30, 47, 50, 57, 58, 79, 84, 85, 87, 95, 103, 107, 124, 141, 180, 181, 184, 185, 186, 187, 191, 193, 210, 219, 221, 252, 254, 255, 258, 268
individuation, 21, 124, 131, 143, 144, 168, 186, 202, 203, 204, 241, 266
insight, 10, 15, 37, 39, 44, 45, 64, 66, 68, 121, 135, 168, 172, 180, 187, 201, 271
intuition, 12, 13, 16, 22, 26, 30, 46, 52, 58, 61, 64, 68, 75, 79, 91, 113, 114, 116, 118, 121, 122, 124, 160, 164, 187, 199, 209, 226, 245, 255, 258, 271
Islam, 1, 3, 11, 15, 25, 134, 231, 253, 268
James, W., 2, 3, 12, 18, 20, 113, 187, 231, 251
jetsunma, 133, 134
Judaism, 1, 3, 9, 11, 15, 25, 28, 64, 77, 96, 134, 150, 160, 183, 193, 200, 231, 232, 253
Jung, C., 3, 4, 19, 20, 21, 29, 31, 39, 79, 84, 87, 96, 124, 131, 135, 143, 153, 159, 163, 170, 182, 183, 184, 191, 203, 204, 225, 241, 247, 252, 261, 266, 268, 270, 272
Kabbalism, 13, 15, 27, 28, 31, 134, 182, 183, 186, 203, 232, 241, 255, 269
"mazeway" configuration, 37, 228
metanoia, 37
mission, 30, 41, 69, 92, 145, 146, 147, 148, 149, 150, 183, 186, 193, 233, 236, 239, 240
monotheism, 1, 8, 25, 27, 33, 98, 165, 187, 201, 267
music, 29, 43, 52, 54, 61, 63, 70, 74, 95, 100, 116, 118, 146, 150, 153, 155, 156, 160, 161, 164, 221, 222, 223, 225, 226, 227, 235, 270
    fairy. *See* fairy music
Native America, 66, 96, 231, 238, 259

nature spirit, 1, 4, 8, 9, 11, 20, 24, 25, 26, 28, 33, 35, 71, 92, 93, 96, 101, 144, 149, 164, 165, 221, 251, 257
neurophenomenology, 225, 231
New Age, 3, 8, 9, 19, 79, 97, 101, 102, 103, 104, 105, 148, 149, 170, 184, 198, 204, 207, 208, 215, 217, 233, 234, 237, 261, 268, 271
Newhouse, F., 39, 40, 97, 100, 101, 134, 135, 149, 208, 212, 213, 214, 217, 234
noesis, 12, 57, 121
other-than-human person, 1, 2, 72, 163, 216
Pagan, (Neo-Pagan), 7, 8, 9, 84, 92, 98, 182, 187, 252, 253
participation mystique, 20, 182
Pathwork, 177, 178, 241
perception, 5, 9, 11, 12, 13, 17, 25, 27, 47, 57, 64, 67, 78, 110, 160, 171, 184, 187, 193, 203, 208, 218, 237, 242, 252, 254, 260, 261, 262, 265, 269, 270, 272
pishogue, 35
polytheism, 9, 68, 187
psychoid, 183, 185, 268, 269
psychological fall, 46
reflexivity, 46, 67, 68, 89, 120, 201, 264
reincarnation, 22, 24, 28, 30, 32, 43, 50, 53, 73, 74, 84, 122, 125, 133, 134, 135, 136, 137, 138, 139, 140, 142, 143, 155, 157, 163, 174, 176, 189, 216, 233, 236, 237, 240, 266, 267
revitalization, 13, 207
shadow, psychological, 20, 115, 135, 136, 190, 204, 270
Shakespeare, W., 92
shamanism, 5, 6, 9, 20, 21, 28, 32, 71, 99, 203, 260
spiritual bypass, 204
spiritual emergency, 204, 269

Sufi, 12, 15, 134, 184, 268, 271
sylph, 29, 35, 42, 85, 92, 97, 101, 153, 154, 155, 156, 160, 218, 236, 237, 239, 240
telepathy, 50, 59, 64
theory of mind, 46
theosophy, 4, 9
Theosophy, 2, 14, 28, 104, 133, 251
Tibetan, 3, 4, 27, 94, 96, 113, 133, 134, 138, 193, 220, 265, 266, 268
tikkun, 150, 186, 232
transcendent function, 143, 225
transformation, 11, 19, 20, 26, 27, 28, 31, 36, 66, 67, 85, 91, 92, 93, 94, 111, 119, 121, 122, 131, 136, 140, 148, 163, 170, 181, 183, 184, 186, 189, 190, 191, 192, 193, 194, 199, 200, 201, 202, 203, 204, 205, 208, 212, 216, 217, 237, 241, 248, 264, 267, 269
transpersonal, 7, 17, 18, 19, 20, 23, 31, 35, 121, 193, 237, 242, 264
    anthropology, 2, 6, 7, 17, 20, 21, 35, 91, 131, 168, 225, 228, 247, 248, 251, 255, 257
    psychology, 6, 16, 20, 21, 23, 68, 121, 182, 185, 187, 201, 202, 204, 231, 269
Tuatha de Danaan, 74, 92, 106, 135
Turner, E., 1, 7, 10, 20, 27, 259
vision, 4, 5, 9, 10, 12, 13, 25, 49, 50, 51, 57, 64, 71, 98, 99, 100, 102, 114, 118, 164, 182, 185, 186, 202, 213, 226, 252, 255, 262
Wilber, K., 18, 20, 31, 46, 91, 121, 163, 193, 231, 263, 265, 269, 270
Yeats, W. B., 2, 9, 91, 97, 98, 100, 146, 251, 261
Yoga, 4, 12, 28, 66, 67, 68, 131, 150, 204, 231, 265
Zen, 18, 66, 110, 122, 201